OXFORD W

THE LIVES OF

HEMACANDRA (1089–1172), v
site of the modern city of Ahmedabad. While he was still a child his parents, who were members of a merchant community, decided that he should become a Jain monk, and handed him over to a monk who supervised his education and initiated him into the monastic life. Hemacandra was an extremely able pupil, and soon mastered many branches of learning; his knowledge of language, grammar, and poetics was particularly profound. Eventually, he came to the notice of the ruler of much of Gujarat, Jayasiṃha Siddharāja (*c.*1094–1143), and was appointed court annalist and poet. At Jayasiṃha's request, Hemacandra compiled a grammar of the Sanskrit and Prakrit languages, and began to compose an epic poem which had the dual purposes of illustrating the rules of his grammar and eulogizing his royal patron. His relationship with Jayasiṃha's successor, Kumārapāla (*c.*1143–72), was particularly close, and through Hemacandra's influence the Jain religion received such a degree of royal patronage that the reign of Kumārapāla is still remembered by Jains as a golden age for their religion. *The Lives of the Jain Elders* was Hemacandra's last major work. Hemacandra died a few months before his royal patron, his vast learning and literary output having made him one of the major figures in the literary tradition of India.

R. C. C. FYNES was educated at the University of Leeds and The Queen's College, Oxford. From 1992 to 1994 he was Junior Research Fellow in Indology at Wolfson College, Oxford. He is now Senior Lecturer in Historical and Political Studies at De Montfort University, Leicester. His major research interests are in the Jain literary tradition and in cultural transmission between India and ancient Greece and Rome.

OXFORD WORLD'S CLASSICS

For almost 100 years Oxford World's Classics have brought readers closer to the world's great literature. Now with over 700 titles—from the 4,000-year-old myths of Mesopotamia to the twentieth century's greatest novels—the series makes available lesser-known as well as celebrated writing.

The pocket-sized hardbacks of the early years contained introductions by Virginia Woolf, T. S. Eliot, Graham Greene, and other literary figures which enriched the experience of reading. Today the series is recognized for its fine scholarship and reliability in texts that span world literature, drama and poetry, religion, philosophy and politics. Each edition includes perceptive commentary and essential background information to meet the changing needs of readers.

OXFORD WORLD'S CLASSICS

HEMACANDRA

The Lives of the Jain Elders

Translated with an Introduction and Notes by
R. C. C. FYNES

Oxford New York
OXFORD UNIVERSITY PRESS
1998

Oxford University Press, Great Clarendon Street, Oxford OX2 6DP
Oxford New York
Athens Auckland Bangkok Bogota Bombay Buenos Aires
Calcutta Cape Town Dar es Salaam Delhi Florence Hong Kong Istanbul
Karachi Kuala Lumpur Madras Madrid Melbourne Mexico City
Nairobi Paris Singapore Taipei Tokyo Toronto Warsaw
and associated companies in
Berlin Ibadan

Oxford is a trade mark of Oxford University Press

First published as an Oxford World's Classics paperback 1998

British Library Cataloguing in Publication Data
Data available

Library of Congress Cataloging in Publication Data
Hemacandra, 1088–1172
[Triśaṣṭiśalākāpuruṣacarita. English]
The lives of the Jain Elders / Hemacandra; translated with an introduction and notes by R.C.C. Fynes.
(Oxford world's classics)
Includes bibliographical references and index.
1. Jaina saints—Poetry. I. Fynes, R. C. C. II. Series.
PK3794.H46A24 1998 891'.21—dc21 97-49971
ISBN 0-19-283227-1

1 3 5 7 9 10 8 6 4 2

Typeset by Best-set Typesetter Ltd., Hong Kong
Printed in Great Britain by
Caledonian International Book Manufacturing Ltd.
Glasgow

IN PARENTUM MEMORIAM

CONTENTS

ACKNOWLEDGEMENTS

THANKS are due to Kate Crosby and Andrew Skilton for their encouragement when this translation was in its early stages and for their suggestion that I should submit it for publication in the World's Classics series. Judith Luna and the editorial staff at Oxford University Press were patient and helpful. Professor Richard Gombrich read the first draft of the translation with me. Special thanks are due to Richard's wife, Dr Sanjukta Gupta; whenever Richard and I were stumped by a difficult passage, Sanjukta invariably found the solution. Richard and Sanjukta also checked my translations of the names in the Index of Principal Characters and Places. Dr Will Johnson read the Introduction and the text; I was encouraged by his comments. The Librarian, Dr Gillian Evison, and the staff of the Indian Institute Library, Oxford, were, as ever, helpful and courteous. De Montfort University helped by providing a research grant which enabled me to visit libraries in Oxford, and I wish to acknowledge the support of my colleagues at that institution; special thanks are due to Professor Michael Scott, Pro-vice Chancellor, De Montfort University. Most of all, thanks are due to my wife, Michelle, for her patience and support while I was working on this translation.

I have received much help, but no doubt many defects remain; I take sole blame for them.

INTRODUCTION

THE literature of the Jains, written for the most part in ancient Indian languages, is full of interest, yet relatively little of it has been translated into English or even modern Indian languages. *The Lives of the Jain Elders* is an epic poem in Sanskrit, the classical language of India, written by the Jain scholar-monk Hemacandra (1089–1172). It is lively reading, being full of racy folk-tales which provide a fascinating insight into the social life of medieval India. This introduction is intended to do no more than provide sufficient information to enable the non-specialist reader to enjoy Hemacandra's poem. Those who wish to deepen their knowledge of Jainism should turn to the specialist books and articles listed in the Bibliography.

Jainism already had a history of some 1,500 years when Hemacandra wrote *The Lives of the Jain Elders*, and today it remains a living religion, actively responding to challenges of a new millenium. Jainism is not a monolithic religion; it has developed in response to changing social conditions, and within it there are several sects or traditions who share the central beliefs of Jainism but have differing views about religious practice. The main division is between the White Clad (Śvetāmbaras), whose ascetics wear white robes, and the Sky Clad (Digambaras), whose fully initiated monks go naked. Hemacandra belonged to the White Clad tradition, and he does not concern himself with the practices of the other traditions in *The Lives of the Jain Elders*. Consequently, the reader should be aware that the beliefs and practices described in the text, notes, and introduction are not necessarily normative for the whole of Jainism.

The life and works of Hemacandra

Hemacandra is one of the key figures in the cultural tradition of the White Clad Jains. So striking was his personality and so pervasive was his influence that very soon after his death he became a figure of legend, endowed with supernatural powers. There are several accounts of his life, but, with their stress on the marvellous, they are hagiographical; hence it is not possible to reconstruct Hemacandra's life story in a way that would satisfy the criteria of scholarly historical biography. However, there is sufficient information, derived chiefly from his own works, to allow the key events of his life to be related.

The child who was to become known as the Omniscient One of the Dark Age (i.e. the present) was born in November/December 1089 in the town of Dhandukā in Gujarat, not far from the site of the present city of Ahmedabad. His parents, who belonged to a merchant caste, were devout Jain laypeople. They named the boy Caṅgadeva. When he was 8 years old his parents decided that he should become a Jain monk. They entrusted him to a White Clad monk named Devacandra who initiated the boy, giving him the name Somacandra. He remained Devacandra's pupil for the following twelve years. Somacandra was highly intelligent. During the time he spent as Devacandra's pupil, he mastered many branches of knowledge, both Jain and non-Jain. His knowledge of language, grammar, and poetics was particularly profound. Devacandra nominated him as his successor, and in 1108 he was awarded the title of Teacher (Sūri or Ācārya), giving him the right to lead his own group of monks and to expound scriptural doctrine. On being ordained with the rank of Teacher, in accordance with ascetic custom he again changed his name, assuming the name by which he is remembered, Hemacandra.

In the latter part of the eleventh century a dynasty of rulers known as the Caulukyas had established a flourishing kingdom in Gujarat, and the dominant concern of sources for Hemacandra's life is his relationship with two rulers of this dynasty, Jayasiṃha Siddharāja (*c.*1094–1143) and Kumārapāla (*c.*1143–1172). Jayasiṃha's policy of warlike aggression made his the dominant power in western India, and through his patronage his capital at Patan in northern Gujarat became a centre for learning and the arts. Hemacandra was appointed court scholar and annalist, and at the king's request composed a grammar, *The Siddhahemacandra* or *Siddhahaima*, named after its author and its patron. The grammar contains the rules for Sanskrit and for several Prakrits; the latter are literary vernaculars closely related to Sanskrit in their vocabulary and morphology. He then composed *The Epic Poem with a Dual Purpose* (*Dvāśrayamahākāvya*), so called because it is both an illustration of the rules of his grammar and a eulogistic history of the Caulukya rulers. He also compiled dictionaries and wrote handbooks on composition, poetics, and metrics.

The Epic Poem with a Dual Purpose was completed in the reign of Jayasiṃha Siddharāja's nephew and successor, Kumārapāla.

Hemacandra may have been instrumental in helping Kumārapāla win the throne on his uncle's death. According to some sources, Kumārapāla was only saved from being put to death by his jealous uncle through the intervention of Hemacandra, who sheltered the fugitive prince under a pile of manuscripts. This story probably owes more to romantic fiction than to historical fact. What is certain is that a close relationship developed between the scholar-monk and the young ruler, who appears to have regarded Hemacandra as his mentor. Hemacandra's teaching led Kumārapāla to embrace Jain ideals and to propagate them in his kingdom. At Kumārapāla's request, Hemacandra composed *The Conduct Manual* (*Yogaśāstra*) which explains the way a Jain should live, and in *The Epic Poem with a Dual Purpose* Hemacandra states that the king took the vows of a Jain layman.[1] Kumārapāla was certainly eager to promote the Jain ethic of non-violence, and epigraphic evidence confirms that he discouraged the religious sacrifice of live animals. He financed the building of Jain temples and gave favoured treatment to the Jain merchant community. His reign remains proverbial among Jains as a golden age in which the power of the state promoted the ideals of the Jain religion and fostered and protected the Jain community. Hemacandra wrote *The Deeds of Kumārapāla* in praise of his patron; it also has the purpose of illustrating the Prakrit section of his grammar. At Kumārapāla's request Hemacandra composed a massive epic poem in Sanskrit about the chief personages of Jainism, *The Lives of the Sixty-three Illustrious People* (*Triṣaṣṭiśalākāpuruṣacari-tra*). The work here translated, *The Lives of the Jain Elders* (*Sthavirāvalīcaritra*), is a self-contained sequel to the *Lives of the Sixty-three Illustrious People*; for that reason it is also known as *The Appendix* (*Pariśiṣṭaparvan*).

The Lives of the Jain Elders was Hemacandra's last major work. He died in 1172, shortly before Kumārapāla. Hemacandra's vast learning, which earned him the epithet of Omniscient One of the Dark Age, was encyclopedic. His literary activity provided the community of White Clad Jains in Gujarat with a synthesis of existing knowledge which was to remain one of the prime elements of their cultural life.

[1] It was the duty of Indian kings to provide patronage for all priests and ascetics in their kingdoms, and Kumārapāla, despite his personal interest in Jainism, continued to support the state cult which centred on the Hindu god Śiva, whose main temple was at Somnath.

Jainism

Jainism is a soteriology: it provides the means by which the soul (*jīva*) can escape from the bondage of a continual cycle of death and rebirth. Traditional Jain belief holds that truths of the Jain religion have always existed; throughout time they are periodically reactivated by a series of omniscient teachers called Fordmakers (Tīrthaṅkaras) because their preaching of the Jain religion creates the community of ascetics and their lay supporters which is the Ford by which souls are enabled to cross the ocean of existence. The Fordmakers are also known as Jinas, meaning Conquerers, so-called because their omniscience has been gained as a result of their conquering their desires and passions by means of a life of harsh asceticism; hence a Jain is one who follows the religion of the Conquerers. Although they have superhuman characteristics as a result of their superior spiritual status, the Fordmakers are human, born of human parents. Despite the traditional Jain belief in the uncreated and eternal verities of the religion, it is clear that the historical origins of Jainism began with the most recent Fordmaker, Mahāvīra, who lived and preached in the areas bordering the lower Ganges valley in the fifth century BC, and that the other Fordmakers, with the possible exception of the one immediately preceding Mahāvīra, are components of a complex mythology which was not fully elaborated until many years after Mahāvīra's death.

Through his preaching Mahāvīra attracted an ascetic following which was organized into a monastic community of monks and nuns (*saṅgha*). In *The Lives of the Jain Elders* Hemacandra relates the lives of the early leaders of this community, while placing them in the context of the uncreated and eternal Jain universe. To gain a full understanding of the universe in which the lives of the Jain elders were lived, it is necessary first to consider the specific social and cultural conditions in which Jainism originated and developed.

The Āryan people

From about 1500 BC groups of nomadic tribes, who called themselves 'Ārya', to which they ascribed the meaning 'honourable' or 'noble', began to migrate from the regions to the north-west of the Indian subcontinent into the Punjab. Originally nomadic, in time they settled and began to lead a pastoral life. The chronology and the precise nature of their migration remains unclear; there may have been several waves of migration extending over several centuries. The country into which they migrated was not uninhabited; as they migrated south and west from the Punjab they encountered and interacted with various indigenous peoples, and the continued interaction between Āryan and non-Āryan became a dominant factor in the development of Indian society and culture.

Although the material culture of the Āryan people was relatively poor, the social and religious ideas of their priestly class became the dominant ideology in northern India, eventually spreading throughout the subcontinent. Their cultural dominance initially depended on their military dominance. Although the Āryan people may have been fewer in number than the indigenous peoples with whom they first came into contact, the Āryans were able to subjugate them because their skilled use of horses, which drew their war-chariots, gave the Āryans military superiority.[2] Later, when the Āryans had become settled, cattle-owning agriculturalists, rituals centring on the sacrifice of horses remained an important element in the consecration of their ruling classes. Other civilizations in other ages provide examples of the ways in which the social ideology of a cultural élite can dominate and provide a common ideology for very diverse social groups. This is what happened in India: the reaction of indigenous peoples to the social and religious ideology of the Āryan priestly classes was the catalyst for nearly all subsequent developments in Indian religion until the coming of Islam. The Āryan people were responsible for the development of a ranked, fourfold division of society, which is known as the *varṇa* system. The highest class (*varṇa*) was that of the Brahmins (Brāhmaṇas), the priestly class, who were responsible for the performance of sacred ritual. Below them was the ruling or warrior class (Kṣatriyas), whose authority was sanctified by the rituals of the priestly class. Below the warrior class was the class of independent peasant agriculturalists (Vaiśyas), to which those people who engaged in trade were later ascribed. At the bottom of the hierarchy

[2] This model of a diffusion of Āryan culture based initially on the military superiority of a migrating people has been disputed by some scholars. Nevertheless, despite being a simplification of what was surely a long and complex process, it remains the explanation which is most in accordance with the evidence.

was the class of servants and slaves (Śūdras) whose function was to serve the three higher classes. A concept of ritual purity provided the rationale for this social system; not comprehended within it were peoples whose customs diverged so far from those of the Āryans that social contact with them was thought to be polluting. Eventually, membership of a particular class came to be ascribed by birth; there was no place for social mobility in this system, and it became one of the chief duties of rulers to prevent the mixing of the classes.

The Āryans were illiterate, yet the reason why we are able to reconstruct the ideologies of their priestly class is because we possess their sacred literature, which was orally transmitted from generation to generation, and continued to be orally transmitted from teacher to pupil even after the use of writing became widespread in India during the third century BC. Even today there are people in India who can recite by heart vast sections of this literature.

The name given to this sacred literature is Veda, which means knowledge; the Vedas are concerned with sacred knowledge. The earlier strata of the Vedic literature were composed in an early form of Sanskrit known as Vedic Sanskrit, and the later strata were composed in a form of the language which approaches classical Sanskrit, which was codified by grammarians in about the fourth century BC and which is the form of the language in which Hemacandra composed *The Lives of the Jain Elders*. Historians, in the lack of other evidence, have used the Vedic literature and its internal chronological stratification to name and to date a historical period: the Vedic period, which is subdivided into an early Vedic period, beginning with the start of the migrations of the Āryan people in about 1500 BC and lasting to about 1000 BC, and later Vedic period, lasting from 1000 BC to 500 BC. The classification of Vedic literature is complex: in simple terms one can think of the four Vedas themselves which were recited by the Brahmins as they performed the sacrificial rituals,[3] the Brāhmanas which contain mythological material and

[3] The classification is made more complex by the fact that sometimes the number of Vedas is said to be only three: the *Ṛg Veda*, the *Sāma Veda*, and the *Yajur Veda*. The first is a collection of 1,028 hymns, the second consists of excerpts from those hymns arranged for chanting at the sacrifice, and the third contains material to be recited at the sacrifice. The fourth collection, the *Atharva Veda*, consisting mainly of magical spells and incantations, had a more tenuous connection with the sacrificial ritual, and hence a less assured status as a Veda.

instructions for performing the sacrificial rituals, and the Upaniṣads, a collection of texts which contain a variety of speculative material about sacrifice, the universe, and the soul. It is not possible to date this literature in any way approaching precision: the oldest hymn of the *Ṛg Veda* may be as old as 1500 BC, and the earliest Upaniṣads had certainly been composed before 500 BC.

The religious cult of the early Āryans centred on sacrifice. Sacrifice to such gods as Indra, the god of war, was offered on a quid pro quo basis: a slaughtered animal was offered to a god in return for a material benefit. The sacrifice was performed by Brahmins and was sponsored by a householder of one of Brahmin, warrior, or peasant classes who paid the fees of the sacrificing Brahmins. In the course of time, the sacrificial rituals became more complex, and there developed a concomitant elaboration of the theory of the purpose of the sacrifice: the sacrifice was thought to both create and sustain the universe, and to create, sustain, and provide the rationale for the fourfold social system. A late hymn from the *Ṛg Veda* describes the creation of the universe and the social order from the sacrifice of a primeval man: the Brahmins were formed from the man's mouth, the warrior class from his arms, the peasants from his thighs, and the servants from his feet. Thus the ranked social order was implicit in creation, and the Brahmins' performance of the sacrifice guaranteed its continuance.

In the early Vedic period a man was thought to die once only: if he was fortunate, after death he would join his ancestors in heaven, and eventually there developed the idea that the performance of a specific sacrifice would guarantee its sponsor a place in this World of the Fathers. However, by the end of the later Vedic period a belief in a continued process of death and rebirth had become general. The Sanskrit word for this continuous cycle of death and rebirth is *saṃsāra*, meaning 'flowing through'. Together with a belief in reincarnation there developed the theory that the actions of one's present life predetermine the condition of one's future embodiment, the more ethically good the actions of one's present life, the more fortunate the state of one's next embodiment. This is the theory of karma, a word whose basic meaning is 'action'. All life, ranging from the smallest insects or even plants to gods in heaven, was thought to be subject to this process. Even gods were thought to pass away in the course of time, to be replaced in heaven by newly embodied gods who had the same form and name as the ones who had passed away. Rebirth in heaven, although doubtless pleasant, was impermanent. A good rebirth in the future remained an immediate aspiration, but the ultimate goal for the individual became escape from the cycle of death and rebirth altogether. The Sanskrit word for this is *mokṣa*, literally 'liberation' or 'release', that is, release from further embodiment. How to gain liberation became, and remains, a central preoccupation of religious thought in India, and the idea that knowledge of reality, the way things actually are, leads to liberation became a key element in this speculation. In the *Cāndogya Upaniṣad* this knowledge is equated with the realization that the vivifying power which sustains the individual is equivalent to the vivifying and sustaining power of the universe. There were other views, but whatever view was taken about the nature of reality, there seems to have been general agreement that two related elements were necessary to gain knowledge of it: asceticism and meditation.

The ascetic milieu

The idea that supernormal powers and knowledge can be gained through the practice of asceticism is central to the religious thought of India. Fasting, sexual continence, and the performance of harsh bodily mortification are thought to generate power. The Sanskrit word for the practice of asceticism and for the power it brings is *tapas*, literally 'hear'. *Tapas* can give the ascetic practitioner the power to see and hear things which lie beyond the normal range of the senses, to read the minds of others, and to fly; it can also grant knowledge of the true nature of reality, and as such can lead to final liberation. Meditation is closely allied with the practice of asceticism. On one level, meditation can mean nothing more than thinking deeply about a particular religious topic or teaching, but on another level it describes the process whereby the practitioner withdraws to a secluded place, withdraws his senses from their objects, and stills his mind from discursive thought until knowledge of the true nature of reality is gained; thus meditation is also a path to liberation.

By the time of the composition of the early Upaniṣads many people were renouncing the life of a householder in order to practise the techniques of asceticism and meditation. Some of these renunciants wandered alone, seeking religious insight by means of their own ascetic practices and meditation techniques, while others wandered in groups, following the guidance of a teacher. So widespread was the practice of renunciation that a theory was developed to accommodate it within the Brahminical social system. This is the theory of the four stages of life (*āśramas*). According to it, in his youth a member of three twice-born classes would lead a celibate life studying sacred knowledge with his teacher, then he would marry and lead the life of a householder; in late middle age, when his son had in turn given birth to a son, he would, accompanied by his wife, abandon home for a hermitage in the forest; finally, in old age, he would abandon the hermitage and his wife for the life of a homeless wanderer. This theory represents an ideal: many renunciants would abandon home at a relatively early age, before marrying; on the other hand, many householders would never abandon their homes at all. Thus, a place was found for renunciation within the Brahminical value system, and in turn, many renunciants accepted its claims, together with a belief in the authority of the Vedas. Other renunciants, however, were opposed to the Brahminical value system and rejected the authority of the Vedas. Such non-orthodox renunciants believed that birth in a particular class had no relevance for an individual's religious progress. They were opposed to the performance of sacrificial rituals, believing that they were an obstacle to the attainment of liberation. These non-orthodox renunciants were known as Śramaṇas, literally 'Strivers', because they believed that religious progress could be made only by one's own efforts; birth and ritual sacrifice had nothing to do with the matter. The Striver renunciants had a variety of beliefs and practices. Many of them were solitary, seeking an individual path to liberation, but others taught their beliefs to groups of followers. Some, perhaps the majority, of these groups were relatively ephemeral, soon dispersing after the deaths of their founders; others were more persistent, and in some cases religious traditions were created that were able to outlast the lives of their founders by several generations. Two Striver religions have survived and continue to flourish at the present day: Buddhism and Jainism. Both religions offer a path to Liberation, but their paths are very different. For Jainism, the answer to the problem of escape from the cycle of death and rebirth lies in asceticism. Since all actions, even good ones, create karma for the individual soul, the best course is to cease from action and to expunge one's existing karma by undergoing harsh bodily mortification. Severe asceticism leads to omniscience and to liberation from future rebirth. As with all Striver religions, Jainism rejects the claims of the Brahmins, denying that the Vedas contain ultimate knowledge and that the Vedic sacrifice has any efficacy. Indeed, Jainism argues that, since many Vedic rituals involve the sacrifice of animals, those who perform them will go to hell.

Unlike Jainism, Buddhism rejects severe asceticism as a path to salvation. The Buddha, who was Mahāvīra's contemporary and who for a time practised bodily mortification before becoming disillusioned with its effectiveness as a path to salvation, preached a 'middle way' between harsh asceticism and sensual indulgence, with a stress on meditation as a means to salvation. In contrast, it is Mahāvīra's life of unflinching asceticism which provides the motivating dynamic for Jainism, the religion of the Conquerers.

The life of Mahāvīra

The traditional Jain accounts of Mahāvīra's life use the language of myth. His life, as do the lives of all Fordmakers, centres around five auspicious moments: conception, birth, renunciation, gaining of omniscience, and liberation from further rebirth.

According to the accounts of the White Clad Jains, the child who was to become Mahāvīra was first conceived in the womb of a Brahmin lady, but, since Fordmakers are born only in the warrior class, Indra, the king of the gods, knowing that the embryo was to become a Fordmaker, transferred it to the womb of Triśalā, the queen of King Siddhārtha, a member of the Jñātṛ clan. The royal couple lived at Kuṇḍagrāma in the kingdom of Vaiśālī, not far from the site of the modern city of Patna.

The gods came to celebrate his birth. During his mother's pregnancy, the family's wealth began to increase miraculously, and this continued after his birth; hence, he was given the name Vardhamāna, meaning 'increasing'. As a youth and young man Vardhamāna performed the duties of his class, marrying a princess, Yaśodhara, and fathering a daughter. After his parents' death, Vardhamāna, at the age of 30, renounced the world, having uprooted his hair in five handfuls. His initiation was attended by the gods.

The harsh asceticism of his life as a renunciant gained him the name Mahāvīra, which means 'great hero'. After the garment which covered his midriff was torn off on a thorn bush, he went naked, completely exposed to the heat of the sun and the cold of winter. His diet was plain and sparse, and he underwent long periods of fasting, during which he did not even take water. He bore with equanimity the attacks of animals and humans. Eventually, twelve years, six months, and fifteen days after his renunciation, he gained omniscience, absolute knowledge of the true nature of reality (*kevala-jñāna*) and became the twenty-fourth, final Fordmaker of the present era. The gods created an enclosure for him to preach in, and by his preaching Mahāvīra created the fourfold congregation of Jain monks, nuns, laymen, and laywomen.

For the remainder of his life, Mahāvīra wandered through countries bordering the Ganges valley, preaching the Jain religion. Upon his death at the age of 72 at a town called Pāpa, not far from the site of his birth, his soul became liberated from further rebirth, and the gods built a funeral pyre on which they cremated his body.

Despite the mythical framework of Mahāvīra's life story, he is certainly a historical figure. According to the traditional accounts of the White Clad Jains, he lived between 599 and 527 BC; recent research, however, suggests that he probably lived in the following century (see below). By the time of his death, he had established an ascetic community of monks and nuns, which received sustenance and patronage from sympathetic rulers and laypeople, and was guided by the Jain elders whose lives are the subject of Hemacandra's text.

The Jain elders

According to the Jain accounts, Mahāvīra's first converts and chief disciples were a group of eleven Brahmins about to perform a Vedic sacrifice to whom he preached shortly after gaining omniscience. They abandoned their belief in the efficacy of the sacrifice, and became Jain monks. Their names were Indrabhūti Gautama, Agnibhūti, Vāyubhūti, Vyakta, Sudharman, Maṇḍaka, Mauryaputra, Akampita, Acalabhrātṛ, Metārya, and Prabhāsa. Each became the head of a number of ascetic followers, bearing the title Supporter of the Flock (Gaṇadhara), and in due course each gained omniscience. After Mahāvīra's death, the leadership passed to the two Supporters of the Flock who survived him, Indrabhūti Gautama and Sudharman. The former died in the twelfth year after Mahāvīra's death, the latter in the thirteenth.

Sudharman is the only Supporter of the Flock to play an important role in *The Lives of the Jain Elders*. His initiation of his pupil Jambū begins the lineage of pupillary succession which forms the framework of Hemacandra's narrative. Jambū is important in Jain tradition as the last person to gain omniscience and hence final liberation, for some three years after Mahāvīra's final liberation, Bharata (the Indian subcontinent) passed into the present era in which conditions are too bad for people born in it to gain omniscience; some 80,000 years must elapse before conditions are once more propitious for the gaining of omniscience and final liberation (see below and the Appendix on the Jain universe).

The lineage of pupillary succession from Jambū to Vajra, the last of the Jain elders to have his story related in detail by Hemacandra, is given below. The names of the Jain elders mentioned in Hemacandra's narrative are in small capitals.

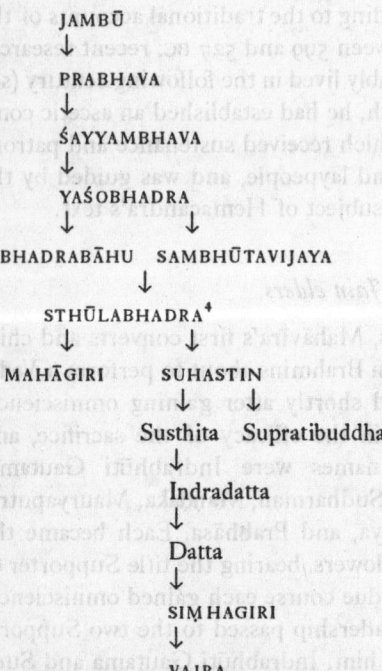

JAMBŪ
↓
PRABHAVA
↓
ŚAYYAMBHAVA
↓
YAŚOBHADRA
↓ ↓
BHADRABĀHU SAMBHŪTAVIJAYA
↓
STHŪLABHADRA[4]
↓ ↓
MAHĀGIRI SUHASTIN
↓ ↓
Susthita Supratibuddha
↓
Indradatta
↓
Datta
↓
SIṂHAGIRI
↓
VAJRA

[4] Sthūlabhadra was initiated by Sambhūtavijaya and taught by Bhadrabāhu after the former's death.

Jain canonical literature in The Lives of the Jain Elders

A defining characteristic of the Jain elders is their knowledge of a body of sacred teachings, known as Old or Original Teachings (Pūrvas) which were preached by Mahāvīra and gathered into fourteen collections by the Supporters of the Flock. The transmission of these sacred teachings from teacher to pupil is an important theme of *The Lives of the Jain Elders*. The Supporter of the Flock Sudharman taught them to his pupil Jambū. Knowledge of all fourteen Original Collections of Teachings died with Sthūlabhadra. His successors down to and including Vajra knew ten, but in the years following Vajra's death they were completely forgotten. They probably contained teachings on the nature of the soul, the cosmos, karma, and criticisms of the teachings of the followers of other religions. More important than their actual content is the status ascribed to them: in *The Lives of the Jain Elders* they are presented as enormous texts containing *all* knowledge; the Original Collections of Teachings thus come to validate the claims of Jainism in precisely the same way as the Vedas validate the claims of the Brahminical religion.

The Original Collections of Teachings were transmitted orally. Their loss is attributed by Hemacandra to the general decay in spirituality which is a necessary consequence of life in the present era (see below). Today, the image-worshipping White Clad Jains have a canon of forty-five texts which was first put into writing as late as the fifth century AD, about 900 years after the death of Mahāvīra.[5]

The texts are arranged in five groups: twelve Limbs (Aṅgas), twelve Subsidiary Limbs (Upāṅgas), seven Demotion Scriptures (Cheda Sūtras), four Basic Scriptures (Mūla Sūtras), ten Miscellaneous Scriptures (Prakīrṇa Sūtras), and two Appendix Scriptures (Cūlikā Sūtras). Some of the material of the Original Collections of Teachings was placed in the twelfth Limb, the *Disputation about Views* (*Dṛṣṭivāda*), but this too had been lost by the fifth century AD. As an added complication, the title Disputation about Views in sometimes used as a synonym for the Original Collections of Teachings in their entirety.

The language of the forty-five canonical texts of the White Clad

[5] The Sky Clad Jains do not accept the authenticity of this canon. They believe that the scriptures were irrecoverably lost in the course of their transmission.

Jains is a special form of Prakrit or Middle Indo-Aryan,[6] called Ardhamāgadhī, found only in those scriptures. Ardhamāgadhī, literally 'half-Māgadhī', takes its name from Magadha, the country in which Mahāvīra spent much of his life, and is probably not very different from the language in which Mahāvīra preached. The scriptures were transmitted orally from teacher to pupil, but in the course of the centuries of their transmission, their language remained fixed while the spoken language of the day developed and altered. Consequently, by the time they were put into writing, their language had become archaic and much of their meaning obscure even to learned ascetics. The texts were accessible only to monks and nuns, since only they had training in their language and understood their technical subject-matter; Jain laypeople had little concern with them. However, in time there developed a body of literature which was accessible to both ascetics and laypeople.

Jain narrative literature

When Jain monks were preaching to laypeople they used popular stories to illustrate the truths of the Jain religion. In many cases the stories were well-known folk-tales to which a Jain moral was added. Eventually the stories were gathered into the written collections to which Western scholars have given the generic name Jain narrative (*kathā*) literature. Similar collections of stories were gathered by Buddhists and Hindus, and it is not unusual for the same story to appear in Jain, Buddhist, and Hindu collections, with its moral changed to suit its context. The primary purpose of Jain narrative literature was to edify through amusement; consequently the stories are racy, and in some cases the moralizing element is rather tenuous. Edifying stories were incorporated into the commentarial literature which developed in exegesis of the canonical texts. In particular, the commentaries on the *Obligatory Duties* (*Āvaśyaka Sūtra*), one of the Basic Scriptures, which contains material on the obligatory ritual actions to be performed by Jain ascetics, became repositories of such stories. The earliest commentary on the text, composed in the second or third centuries AD, consists of about 2,000 mnemonic verses in

[6] Prakrit, meaning 'artless' or 'unrefined', is the generic name given to the various dialects of Middle Indo-Aryan. In contrast, Sanskrit means 'refined' or 'elaborated'.

Prakrit (*niryukti*). Later, commentaries in prose were composed. A prose commentary in Prakrit (*cūrṇi*) is attributed to the monk Jinadāsa (?7th cent. AD) and a prose commentary in Sanskrit (*ṭīkā*) to Haribhadra (?7th or 8th cent. AD). Later authors used the prose commentaries on the *Obligatory Duties* as a source for the preparation of independent anthologies or 'treasuries' (*kośas*) of didactic stories and for the composition of biographies of important figures in Jainism.

Jain biographical literature is concerned with Fordmakers, kings, and exemplary ascetics and laypeople. The biographies are called deeds (*caritras*) or compositions (*prabhandas*); the latter term tends to be applied to the lives of Jain monks or laypeople who lived after Vajra, but the distinction is not rigidly observed. Sometimes the lives of figures who were not directly connected with Jainism came to be incorporated in this literature. The life stories are not historical biographies, although they are set in a historical past. In many cases, the biographies are formed from blocks of shorter stories which cluster around a particular figure and define the significant moments of his life.

Another feature of the biographies is their concern with the past and future lives of their subjects. The fate of the embodied soul is of fundamental importance for Jainism, and there developed a genre of soul biography, in which the adventures of a soul are related through the course of several of its embodiments. The soul biographies usually relate the stories of a pair of souls, which are reunited and react with each other over a series of parallel lifetimes.

Eventually individual biographies of the important figures in Jainism were joined together to form continuous stories covering vast periods of time, hence Western scholars have given the name 'universal history' to the genre. The earliest examples of the genre are written in literary Prakrits, but the latest and fullest version is Hemacandra's Sanskrit *The Lives of the Sixty-three Illustrious People*.

The Lives of the Sixty-three Illustrious People

The Lives of the Jain Elders (*Sthavirāvalīcaritra*) is subtitled *The Appendix* (*Pariśiṣṭaparvan*), because, although complete in itself, it serves as the sequel to a much larger work, Hemacandra's *The Lives of the Sixty-three Illustrious People* (*Triṣaṣṭiśalākāpuruṣacaritra*),[7] which, as its title suggests, relates the stories of key figures in Jainism. Most important are the twenty-four Fordmakers. Bharata is subject to a perpetual time cycle of successive decay and regeneration, and Fordmakers are only born in the period when there is a balance between good and bad conditions, for only then can humans benefit from their preaching; before, conditions are too pleasant, afterwards, as in the present era, too unpleasant. During the period when good and bad are balanced, a series of twenty-four Fordmakers arises, separated from each other by decreasing eras of time; there are billions of years between the first and the second Fordmaker, but only 250 years between the twenty-third and the twenty-fourth. Since the universe is uncreated and eternal, there has been an infinite number of Fordmakers in the past, and there will be an infinite number in the future. Even though *The Lives of the Sixty-three Illustrious People* is concerned only with the lives of the last twenty-four Fordmakers, the time scale covered by the work is immense. During that time, as well as the twenty-four Fordmakers, there also arises a succession of twelve universal emperors (Cakravartins) who each extend their imperium over the whole of Bharata and a succession of nine kings who rule half of Bharata (Vāsudevas). Each of the nine kings has a brother who is lord of the other half of the country. The nine kings are each opposed by an enemy (Prativāsudeva) whom they succeed in destroying. These, together with the twenty-four Fordmakers, are the sixty-three illustrious people.

Leaving aside the Fordmakers, many of the sixty-three illustrious people are well-known characters of Hindu mythology. Indeed, in *The Lives of the Sixty-three Illustrious People* there is both a wholescale appropriation of Hindu mythology, which is placed in a Jain context, and an attempt to validate Hindu social custom in the light of Jain mythology. For example, Hemacandra incorporates into his text a Jain version of the Hindu epic poem the Rāmayaṇa, whose hero, Rāma, is presented as one of the Vāsudevas, and a Jain version of the life of the Hindu god Kṛṣṇa, also a Vāsudeva. Furthermore, according to Hemacandra, even the Vedas were originally a Jain text:

[7] The preparation of an English translation of its immense text was the life's work of the America scholar Helen Johnson, in her *Triṣaṣṭiśalākāpuruṣacaritra or The Lives of Sixty-three Illustrious Persons by Ācārya Śrī Hemacandra* (Baroda, 1931–62: Gaekwad's Oriental Series).

composed by Bharata, the first universal emperor, after whom the Indian subcontinent takes its name of Bharata, they consisted of hymns of praise to the Fordmakers and instruction in the Jain religion; it was only later that their contents were altered and perverted by unscrupulous Brahmin sages.[8]

The Lives of the Sixty-three Illustrious People is thus an all-inclusive history of Bharata over a vast section of the perpetual cycle of time. Since the Fordmakers are omniscient, every event in the past, present, and future of the entire universe is known to them. In the final dedicatory section of *The Lives of the Sixty-three Illustrious People* the reader is informed that it was composed by Hemacandra at the request of his patron, King Kumārapāla. In the main body of the text Hemacandra's meeting with that king is prophesied by Mahāvīra: the Fordmaker informs the son of his patron, King Śreṇika, that Kumārapāla will be prompted by Hemacandra's teaching to become a patron of the Jain religion. Mahāvīra also relates the names of the next sixty-three illustrious people who will arise in the future when the temporal conditions are once more propitious for their existence: the first of the future Fordmakers, Padmanābha, will be the final embodiment of the soul of none other than Mahāvīra's patron King Śreṇika! Thus, the author, the work, and events of the past, present, and future, are all linked in a continuum of unfolding time.

The Lives of the Jain Elders

Mahāvīra's prophecies form a connection between *The Lives of the Sixty-three Illustrious People* and *The Lives of the Jain Elders*; in the last canto of the former he foretells the names of the Jain elders and the gradual decline in religious knowledge and practice, and in the first canto of the latter he narrates to King Prasannacandra the previous lives of the Jain elder Jambū. Thus, there is continuity between the two works, but *The Lives of the Jain Elders* can be read and enjoyed without any prior knowledge of the contents of *The Lives of the Sixty-three Illustrious People*.

The earliest listing of the lineage of Jain elders is given in *The Guide Book* (*Kalpa Sūtra*), a chapter of the *Ten Chapters of*

[8] Ibid. i. 344f.

Teachings (*Daśāśrutaskandha*), one of the Demotion Scriptures. *The Guide Book* is a guide for monastic observance during the retreat held in the monsoon season, and it is still recited annually at the Abiding Festival which is held at that time of the year. It contains the rules which monks have to observe during the festival, lives of the Fordmakers, and lineages of the Jain elders who succeeded the Supporters of the Flock. The lineages of Jain elders given in *The Guide Book* are bare lists of pupillary succession devoid of any biographical material. Nevertheless, the lists of Jain elders are of great importance for White Clad ascetics. By the time Hemacandra was writing, the ascetics of the White Clad tradition were divided into small groups or chapters (*gacchas*) which traced their origins to one of four lineages of 'families' (*kulas*) of monastic succession, each founded by one of the four pupils of Vajra.[9] Validation of the groups' beliefs and practices was provided by their possession of a lineage of pupillary succession which linked them to one of Vajra's pupils, and hence through the lineage of Jain elders to the Supporter of the Flock Sudharman, who transmitted the sacred teachings to his pupil the Jain elder Jambū.

Hemacandra's continuous narrative of the Jain elders' lives is formed from stories which he links to the lineage of their pupillary succession. His two main sources were *The Life of Jambū* (*Jambucariyaṃ*) of Guṇapāla (?8th–9th cent. AD) and stories taken from the commentaries on the *Obligatory Duties*.[10] *The Life of Jambū* is written in a literary Prakrit in a mixture of verse and prose, and is itself based on earlier source material, in particular the material taken from *The*

[9] The terminology of monastic organization is complex. The original term for a group of monks was *gaṇa*, but *gaccha* had become the more usual term by the time of Hemacandra. See the discussion in S. B. Deo, *History of Jaina Monachism* (Poona, 1956: Deccan College), 337 ff. For lists of the various groupings of both the White Clad and the Sky Clad Jains, see M. U. K. Jain, *Jaina Sects and Schools* (Delhi, 1975: Concept Publishing Company).

[10] Guṇapāla, *Jambucariyam*, ed. Muni Jinavijaya (Bombay, 1959: Singhi Jain Series). Jacobi, in the introduction to his edition of Sanskrit text, gives a synoptic table of the contents of *The Lives of the Jain Elders* with references to the sources of the stories (*Sthavirāvalīcarita* (Calcutta, 1932: Asiatic Society of Bengal), pp. viii–x). Jacobi's table is based on Leumann's analysis of the *Obligatory Duties* stories (E. Leumann, 1897). However, neither Jacobi nor Leumann was aware of Hemacandra's debt to Guṇapāla's *Jambucariyam*, which is known only from a single manuscript which had not been published at the time they were writing.

Wanderings of Vasudeva (*Vasudevahiṇḍi*),[11] a vast work in Prakrit prose, dating perhaps from as early as the third century AD, which is also the original source of much of the material eventually incorporated into *The Lives of the Sixty-three Illustrious People*. *The Life of Jambū* is Hemacandra's immediate source for the first four cantos of *The Lives of the Jain Elders*, that is, for nearly one-half of the entire work. Nevertheless, despite his reliance on earlier sources, Hemacandra is no mere scissors and paste author, for he continually enlivens his often rather drab source material with the deft skill of a highly competent literary stylist.

The historical background of The Lives of the Jain Elders

Hemacandra's biographies of the Jain elders are hagiographies in which the significant moments of the elders' lives are defined by legend, not by historical fact. However, Jain tradition preserved the memory of the kingdoms in which the Jain elders preached and of the rulers who gave them patronage. From this traditional material Hemacandra was able to form an idealized reconstruction of the society in which the Jain elders lived. Hemacandra depicts an urban society; the Jain elders wander from town to town, where they receive patronage from kings and wealthy merchants. This accords with the historical evidence; at the time when Mahāvīra was preaching, the Ganges valley region had not been long urbanized, and it has been argued persuasively that Jainism, Buddhism, and the other Striver religions had particular appeal for the newly rich traders and craftsmen of the new towns, people who failed to find affirmation for their social and religious aspirations in the hierarchical system of the Brahminical religion.[12]

Mahāvīra visited and preached in a number of kingdoms which bordered the Ganges valley. One of these kingdoms, Magadha, was

[11] For discussions of the contents of the *Vasudevahiṇḍi*, see L. Alsdorf, 'The Vasudevahiṇḍi, A Specimen of Archaic Jaina-Mahārāṣṭrī', *Bulletin of the School of Oriental and African Studies*, 8 (1935–7), 319–33; and J. Jain, *The Vasudevahiṇḍi: An Authentic Jain Version of the Bṛhatkathā* (Ahmedabad, 1977: L. D. Series).

[12] For a discussion of the connection between urbanization and the rise in popularity of the Striver religions, see Richard F. Gombrich, *Theravāda Buddhism: A Social History from Ancient Benares to Modern Colombo* (London, 1988: Routledge and Kegan Paul), 49–59.

to conquer the others and develop into an empire which dominated the whole of the Indian subcontinent except for the extreme south of the peninsula. The empire is known as the Mauryan empire from the name of its ruling dynasty. The bulk of *The Lives of the Jain Elders* is set in the period which saw the growth of Magadha and the heyday of the Mauryan empire, that is from about 480 to 220 BC. There is insufficient evidence to allow the dating and the course of political events of the earlier part of the period to be reconstructed with any certainty; for the Mauryan empire evidence provided by epigraphy and information related by Greek and Roman historians suggests that Candragupta, the first of the Mauryan emperors, came to power in about 318 BC, and that his grandson, Aśoka, ruled between about 268 and 235 BC.

In the first canto of *The Lives of the Jain Elders* Mahāvīra visits Rājagṛha, the capital of Magadha, where the king, Śreṇika, comes to pay him honour. Śreṇika, whose surname was Bimbisāra, is mentioned in Buddhist texts, in which he is portrayed as a patron of the Buddha. The contemporaneity of Śreṇika, the Buddha, and Mahāvīra is firmly attested, yet it is not possible to date them precisely. According to the traditional accounts of the White Clad Jains, Mahāvīra lived between 599 and 527 BC. The Buddha died at the age of 80, and historians used to think that event took place in either 486 or 483 BC. However, recent research shows that the Buddha died some eighty years later, in about 404 BC. Since the dating of Mahāvīra and King Śreṇika depends on a synchronicity with the dating of the Buddha, then they too must have lived in the fifth century BC. This later dating accords with the archaeological and numismatic evidence. Interestingly, a later dating for Mahāvīra is partially supported by Hemacandra, who does not follow the traditional dating of the White Clad Jains: in Canto Eight, verse 339, he states that Candragupta, the first Mauryan emperor, came to power 155 years after the death of Mahāvīra, thus placing that event in the 470s BC.

Jain, Buddhist, and Hindu sources all agree that the successors of Śreṇika were supplanted by the Nanda dynasty, and that the Nanda dynasty was in turn replaced by the Mauryans. However, although the sources are in agreement about the broad sequence of events, they give variant listings of rulers and assign different dates to them, thus making it impossible for the historian to reconstruct an exact chronology.[13] Hemacandra gives the following sequence of rulers: Śreṇika, Kūṇika, Udāyin, the nine Nandas, Candragupta, Aśoka, Samprati. The Jain elders, with the exception of the last two, lived during the period of these rulers, so the bulk of *The Lives of the Jain Elders* has a dramatic dating of roughly 480 to 200 BC.

The stories which Hemacandra tells about the kings who patronized the Jain elders are legend not history; historical reality may or may not underlie the legend. For instance, Buddhist tradition agrees with Hemacandra's statement that Udāyin transferred the capital of Magadha from Rājagṛha to Pāṭalīputra. Since the latter city is well attested as the capital of the Mauryan empire, Hemacandra's story may be based on historical fact. On the other hand, Hemacandra and some Buddhist sources agree that Aśoka's son Kuṇāla was blinded on the orders of his wicked step-mother; this story is probably legend.

Certainly historical is the spread of the Striver religions throughout the Indian subcontinent in the time of the Mauryas. Aśoka is remembered by the Buddhist sources as a patron of Buddhism, and the inscriptions which he had inscribed on rocks on pillars throughout his kingdom, in which he is concerned to promote the Striver ethic of non-violence, provide firm historical attestation of his patronage of the Striver religions and the spread of those religions throughout India. Aśoka probably learnt about the Striver religions through conversations with Buddhist monks. On the other hand, Jain legend remembers Aśoka's grandfather, Candragupta, and grandson, Samprati, as patrons of Jainism. According to Hemacandra, Samprati was responsible for sending missionaries to spread the Jain religion in the south. With Samprati the dramatic setting of *The Lives of the Jain Elders* moves from the Ganges valley to the west of India; most of the remainder of the poem is set in Avanti, a country in western India. This too reflects historical reality; after the time of the Mauryas, Jains began to migrate from their original heartland around the Ganges valley to the west and south of India,[14] areas which remain strongholds of the Jain religion to this day.

[13] For a synopsis of information given by the various sources, see É. Lamotte, *History of Indian Buddhism: From the Origins to the Śaka Era* (English trans., Louvain, 1988: Institut Orientaliste Louvain-la-Neuve), 85 ff.

[14] This migration was probably due to economic and political reasons. The successors of the Mauryas are remembered in Buddhist tradition as Brahmins who were

Death, rebirth, and liberation in The Lives of the Jain Elders

The ultimate goal of Jainism is the liberation of the soul (*jīva*) from the everlasting cycle of death and rebirth. Upon death, the soul is re-embodied almost immediately; in one of Hemacandra's stories a man is reborn in his own semen! There are four possible classes of embodiment for a soul: that of a god, a human, a hell being, or an animal or plant (animals or plants form a single class of embodiment). The condition of the soul's embodiment is determined by the amount and type of karma that has accrued to it in its previous life. Karma means action, and the Jains shared the belief that the ethical content of one's actions predetermined the status of one's future embodiment. In amplification of this belief, however, they developed the theory, unique to them, that karma is a fine material substance that somehow 'flows in' and clings to the soul, obscuring its natural qualities of bliss and omniscience, and causing and determining the nature of its embodiment. To gain final liberation from death and rebirth it is necessary to 'expunge' all the karma from one's soul; the only way to do this is through asceticism.

The drama of the soul's embodiment is played in the Jain universe: uncreated and eternal, it is a vast three-dimensional structure in the shape of a gigantic man standing with his arms akimbo. At the level of its chest and neck is the upper world, where the heavens are situated, the homes of the gods; at the level of its waist is the middle world, a flat disc on which are innumerable concentric rings of land separated from each other by oceans, its inner land masses being the home of human beings and animals and plants; below its waist are the hell grounds, the homes of the hell beings. The central island of the middle world is Rose-apple Tree Island, in which the continent of Bharata is situated; Bharata, the Indian subcontinent, is where the action of *The Lives of the Jain Elders* is set. Over the upper world is an upturned canopy above which the liberated souls (*siddhas*) live, in a state of permanent bliss and omniscience, never to be reborn.

persecutors of the Striver religions. Religious persecution may have stimulated the migration of Jains along the caravan routes which led from the Ganges valley to the west and south. Archaeological evidence from Mathurā, a city on the western caravan route, attests the popularity of Jainism and the wealth of its lay community in the first century AD. For a discussion of Mathurā in this period, see D. M. Srinivasan (ed.), *Mathurā: The Cultural Heritage* (New Delhi, 1989: Manohar).

The rules of rebirth are fairly simple: a human being can be reborn as another human being, or animal or plant in the middle world, as a god, or as a hell being. Life as a god or as a hell being is not permanent. Since the Jain universe is uncreated and self-existent there are no permanent, creator gods. A god may enjoy countless blissful years in heaven, but the time it spends there is determined by its karma; once the fruit of its karma has been used up, it falls from heaven to be reborn in the middle world. Likewise with hell beings; they may spend countless years in a hell, but once their time there is through, they too are reborn in the middle world. Even though life as a god is pleasant, it is not permanent and is not conducive to liberation. Only human beings can gain liberation, and the way for them to gain it is to lead the life of a Jain ascetic.

Ascetics and laypeople in The Lives of the Jain Elders

The purpose of the monastic life is to prevent the influx of new karma and to expunge the existent karma from the soul by means of asceticism. At his initiation ceremony the renunciant uproots his hair in five handfuls in imitation of Mahāvīra's renunciation, and takes five Great Vows which he has to follow for the rest of his life. The five vows are to avoid harming living beings, to abstain from falsehood, not to take what has not been given, to renounce sexual activity, and to abandon all possessions and attachment to sense objects. After taking the vows, the White Clad monk is given his characteristic white robe, a whisk-broom with which gently to remove living insects from his path, and a begging bowl in which to collect the gifts of food on which he will live. Having abandoned a fixed abode, Jain ascetics travel together in groups headed by a Teacher (Ācārya) who is responsible for monastic discipline and for the instruction of the monks. A life of harsh asceticism is not only the one path leading to final liberation from further rebirth; supernatural powers can also accrue to the monk who practises particularly harsh austerities, and the supernatural and magic powers possessed by Jain monks are the subject of many of the stories in *The Lives of the Jain Elders*.

The first of the five Great Vows, the vow of not harming (*ahiṃsā*), is the most important ethical precept in Jainism. The concern to avoid harm to living beings does not only apply to human beings and the higher animals; it is extended to insects, vegetable life, and even submicroscopic forms of life. Jain ascetics have to take great care in walking, lest they trample on plants, since they are thought to be inhabited by souls. In the monsoon season, when the ground teems with newly sprouting vegetation, Jain monks are forbidden to travel, because at that time it is impossible for them to avoid harming plants. Jain ascetics must avoid harming the invisible creatures which are thought to cluster together in the elements of earth, fire, water, and air; consequently they are forbidden to dig in the earth, to kindle or extinquish fires, to bathe in or to draw water, or to fan themselves. Severely circumscribed in their actions, Jain ascetics are thus absolutely dependent upon laypeople for the means of supporting life.

Jain laypeople provide subsistence for the ascetics, but it is the ascetics who confer a benefit on the laypeople, for the ascetics' begging for food allows the laypeople to display the primary lay virtue of religious generosity (*dāna*). From a very early period Jainism became a favoured religion of wealthy merchant communities, and the making of lavish donations for religious purposes allowed members of those communities to gain reputations for piety and probity. The building of Jain temples was funded by the donations of the lay community, and the worship of the images of the Fordmakers within the temples is largely a lay activity, since, lacking all possessions, Jain ascetics are unable to make gifts of worship to the images of the Fordmakers. In *The Lives of the Jain Elders* the poverty of the ascetics is contrasted with the wealth of the laypeople. Indeed, many of the names Hemacandra gives to the laypeople are formed with the element *dhana* meaning 'wealth'. Many of the laypeople in *The Lives of the Jain Elders* are stated to have taken lay vows, which are versions of the vows taken by ascetics modified in a way enabling them to be followed in the context of lay life. The virtues which the vows inculcate are those of abstinence, charity, and probity, and in later life the layperson is encouraged to gradually withdraw from worldly affairs, leading a life modelled on that of the ascetic. Nevertheless, the religious life of Jain laypeople centres on worship in the temple, pilgrimage, and festivals rather than on asceticism. Even though it is lived with abstinence and piety, the life of the layperson remains inferior to that of the ascetic, since only the life of the latter leads to final liberation.

The Lives of the Jain Elders *as literature*

The Lives of the Jain Elders is an epic poem, a *mahākāvya*, written in 3,460 verse couplets (*ślokas*) divided into thirteen cantos of unequal length.[15] Although much of his source material was found in popular stories which must have been familiar to all levels of society, Hemacandra, as a court poet, was writing for a learned, highly sophisticated audience. This is evident in his choice of language: Sanskrit had long ceased to be a natural language, acquired as a mother tongue; it had to be mastered by consciously learning the rules of the language as codified by the Sanskrit grammarians. Thus Sanskrit in the time of Hemacandra occupied a similar position in Indian culture to that of Latin in the European Middle Ages. Sanskrit, although a learned language, was by no means a 'dead' one; there developed complex theories of poetic technique and aesthetic appreciation, supported by a vast vocabulary which was particularly rich in synonyms and homonyms.

Hemacandra, a grammarian, lexicographer, and author of works on poetic theory, was able to make full use of the copious resources of the Sanskrit literary tradition. In *The Lives of the Jain Elders* he employs all the techniques of what the theorists called 'ornamentation' (*alaṃkāra*), a term which describes the poetic repertoire of simile and metaphor, punning, euphony, alliteration, gnomic generalization, and allusion. Allusion or reverberation (*dhvani*) is the name given to the process whereby the poet's skilful handling of assonance and the secondary meanings which cluster around Sanskrit words enables him to suggest more than the bare meaning of his words; Hemacandra is a master of this art. As a grammarian, Hemacandra is eager to display his knowledge of recondite grammatical forms, and as a lexicographer, he flaunts his knowledge of rare words, some of which are not otherwise attested in the entire corpus of Sanskrit literature. Hemacandra's mastery of the techniques of Sanskrit poetics is fully displayed in his ornate descriptions of such stock

[15] Sanskrit metres were quantitative, like the metres of classical Greek and Latin poetry, that is their rhythms were based on the order of long and short syllables and not on stress, as in most modern English verse. The *śloka* of thirty-two syllables divided into four feet of eight syllables was the usual metre of Sanskrit epic poetry. Hemacandra is innovative in his use of this metre in that he often omits the usual caesura or pause after the first and third feet, and sometimes uses unusual patterns of short and long syllables. See Jacobi, *Sthavirāvalīcarita*, pp. xxiff.

topics as cities, mountains, the seasons, sunrises and sunsets, and weddings, with which an epic poem was supposed to be embellished. In contrast to the flowery language of the more ornate parts of the poem, Hemacandra's language in the narrative portions is swift, terse, and humorous, and he creates an immediacy of situation which his often rather colourless source material tends to lack.

Of Hemacandra's literary skills, the one most readily appreciated by the modern reader, and certainly the easiest to convey in translation, is his skill in characterization. The stories in *The Lives of the Jain Elders* abound in memorable characters: Valkalacīrin who was so unworldly that he thought prostitutes were monks, crafty Durgilā who, although seen sleeping with another man by her father-in-law, was still able to deceive her husband, the Jain elder Jambū who, although surrounded by his eight beautiful newly married wives, preserved his vow of chastity, and many others besides.

With Hemacandra, the genre of Jain story literature reaches its culmination, and, for the White Clad Jains, *The Lives of the Jain Elders* became the standard synthesis of source material for the early history of Jainism. A formative influence in the cultural tradition of the White Clad Jains, Hemacandra is a key figure in the wider context of Sanskrit literature. *The Lives of the Jain Elders* is the work of one whose knowledge of Sanskrit, its language, literature, and literary techniques, has probably never been surpassed; as such it fully justifies its claim to be a World's Classic.

NOTE ON THE TEXT AND TRANSLATION

NO translation could possibly do justice to the richness of Hemacandra's language; to explain his puns and his use of the technique of reverberation would require such a vast array of notes that my object of preparing a translation for the non-specialist reader would be defeated. The full subtlety of Hemacandra's language can only be appreciated in the Sanskrit.[1] In my translation, I have attempted to reproduce the learned effect of Hemacandra's language by writing in a rather formal, Latinate idiom, while also trying to capture some of the speed and directness of his narrative. I have not attempted to write in verse. However, I have reproduced the verse format of Hemacandra's original text. Hemacandra's sense units are usually contained within a single verse, so I felt that a verse-format translation would give a truer impression of the original text than one in continuous prose.

The translation is based on Hermann Jacobi's second edition of the Sanskrit text, published in 1932.[2] By and large, the translation follows the order of Hemacandra's verse couplets. However, in some parts, in order to write intelligible English, I have deviated from Hemacandra's order, and this is indicated in the numbering of the verses; 'a' and 'b' refer respectively to the first and second lines of a verse couplet.

[1] I hope that this translation will inspire some readers to begin the demanding, but not impossible, task of learning Sanskrit. D. Killingley's Sanskrit course (*Beginning Sanskrit*, vol. i, Munich, 1996: Lincom Europa) provides a gentle introduction to the language. For those who prefer a brisker pace, there is M. Coulson, *Teach Yourself Sanskrit* (2nd edn., London, 1992: Hodder and Stoughton).

[2] Hermann Jacobi (ed.), *Sthavirāvalīcarita or Pariśiṣṭaparvan, being an Appendix of the Triṣaṣṭi-śalākāpuruṣacrita by Hemacandra* (2nd edn., Calcutta, 1932: Asiatic Society of Bengal).

NOTE ON THE PRONUNCIATION OF SANSKRIT WORDS AND PROPER NAMES

THE grammarians of ancient India developed systems of writing which are far more scientific than the relatively crude Roman alphabet, which has to be adapted to give an accurate representation of the Sanskrit sound system. The Sanskrit words and proper names in the text, notes, and introduction are printed with a system of diacritic marks devised by Western scholars to represent the sounds of Sanskrit when printed in Roman letters. I have followed the usual, but philologically suspect, practice of forming plurals of Sanskrit words by adding the English plural suffix '-s'. For fuller discussions of the Sanskrit sound system, see the Sanskrit courses by M. Coulson and D. H. Killingley listed in the bibliography.

Vowels

Long vowels are distinguished from short by the addition of a macron.

Pronounce Sanskrit	as in English
a	as in northern English *cat*
ā	as in *far*
i	as in *sit*
ī	as in *me*
u	as in *put*
ū	as in *too*
ṛ	as in *risk*
e	as in *pray*
ai	as in *aisle*
o	as in *hope*
au	as in *sound*

ḥ indicates a slight aspiration with an echo of the preceding vowel.

ṃ nasalizes the preceding vowel, as in French *bon*

Consonants

g	as in *go*
ṅ	as in *hang*
c	as in *church*
ñ	as in *punch*
ś	as in *shame*
ṣ	as in *dish*
s	as in *snake*

Dental and retroflex consonants

Indian languages distinguish between dental consonants, pronounced with the tongue striking the back of the teeth, and retroflex consonants, pronounced with the tongue striking the roof of the palate above the teeth. The dental consonants are t, th, d, dh, and n; the retroflex consonants are differentiated from the dental by the addition of a dot: ṭ, ṭh, etc.

Aspirated consonants

Aspiration is indicated by an 'h' following the consonant: the 'h' is not pronounced as a separate letter. Thus 'kh' is pronounced as in *inkhorn*; 'th' as in *hothouse* and not as in *with*; and 'ph' as in *shepherd* and not as in *phone*. The aspirated consonants are kh, gh, ch, jh, ṭh, ḍh, th, dh, ph, and bh.

Masculine proper names usually end with a short vowel, female with a long. Thus, Kuberadatta is a boy and Kuberadattā a girl.

SELECT BIBLIOGRAPHY

Text and translation

The edition of the Sanskrit text of the *Lives of the Jain Elders* used in preparing this translation is: H. Jacobi (ed.), *Sthavirāvalīcarita or Pariśiṣṭaparvan, being an Appendix of the Triṣaṣṭi-śalākāpuruṣacrita by Hemacandra* (2nd edition, Calcutta, 1932: Asiatic Society of Bengal).

This Oxford World's Classics translation is the first complete translation of *The Lives of the Jain Elders* into any European language. Jacobi's edition of the Sanskrit text contains a short English précis. There is a German translation, based on Jacobi's first edition, of selected portions of the text: J. Hertel, *Ausgewählte Erzählungen aus Hemacandras Pariśiṣṭaparvan* (Leipzig, 1908: Bibliothek morganländischer Erzähler). There is an English translation of the section relating the story of Candragupta and Cāṇakya (8. 194 to 9. 13): R. Lefeber, 'Hemacandra's Pariśiṣṭaparva: The Story of Cāṇakya', in P. Granoff (ed.), *The Clever Adulteress and Other Stories: A Treasury of Jain Literature* (Oakville, Ont., 1990: Mosaic Press), 189–207.

A précis of the same section can be found in T. R. Trautmann, *Kauṭilya and the Arthaśāstra: A Statistical Investigation of the Authorship and Evolution of the Text* (Leiden, 1971: E. J. Brill), 21–5.

Hemacandra's other works

References to *The Lives of the Sixty-three Illustrious People* are to Helen Johnson's English translation: H. M. Johnson, *Triṣaṣṭiśalākāpuruṣacaritra or The Lives of Sixty-three Illustrious Persons by Ācārya Śrī Hemacandra* (Baroda, 1931–62: Gaekwad's Oriental Series). For an English translation of *The Conduct Manual* (*Yogaśāstra*), together with its Sanskrit text, see A. S. Gopani, *The Yoga Shastra of Hemacandracharya: A 12th Century Guide to Jaiṇ Yoga* (Jaipur, 1989: Prakrit Bharti Academy).

For bibliographical details of Hemacandra's other works, see: M. Maji, 'A Comprehensive List of the Published Works of Hemacandra', *Jain Journal*, 2 (1968), 262–74.

The life of Hemacandra

The standard work is: G. Bühler, *Über das Leben des Jaina Mõnches Hemacandra* (Vienna, 1889: Kaiserlichen Akademie der Wissenschaften). There is an English translation of the above which contains additional prefatory material: M. Patel (trans.), *The Life of Hemacandrācārya by Professor Dr. G. Bühler* (Śāntiniketan, 1936: Singhi Jaina Series). See also J. P.

Sharma, 'Hemacandra: The Life and Scholarship of a Jaina Monk', *Asian Profile*, 3 (1974), 195–215.

Jainism

There are two standard introductions. Both contain excellent bibliographies: P. Dundas, *The Jains* (London, 1992: Routledge); P. S. Jaini, *The Jaina Path of Purification* (Berkeley, 1979: University of California).

Long before the time of Hemacandra, Jain doctrine had been summarized into 350 short mnemonic sentences in Sanskrit by Umāsvāti, who lived sometime between AD 150 and 350. Later commentaries on and amplifications of Umāsvāti's *Mnemonic Rules Concerning the Nature of Reality* (*Tattvārtha Sūtra*) provide encyclopedic surveys of every aspect of Jain doctrine. An accessible modern commentary, which gives the Sanskrit text of the *Tattvārtha Sūtra*, is: K. K. Dixit (trans.), *Pt Sukhlalji's Commentary on Tattvārtha Sūtra of Vācaka Umāsvāti* (Ahmedabad, 1974: L. D. Series). For the doctrinal development of early Jainism, see: W. J. Johnson, *Harmless Souls: Karmic Bondage and Religious Change in Early Jainism with Special Reference to Umāsvāti and Kundakunda* (Delhi, 1995: Motilal Banarsidass). For Jain monastic organization, see: S. B. Deo, *History of Jaina Monachism* (Poona, 1956: Deccan College); M. U. K. Jain, *Jaina Sects and Schools* (Delhi, 1975: Concept Publishing Company). Jain texts which describe the religious duties to be undertaken by Jain laypeople are discussed in: R. Williams, *Jaina Yoga: A Survey of the Mediaeval Śrāvakācāras* (Oxford, 1963: Oxford University Press). For a beautifully illustrated description of the Jain universe, see: C. Caillat and R. Kumar, *The Jain Cosmology* (Basle, 1981: Ravi Kumar).

The following are English translations of Jain canonical texts cited in the notes and introduction: H. Jacobi (ed.), *Jaina Sutras*, 1 and 2 (Oxford, 1884, 1895: Sacred Books of the East; reprinted Delhi, 1989: Motilal Banarsidass); K. C. Lalwani (trans. and ed.), *Ārya Sayyambhava's Daśavaikālika Sūtra* (Delhi, 1973: Motilal Banarsidass).

Jain story literature

For a selection of lively English translations of excerpts from Jain story literature, see: P. Granoff (ed.), *The Clever Adulteress and Other Stories: A Treasury of Jain Literature* (Oakville, 1990: Mosaic Press). For a discussion of the stories in the prose commentaries on the *Obligatory Duties*, see: E. Leumann, *Übersicht über die Āvaśyaka-Literatur* (Hamburg, 1934: De Gruyter). For the Prakrit text of *The Life of Jambū*, important as one of Hemacandra's major sources for *The Lives of the Jain Elders*, see: Guṇapāla, *Jambucariyam*, ed. Muni Jinavijaya (Bombay, 1959: Singhi Jain Series). For the *Wanderings of Vasudeva*, another important source, see: L.

Alsdorf, 'The Vasudevahiṇḍi, A Specimen of Archaic Jaina-Mahārāṣṭrī', *Bulletin of the School of Oriental and African Studies*, 8 (1935–7), 319–33; J. Jain, *The Vasudevahiṇḍi: An Authentic Jain Version of the Bhatkathā* (Ahmedabad, 1977: L. D. Series).

Ancient and medieval India

The best one-volume survey of the history and culture of ancient and medieval India is: A. L. Basham, *The Wonder that was India: A Survey of the History and Culture of the Indian Subcontinent before the Coming of the Muslims* (3rd edn., London, 1985: Sidgwick & Jackson). There is a good discussion of the social background of the origins and early development of the Striver religions in: R. F. Gombrich, *Theravāda Buddhism: A Social History from Ancient Benares to Modern Colombo* (London, 1988: Routledge and Kegan Paul).

For a very full survey of the various sources for the dynastic and political history of ancient India, see: É. Lamotte, *History of Indian Buddhism: From the Origins to the Śaka Era* (English trans.), Louvain, 1988: Institut Orientaliste Louvain-la-Neuve).

For the archaeological evidence for the patronage of Jainism in an ancient city of north-western India, see: D. M. Srinivasan (ed.), *Mathurā: The Cultural Heritage* (New Delhi, 1989: Manohar).

For Gujarat in the time of Hemacandra, see: A. K. Majumdar, *Chaulukyas of Gujarat* (Bombay, 1956: Bharatiya Vidya Bhavan); M. R. Majmudar, *Cultural History of Gujarat from Early Times to the Pre-British Period* (Bombay, 1964: Popular Prakashan).

Sanskrit: language and literature

There are excellent introductory chapters on Sanskrit language and literature in A. L. Basham's *The Wonder that was India* cited above. While working on his edition of the Sanskrit text of *The Lives of the Jain Elders*, Jacobi prepared a list of Hemacandra's more unusual words and usages. The translator is grateful that Jacobi's list was incorporated into the standard Sanskrit–English dictionary, which is: M. Monier-Williams, *A Sanskrit–English Dictionary* (Oxford, 1899: Oxford University Press). The most comprehensive Sanskrit grammar in English is: W. D. Whitney, *Sanskrit Grammar* (5th edn., Leipzig 1924, repr. Delhi, 1983: Motilal Banarsidass). More concise is: A. A. Macdonell, *A Sanskrit Grammar for Students* (Oxford, 1927: Oxford University Press; repr. 1987).

For a philological history of Sanskrit, see: T. Burrow, *The Sanskrit Language* (London, 1955: Faber and Faber). For Sanskrit poetical theory, see: P. V. Kane, *History of Sanskrit Poetics* (Bombay, 1961: Authore); P. K. Panda, *Concept of Dhvani in Sanskrit Poetics* (Delhi, 1988: Penman Publications). For learning Sanskrit, the following book is suitable for those who find assimilating the grammatical structure of languages a fairly easy task: M. Coulson, *Teach Yourself Sanskrit* (2nd edn., London, 1992: Hodder and Stoughton). For those whose grammatical skills are less sure, the following book is highly recommended: D. Killingley, *Beginning Sanskrit*, vol. i (Munich, 1996: Lincom Europa).

THE LIVES OF THE JAIN ELDERS

CANTO ONE

The main subject of Canto One is a description of the former lives of Jambū, the last person to gain omniscience. His final life is the subject of Cantos Two and Three.

The stories of the successive embodiments of the souls of the brothers Bhavadatta and Bhavadeva, related in this Canto, are an example of the Jain genre of soul biography mentioned in the introduction. This is a schematic representation of the course of the embodiments:

Bhavadatta	Bhavadeva
↓	↓
A god in the Saudharma heaven	Śakra, king of the Saudharma heaven
↓	↓
Prince Sāgaradatta	Prince Śiva
	↓
	Vidyunmālin, king of the Indra heaven
	↓
	Jambū

The structure of Canto One is complex; much of it is in the form of stories told by the Fordmaker Mahāvīra to Śreṇika, king of Magadha. The reader may find the following précis a useful guide:

1–6 After a short salutation and blessing, Hemacandra announces his intention of relating the Lives of the Jain Elders.

7–28 There follows an elaborate description of Magadha, its capital Rājagṛha, and its king, Śreṇika.

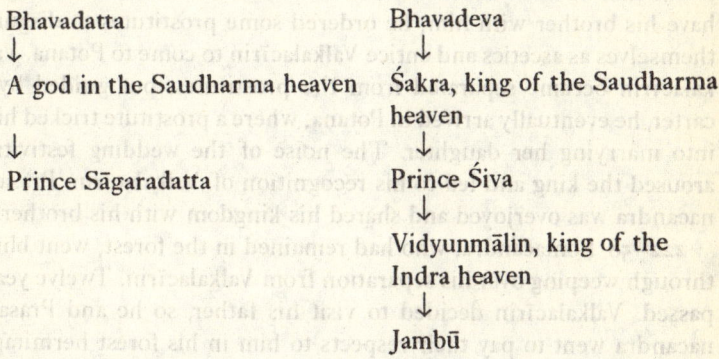

29–65 One day, the Fordmaker Mahāvīra held a preaching assembly near Rājagṛha, which Śreṇika set out to attend. On the way, two of Śreṇika's guards saw the former king Prasannacandra, who had abandoned his kingdom to become a monk, standing in a trance of meditation. When Prasannacandra overheard one of the guards say that the son to whom he had entrusted his kingdom would be murdered by his ministers, his meditation trance was broken, and he imagined that he was slaying the treacherous ministers. However, Prasannacandra recovered himself, and regained his equanimity.

66–128 After Śreṇika had paid his respects to Mahāvīra, the Ford-maker related the story of Prasannacandra's former life:

Somacandra was king of Potana. One day, after his wife Dhāriṇī had noticed a grey hair on his head, he decided to hand over his kingdom to his son Prasannacandra and to live the life of an ascetic in the forest. Dhāriṇī accompanied Somacandra to the forest, where she gave birth to a son, Valkalacīrin. Unfortunately, his mother died while giving birth to him, so Valkalacīrin grew up without seeing any women and knowing little of the world.

129–221 Meanwhile, Prasannacandra, who was ruling in Potana, learnt that he had a brother who was living in the forest. Wishing to have his brother with him, he ordered some prostitutes to disguise themselves as ascetics and entice Valkalacīrin to come to Potana. Valkalacīrin became separated from the prostitutes, but guided by a carter, he eventually arrived in Potana, where a prostitute tricked him into marrying her daughter. The noise of the wedding festivities aroused the king and led to his recognition of Valkalacīrin. Prasannacandra was overjoyed and shared his kingdom with his brother.

222–58 Somacandra, who had remained in the forest, went blind through weeping over his separation from Valkalacīrin. Twelve years passed. Valkalacīrin decided to visit his father, so he and Prasannacandra went to pay their respects to him in his forest hermitage. As Valkalacīrin cleaned his father's ascetic implements, he suddenly remembered that he had been a Jain monk in his former life. He suddenly gained omniscience, and a god presented him with the habit of a Jain monk. Valkalacīrin then instructed his father and his brother in the Jain religion. Mahāvīra concluded the story of Prasannacandra by informing King Śreṇika that he himself initiated Prasannacandra as a Jain monk, who then entrusted his kingdom to his young son.

259–66 As Mahāvīra finished speaking, Śreṇika saw a great assembly of gods in the sky and asked the reason for it. Mahāvīra replied that it was to celebrate Prasannacandra's gaining of omniscience. Śreṇika then asked who would be the last to gain omniscience, and Mahāvīra replied that in seven days' time the god Vidyunmālin, accompanied by his four wives, would fall from heaven and be reborn in Rājagṛha as Jambū, the son of the merchant Ṛṣabhadatta, and that Jambū would be the last to gain omniscience.

267–85 Suddenly, a god called Anādṛta, the lord of Rose-apple Tree Island, began to praise his family in a very loud voice. When Śreṇika asked the reason for this, Mahāvīra explained that in Rājagṛha lived a merchant who had two sons, Ṛṣabhadatta and Jinadāsa. The former was sensible, but Jinadāsa was addicted to gambling so Ṛṣabhadatta renounced him. Jinadāsa was mortally wounded in a gamblers' quarrell. As Jinadāsa lay dying Ṛṣabhadatta gave him instruction in the Jain religion as a result of which Jinadāsa was reborn as the god Anādṛta. He began to praise his family when he overheard Mahāvīra say that Ṛṣabhadatta, his brother in his former life, would be the father of the last omniscient one.

286–389 Then Śreṇika asked why the appearance of Vidyunmālin, who was among the gods assembled in the sky, was so splendid. Mahāvīra related:

In a village in Magadha lived two brothers Bhavadatta and Bhavadeva. Bhavadatta had become a Jain monk while still a young man. As a result of a challenge of his fellow monks, Bhavadatta tricked Bhavadeva into becoming a monk, just as he was about to be married. Years passed. Bhavadatta died and became a god in the Saudharma heaven. Then Bhavadeva remembered the girl he had abandoned on his wedding day, and decided to seek her out and live the life of a householder with her. However, when they were reunited, she convinced Bhavadeva to remain steadfast in his vows. Bhavadeva died and became the chief god of the Saudharma heaven.

390–418 When Bhavadatta's time as a god was over, he was reborn as Sāgaradatta, the son of Vajradatta and Yaśodharā, the king and queen of Videha. He enjoyed the pleasures of a prince, but one day he realized that human pleasures were transient, and became a Jain monk.

419–69 When Bhavadeva's soul fell from heaven, he was reborn as Śiva, son of King Padmaratha and Queen Vanamālā. One day, the monk Sāgaradatta was preaching in the vicinity, and told Śiva about their former lives. Śiva wanted to become a Jain monk, but his parents refused their permission, so he remained at home, living the life of an ascetic. When Śiva died, he became the god Vidyunmālin, the king of the Brahma heaven. Mahāvīra concluded his narrative by once more informing Śreṇika that in seven days' time

Vidyunmālin would fall from heaven to be reborn as Jambū, the last omniscient one.

470–4 Then, as the god Vidyunmālin paid his respects to Prasannacandra, Vidyunmālin's four wives asked the ascetic whether they would be reunited with their husband in their next lives. Prasannacandra confirmed they would. Mahāvīra then left to go elsewhere.

1 Salutation to holy Mahāvīra the Worthy, whose glory is wonderful, a royal flamingo on the lake of joy at final emancipation!

2 We reflect upon blessed Mahāvīra, the omniscient one, god over gods, the original inspiration for the holy beings in the highest stages.*

3 I bow to the holy scion of the Jñātṛ clan, a grove of auspicious wish-granting trees, a Himalaya and a Ganges of religious learning, a sun for the day-lotus of the world.

4 May the words of holy Lord Mahāvīra's teachings protect you; they are like waters washing away impurities from the hearts of sentient beings.

5 Having composed the Lives of the Sixty-three Great People, I shall now continue with its Appendix.

6 In it is related the story of the Jain elders from Jambū onwards; it is like a string of pure white pearls to adorn the neck of the universe.

7 In the southern part of Bharata, here in this Rose-apple Tree Island, is a country called Magadha, an ornament for the face of the earth.

8 In that country, the cowsheds are like villages, and the villages are like towns. The cities rival the cities of the gods in their remarkable prosperity.

9 In that country, when the crop has been cut one time and harvested by the farmers, it immediately grows again, like grass.

10 In that country, the people live contentedly, free from ill-health and free from fear. They are very handsome, as if born at auspicious moments.

11 In that country, the cows are docile, their udders always full of flowing milk. They yield milk day and night; they are like wish-granting cows.

12 In that country, the earth is everywhere fertile, since the clouds produce rain in the proper season. The people are very pious; the country is like an abode of religion.

13 In that country the capital city, a pleasure house of prosperity, is called Rājagṛha. It is as if the entire wealth of the southern part of Bharata were deposited there.

14 In that city, the flashes of light from the golden banners and vessels in the temples kindle the rivalry of the lightning in the clouds which settle during the rainy season.

15 In that city, at night the moon as it beams into the houses which are like moonstones is like an open silver dish full of musk unguent.

16 In that city, the city wall shines like gold. It is like the preaching enclosure built by the gods when a Worthy gains omniscience.

17 In that city is an oblong lake with fresh flowing water. The rays of light flashing from the jewelled steps at two of its sides meet together; it looks as if a bridge had been built over the lake.

18 In the mansions of that city, whose sole government is the Jain religion, young girls even teach the parrots which they keep for their amusement to recite hymns of praise to the Worthies.

19 In that city, at night the light of the stars as it touches the pinnacles of the lofty Jain temples is divided among their golden pots.

20 In that city, the city wall shines with its coping of gold and silver like a mountain which transcends the world of mortals, with the light of the moon reflected on it.

21 In that city, the breeze perfumed by the fragrance of the incense burnt in the dwelling houses delights the magical nymphs, as it clings to their bodies like a lover.

22 In that city, his glory formed by his merchant guilds, ruled King Śreṇika. Like a skilled guide, he brought prosperity to the earth by means of his excellent qualities.

23 The light of truth spread within his heart; there was not the slightest room for the gloom of falsehood.

24 The hymn of his praises gives joy to the gods, like another kind of nectar to be drunk by the ear, when it is sung in their assembly by the nymphs.

25 As he moved against them in a contrary direction, like a malevolent planet, everywhere the hostile attempts of his antagonists came to naught.

26 The king's power was unbroken, he was like Indra the king of the gods. The earth was under his sole dominion, as the sky is under that of the moon.

27 He was naturally endowed with such virtues as nobility, constancy, depth of character, and valour; they were like auspicious birthmarks on his body.

28 A mighty hero, he established his sole rule over the earth. No one failed to obey his command, which was like the thunderbolt of Indra.

29 One day, by the shrine called 'Rock of Excellence' which is near that city, holy Mahāvīra, attended by gods and demigods, held a preaching assembly.

30 There the gods built an assembly place adorned with three concentric walls made of silver, gold, and jewels.

31 At its centre the gods fashioned an Aśoka tree; as its branches were wafted upwards by the breeze, it seemed to be issuing an invitation to all living creatures.

32 Looking like Mount Meru in human form, shining with the luster of pure gold, Lord Mahāvīra entered the assembly place by its eastern entrance.

33 As was fitting, the Lord, as a swan graces a lotus, graced the lion-throne which, at the desire of the gods, had been placed under the Aśoka tree.

34 The fourfold congregation* sat in their appropriate places, and the Lord began to preach the doctrine of the Jain religion; it was like a shower of nectar.

35 The inhabitants of that place ran as quickly as leaping deer to inform the king that the Lord was holding a preaching assembly there.

36 When the king drank the nectar of the news of the Lord's arrival, the hairs of his body bristled with joy; it looked as if it had been pierced by thorns.

37 The king of Magadha rose from his throne and removed his shoes. He bowed his head to the ground, and concentrated on the Lord.

38 Then the king rewarded the people who had told him of the

Lord's arrival with a heap of gold in payment of the debt he owed them.

39 The king put on a pair of fringed upper and lower garments, suitable for paying a visit to a Worthy; they looked as if they had been woven with billows from an ocean of milk.

40 Resplendent in his crown and many other jewelled ornaments, the king of Rājagṛha looked like a wish-granting tree.

41 The horses and elephants which stood ready at the palace gates quickly approached at the king's command, like kinsmen attracted by prosperity.

42 The eminent king mounted his chief elephant, the maker of good fortune. The glorious king looked like the sun mounting the eastern mountain.

43 The king's elephant was escorted by the other elephants; their temples were red with fresh vermilion and their trunks decorated with patterns of red chalk.

44 The lord of the earth filled the sky with the sound of elephant bells as he set forth, eager to visit the Lord of the Ford.

45 The sound of the trumpeting elephants, neighing horses, and rattling carriages reached the surface of the sky, so that the atmosphere became its own characteristic.*

46 Two guards were advancing in front of the king. They saw a monk. He was alone, single-minded in concentration, standing on one foot, like a tree supported by its single trunk.

47 His two arms were raised aloft, as if to drag down the home of the perfected souls,* and his downcast eyes were fixed motionless on the sun, as if on a mirror.

48 Because of the drops of sweat produced by the heat of the sun, he looked as if he were covered in boils. His essence was freedom from passion; he was like an image of tranquillity.

49 One of the guards said, 'Ah, this is an elephant of a monk! We must pay our respects to this great soul who is practising harsh austerities.

50 Who would stand on one foot? Who would constantly gaze at the disc of the sun like that? Oh, what a performer of difficult austerities!

51 This great-souled one is not far from final emancipation or heaven. What does harsh asceticism not achieve! It even attains the unattainable.'

52 But the other said, 'You don't understand, comrade. This is

King Prasannacandra. He has no religious merit; his asceticism is vain.

53 He has entrusted his kingdom to his young son, but the king's ministers will make the boy fall from power, like an unripe fruit falling from a tree.

54 And the king has left his kingdom to the protection of those wicked ministers, as if leaving cream to the protection of cats.

55 With the extirpation of this child, this king's lineage will be completely finished, for he sinned irremediably by murdering his own elder brothers.

56 As for his wives whom he abandoned in his eagerness to become a wandering ascetic, I don't know how they will survive, deprived of their husband.'

57 These words carried by the wind entered the cavity of the ascetic Prasannacandra's ear, and his meditation trance was broken.

58 The royal ascetic thought, 'Ah, the faith I placed in my wicked ministers turns out to be an offering placed in flames!

59 My young son is about to be deprived of his kingdom by these false, malevolent ministers. Fie upon these murderers in whom I placed my confidence!

60 If I were there now, I would chastise these wicked ministers with ever-renewed punishments.

61 What use is my life? What use is this harsh asceticism of mine, now that I have heard that my son is to be overthrown?'

62 In this way the royal ascetic's thoughts became increasingly malevolent. Full of anger, he forgot about his vows of asceticism.

63 Following the maxim of the lion's backward look,* lapped by the flames of his military glory, he visualized those ministers, the enemies of his son, as if they were actually present.

64 The only protagonist in the theatre of battle, as in the old days he imagined that he was slicing them into pieces with his sword, as if they were cucumbers.

65 Blinded by anger, the royal ascetic sliced and chopped them. What cruel punishments did he not inflict upon the ministers?

66 At that moment, the king of Rājagṛha, a bird for the tree of religion taught by the Jina, came to that place.

67 When that elephant of kings saw the monk, he alighted from his

elephant, and, as he bowed before him, decorated his forehead with the dust from the ground.

68 Seeing the monk standing on one leg with his arms in the air, the king was absolutely delighted and loudly applauded his unrivalled asceticism.

69 Then, thinking that King Prasannacandra the ascetic was engaged in a remarkable trance of meditation, the king came to the presence of the Jina, the Teacher of the Universe.

70 The king of kings bowed to the Lord, touching the earth with his head, hands, and feet. He sat in an appropriate place, and placed his hands together in respectful salutation, his fingers arranged like the petals of a lotus flower.

71 Then, at a suitable moment, the crest-jewel of lords of the world bowed to the Lord of the Universe. He covered his mouth with the edge of his garment, and asked:

72 'If the royal ascetic Prasannacandra had died while absorbed in meditation at the time when I saw him, please tell me in what state would he have been reborn?'

73 The Lord replied, 'If he had died at that moment, King Prasannacandra, the royal ascetic, would have gone to the seventh hell ground.'

74 The right-minded royal Jain layman thought, 'What! Can such a rebirth accrue to that great ascetic whose austerities are so harsh?'

75 Once more, the king asked, 'If that great ascetic were to die now, what rebirth would he attain?'

76 The Lord replied, 'Your majesty, that royal ascetic whose austerities are so harsh is now in every respect fit to attain final emancipation.'

77 The king said, 'Reverend sir, what does this twofold answer mean? Explain it to me in my ignorance. How can the words of an omniscient one be in vain?'

78 The Lord replied, 'Your majesty, at the time when you paid your respects to that royal ascetic, he was engaged in violent meditation, but now his meditation is pure.

79 At that time, engrossed in violent meditation, he was worthy of hell, but now, engrossed in pure meditation, he is certainly worthy of final emancipation.'

80 Then Śreṇika asked the Worthy, that sun for the enlightenment

of the world, 'How did his meditation become violent, why is it now pure?'

81 The Lord replied, 'He learnt from a soldier in your advance guard that his son would be overcome by his own ministers.

82 Affected by his attachment for his son, Prasannacandra forgot his vow, and imagined that he was fighting with those cruel ministers.

83 Imagining that he was actually fighting with them sword in hand, Prasannacandra's tranquillity was dissolved by anger.

84 He examined his weapons, and thought angrily, "I'll kill them with my helmet. Everything is a weapon against the wicked."

85 As he put his hand on his head in order to remove his helmet, he felt the stubble of his plucked-out hair and remembered the vow he had taken.

86 He thought, "Alas, I've become engaged in violent meditation! What is my son and what are those ministers to me, since I am free from the ties of attachment?"

87 As he thought this, the brilliant sun of true discrimination appeared once more in the gloom of the delusion in which he had been absorbed.

88 In that very place he bowed devotedly, as if I were standing before him. He reflected, and returned to a state of auspicious meditation.

89 The firebrand of the royal ascetic Prasannacandra's pure meditation quickly burned the dead wood of his karma which had grown in the forest of violent meditation.'

90 Perfumed by the fragrance of the royal ascetic's behaviour, Śreṇika, strong in religion, asked holy Mahāvīra:

91 'Reverend sir, why did King Prasannacandra set his young son over his kingdom and take initiation as a monk?'

92 Holy Mahāvīra said, 'Your majesty, in the city of Potana a king called Somacandra ruled. He was a moon of benevolence.

93 His virtuous wife was named Dhāriṇī. Morality was her ornament; she was a lake full of the waters of intelligence.

94 One day, she was sitting by a window when she began to stroke her husband's hair with her lotus-hands.

95 Dhāriṇī saw a grey hair on her husband's head. It was as if Old Age had claimed the place with a token of his arrival.

96 She said to the king, "Husband, a messenger has arrived." The king looked round, and said, "I can't see anyone here."

97 The queen showed the king the grey hair on his head, and said, "Lord of my life, this shade of hair is excellent, for it brings a message of religion."

98 When the king saw the grey hair, looking like the sword of the third stage of life slaughtering youth,* he became sad.

99 Dhāriṇī said, "Are you ashamed to grow old, husband? Why are you depressed to see one grey hair?

100 Proclaim at the beat of the drum that none of your subjects is to allude to your old age even in casual talk!"

101 The king replied, "I don't feel shame at the sight of my grey hair, queen of my life. It is rather this which is the cause of my depression:

102 My forefathers took the vow to lead the life of a wandering ascetic before they saw their grey hairs, but I, my dear, remain addicted to sensual pleasures, even though I have grey hairs.

103 I shall take the vow forthwith, but how can I set my son over the kingdom? He still drinks his mother's milk.

104 I wish to take the vow; what concern is my kingdom or my son to me? You are intelligent; bring up your son!"

105 Dhāriṇī said, "I cannot stay here without you. True wives follow their husbands in every situation.

106 So you should entrust the kingdom to your son, although he is a child. But I want to be your servant even in the forest, following by your side like your shadow.

107 Although our son Prasannacandra is a boy, let him flourish according to his karma, like a tree in a forest. What need does he have of me?"

108 Thereupon Somacandra gave his kingdom to his son, and became a homeless ascetic, wandering with his wife and a nurse.

109 Somacandra came to a long-abandoned hermitage, and there practised harsh austerities, living only on leaves and suchlike.

110 He gathered leaves of the Pataśa tree, and built a rest hut where forest animals and travellers could drink the nectar of the cool shade.

111 Somacandra would bring sweet, sweet waters and fruits of forest trees for his wife. He was sown with threads of affection for her.

112 Even there, Dhāriṇī remained passionately devoted to her

husband. In the rest hut, she prepared a couch of soft grass for him.

113 In the daytime, Dhāriṇī pressed oil from ripe iṅguda fruit, which she used to fuel lamps in the evening.

114 For the comfort of her husband, she repeatedly cleaned the yard of the hermitage, smearing it with cow dung.

115 In the hermitage husband and wife cared for the young deer, and passed the time together without infringing their asceticism.

116 As Dhāriṇī lived in comfort and joy, an embryo, which had previously been produced in her womb, was developing, without causing her any discomfort.

117 One day, Dhāriṇī gave birth to a son endowed with all the auspicious marks. He was like an oil-less lamp illuminating his birth chamber with his loveliness.

118 Only birch bark (valkala) was available in the hermitage, so his father clothed him in it and named him Valkalacīrin (clothed in birch bark).

119 Dhāriṇī had died in childbirth. Her son had not seen his mother; he was like an illiterate man.*

120 Somacandra assiduously nourished Dhāriṇī's son on the milk of wild buffaloes, and gave him to the nurse to look after.

121 The nurse too happened to die some time afterwards; it was as if she wanted to follow Dhāriṇī.

122 So Somacandra himself fed the child on buffalo milk, and whether he was walking, sitting, or lying down, bore the infant on his hip.

123 Eventually the child grew into the stage where he was able to walk. Each day he would play in the dust with the cubs of the forest animals.

124 Somacandra fed the child on meals which he had prepared himself with kindling which he had fetched himself and wild rice which he had gathered himself.

125 Somacandra reared the child on grains of wild rice and forest fruits, and made the boy his companion in his ascetic way of life.

126 Valkalacīrin became an adolescent, fit for every kind of activity. He fully understood his father's way of life.

127 Every day he served his father by bringing fruit and other kinds of food and by massaging his body. Serving others is the finest of all holy practices.

128 From his birth, Valkalacīrin lived as if following a vow of chastity; he did not even understand the name of woman, since he lived in the forest, where there were none.

129 One day, Prasannacandra learnt that Dhāriṇī had born a son to his father, who was living in the forest, and a brother to himself.
130 Thinking, "What is my brother like? How can we meet?" the king found it difficult to contain his joyful anticipation.
131 He ordered his court painters, "Go to that forest wilderness which is ornamented by the lotus-feet of my respected father,
132 and paint a portrait of my younger brother who lives in that forest, a swan for the lotus of my father's feet, and bring it to me quickly."
133 The painters said, "As your majesty commands," and went to that forest wilderness which was sanctified by the presence of Valkalacīrin.
134 Such was their skill, they were like new forms of Viśvakarman.* They portrayed him so truly, that the painting was like Valkalacīrin's reflection in a mirror.
135 The court painters quickly took the portrait to the king and showed it to him. It was like an eye-bath of nectar to his eyes.
136 The king thought, "He's the image of my father. The saying that one is born in one's son is absolutely right."
137 The king exclaimed repeatedly, "How fortunate I am to see you, dear brother!", and embraced his picture, kissed him on the head, and refused to take him from his lap.
138 When the king noticed that Valkalacīrin was wearing a covering of birch bark, tears, like a mountain waterfall, immediately fell from his eyes.
139 He said, "My father is advanced in years. It is right for him to lead an ascetic life, but my brother is only a child. Living in a forest is not appropriate for him.
140 Immersed in the lake of royal pleasures, I play like a swan, while my brother lives a forest life like a barbarian.
141 As with an animal born in the forest, it will be difficult to entice him to come to the city."
142 Thinking that life in the forest must be harsh, the king felt compassion for his brother. So he ordered some prostitutes, distinguished for their skills:

143 "Disguise yourselves as monks, and go beguile my brother with physical contact, lively conversation, and candied fruits, and bring him here."

144 At the king's command, the prostitutes quickly disguised themselves as monks, and travelled to the hermitage in which Somacandra was living.

145 The fawn-eyed women saw the ascetic's son approaching, dressed in birch bark and carrying wood apples and other kinds of fruit.

146 His thoughts were guileless. Since they were dressed as ascetics, he greeted them respectfully, and asked, "Who are you? Where is your hermitage?"

147 The prostitutes replied, "We are ascetics. We live in the hermitage called Potana. We have come as your guests. Will you offer us hospitality?"

148 He replied, "Eat these fruits which I have gathered in the forest, great ascetics. They are ripe and sweet."

149 The prostitutes said, "In our hermitage no one would be so tasteless as to eat such tasteless fruit.

150 See the kind of fruit that grows on the trees in our hermitage!" With these words, they sat beneath a tree and invited him to join them.

151 They fed him the candied fruits, and their hopes were not in vain. As soon as he tasted them, he became disgusted with wood apples and the other forest fruit.

152 As he stood among them, they invited him to touch their bodies, placing his hands on the large, fleshy protuberances on their chests.

153 He asked, "Why are your bodies so soft, great ascetics, and why are those two parts of your chests so swollen?"

154 Stroking him with their tender fingers, they replied, "The body becomes soft when one eats the fruit of our forest.

155 And eating the delicious fruits of our forest makes these parts of our chests grow very big.

156 So leave this hermitage and its bitter fruit. Come to our hermitage, and be like us!"

157 Valkalacīrin, greedy for the taste of the candied fruit, agreed to meet and leave with those women who had deceived him.

158 Valkalacīrin collected his ascetic implements, and went to the place where the women had told him to meet.

159 Meanwhile, spies whom the women had placed in trees had informed them that Somacandra the ascetic was coming.

160 The women were frightened that he would curse them. They fled in all directions like deer from a hunter.

161 By the time that his father returned, the young man had begun to search the whole forest for those prostitutes, as if he were seeking his lost wealth.

162 As he was running like a deer in the forest, he saw a man driving a wagon. He thought that the man was an ascetic, and said, "Father, I salute you respectfully."

163 The carter said, "Where are you going, young man?" He replied, "I'm going to the hermitage called Potana, great ascetic."

164 The carter said, "I'm going to the hermitage Potana myself", so Valkalacīrin followed him as if he were his leader.

165 On the way, the young ascetic talked with the carter's wife, who was seated on the cart, and continually addressed her as "father".

166 She asked the carter, "What form of politeness is this? This young ascetic keeps addressing me as father."

167 The carter said, "The fool lives here in the forest where there are no women. He does not know the difference between men and women. He thinks you are a man."

168 Seeing the horses being driven forward, Valkalacīrin said, "Father, why are these deer being used as a means of transport? Surely ascetics are not allowed to do this."

169 The carter smiled at Valkalacīrin, and said, "Oh, this is the job of these deer; there's no harm in it."

170 The carter gave Valkalacīrin some delicious sweets. As soon as he tasted them, he was immersed in bliss. He exclaimed:

171 "I've eaten such forest fruits before! The great ascetics who live in the hermitage called Potana gave them to me."

172 The taste of the sweets stimulated his longing to arrive at Potana. He was disgusted with the dry and bitter wood apples, myrobalan, and the other forest fruits.

173 A fight broke out between the carter and a strong-armed robber, but the carter struck him a mighty blow.

174 The robber said, "A good blow must be praised even when it comes from an enemy. You've defeated me. I'm pleased with your blow, good fellow.

175 I have here a rich booty. Take it, good sir." So the three took his money and loaded it onto the wagon.

176 Eventually, they arrived at Potana. The carter told Valkalacīrin, "This is the hermitage Potana which you were so eager to reach."

177 The carter gave some money to the ascetic's son, who had been his companion on the journey, saying with a smile:

178 "An ascetic cannot stay in this hermitage without money. Whoever wants to stay must pay money to someone as rent."

179 The excellent ascetic wandered through the whole city, looking at the big houses, wondering, "Should I go in here, or should I go in here?"

180 He was so naïve he thought that the men and women were ascetics, and saluted them with devoted reverence. The citizens laughed at him.

181 As he wandered through the city, he saw a prostitute's house. He went straight in, like an arrow from a bow.

182 He mistook the house for an ascetic's hut, and the prostitute for a monk. He said to her, "My respectful greetings, father!"

183 He asked her, "Give me a hut to stay in, great ascetic. Take this money as rent for it."

184 She said, "This is now your hut; take possession of it." Then she summoned a barber to clean and dress him properly.

185 Although the ascetic was unwilling, the barber, at the prostitute's command, cut his toenails; they looked like winnowing fans.

186 The prostitute removed his covering of birch bark, and wrapped the young man in a fine robe, prior to bathing him.

187 He cried like a child, "Great ascetic, don't take away my birch bark covering! I've worn it since my birth!"

188 The prostitute said, "In this hermitage, this is a courtesy which we pay to the ascetics who come as our guests. Why won't you accept it?

189 If you follow the customs of our hermitage, ascetic's son, then you will have a hut to stay in."

190 Since he wanted to stay there, he stopped crying and became as still as a snake charmed by a spell.

191 The beautiful woman dressed his hair with sesamum oil, and gently combed it, as if it were a ball of wool.

192 She washed and oiled Somacandra's son's body. He closed his eyes in pleasure like a cow when it is being groomed.
193 After the prostitute had bathed him in tepid perfumed water, she dressed him in fine clothes and ornaments.
194 Then the prostitute married him to one of her daughters. As the bride took his hand, she looked like the embodiment of the household goddess of prosperity.
195 As all the other prostitutes sang to the bride and groom, the young ascetic's son wondered, "What are all these monks reciting?"
196 A prostitute beat the lucky drum. He was perplexed. He covered his ears, and thought, "What is this?"
197 Meanwhile, those prostitutes who, disguised as ascetics, had gone to fetch the young man returned by the way they had travelled, and informed the king:
198 "We enticed that young forest dweller in all kinds of ways, and he made an agreement with us to come here.
199 But we saw his father coming in the distance, and, fearing his curse, we ran away. Faint-heartedness is a characteristic of women.
200 Since he was now addicted to our charms, he searched for us, passing from wood to wood, but he did not return to his father's hermitage."
201 The king felt remorse. He thought, "I've been stupid. I've separated father and son, and I've not found my brother.
202 Now how will he survive, separated from his father? He'll last just as long as a fish out of water."
203 The king's distress deprived him of all pleasure. He tossed up and down on his couch, like a fish in a dry pond.
204 At that moment the sound of the drumming in that prostitute's house became an unwelcome guest to the king's ears.
205 The king said, "The whole city shares in my sorrow. Who is so superhumanly fortunate that he has a drum sounded before him?
206 But rather, everyone is intent on his own business, and these beats of the drum signal someone's happiness; but to me they sound like blows of a hammer."
207 Carried by the people's ears like water by a channel, the king's words quickly came to fill the irrigation basin of that prostitute's ears.

208 The prostitute went to King Prasannacandra. She folded her hands in salutation, and in a confident voice said impudently:

209 "Your majesty, a fortune teller once told me that if a young man dressed as an ascetic were to come to my house, I should marry him to my daughter.

210 Today, a young man dressed as an ascetic, knowing as little of worldly affairs as an ox, came to my house. I've just married him to my daughter.

211 Your majesty, the marriage festival is being celebrated in my house with singing and with the beating of the drum. I did not know you were depressed. If I have annoyed you, please forgive me."

212 So then the king ordered some men who had seen Valkalacīrin before to inspect the young man, and they went and looked at him.

213 They returned and told the king that it was he, and the king was as happy as if he had had an auspicious dream.

214 The king had Valkalacīrin and his bride mounted on an elephant and brought to his palace.

215 In time, the king taught him all the ways of the world. Even animals learn from their trainers; how much more so men!

216 The king was pleased to have accomplished his purpose. He shared his kingdom with Valkalacīrin and married him to princesses who were as beautiful as the women of heaven.

217 Valkalacīrin enjoyed every desire with these women. He was like an elephant in the waters of the ocean of pleasure.

218 One day, the carter who had been Valkalacīrin's travelling companion came to the city to sell the gold and the other property which the thief had given him.

219 Various people recognized their own property which had been stolen by the thief. Waving their arms, they kept complaining to the police.

220 The police arrested the carter and took him to the palace gates. The king's brother saw him there; his glance was like a life-giving medicine.

221 Valkalacīrin recognized the man who had helped him on his journey, and ordered him to be released. Good people do not forget their benefactors.

222 Meanwhile, Somacandra wandered in that forest without seeing his son, passing from tree to tree, continually watering them with his tears.

223 When messengers came from Prasannacandra bringing him the news about Valkalacīrin, he had become blind.

224 His copious weeping over his separation from his son had made him blind and made his day night.

225 The other ascetics used to bring the old ascetic various fruits when he had finished meditating.

226 Twelve years passed by. One night, Prasannacandra's brother awoke at midnight, and thought:

227 "My mother died while giving birth to me, and my father brought me up, even though he lived in the forest.

228 Day and night he carried me on his hip, and I have caused him a pain far worse than the pains of asceticism.

229 As soon as I became a young man able to repay my father's care, fate made me a sinner with uncontrolled senses, and I came here.

230 I am not able to repay the debt I owe my father in this one lifetime, who has suffered so many trials and tribulations to turn me from a tiddler into an elephant."

231 Thus thinking, he went to the king, and said, "Your majesty, I'm absolutely longing to pay my respects at my father's feet."

232 The king said, "Dear brother, we have the same father. I have the same longing as you to pay my respects at his feet."

233 So the king and the king's brother went with their entourage to the hermitage which was adorned by their father's feet.

234 The two alighted from their carriage, and Valkalacīrin said, "Seeing this hermitage makes the fortune of my royal position seem like grass.

235 These are the ponds in which I played like a swan. These are the trees whose fruit I would eat like a monkey.

236 These are the deer who, like my brothers, used to play with me in the dust. These are the cow buffaloes who, like mothers, used to provide me with milk.

237 Sire, how can I tell you of the many pleasures of this forest? Where in my kingdom is the unique pleasure of serving my father?"

238 The two brothers entered the hermitage, and beheld their father, a sun for the lotus of their eyes.

239 The king bowed before Somacandra the ascetic, saying, "Here is your son, Prasannacandra, bowing before you, father."

240 As the king bowed before him, Somacandra felt him with his hand, as if washing from his body the dust that had collected on him.

241 When the king felt the touch of his father's lotus-hand, his bodily hair bristled with joy; he looked like a blossoming kadamba tree.

242 Then the king's brother bowed before Somacandra, and said, "Here is Valkalacīrin, come as a bee to the lotus of your feet."

243 Somacandra joyfully kissed Valkalacīrin's head, as if sniffing a lotus, and embraced his whole body, like a young cloud clinging to a mountain.

244 Warm tears appeared in Somacandra's eyes, which immediately became a medicine for the final destruction of his blindness.

245 That very moment, the ascetic regained his faculty of sight and saw his two sons. He became bound with those fetters of familial affection which he had previously cast off.

246 He asked, "My dear boys, have you passed your time pleasantly?" They replied, "Yes, thanks to your grace, which is like a wish-granting tree of prosperity."

247 Thinking, "What has become of those vessels for his ascetic life, which my father was unable to see?", Valkalacīrin quickly entered the hut.

248 He began to polish those vessels of asceticism with the edge of his robe, following the pursuit of a former life.

249 He thought, "Have I not cleaned the vessels of ascetics somewhere before?"

250 As he thought this, he gained knowledge of his previous births, and he remembered his previous divine and mortal lives, as if they had been yesterday.

251 He remembered his former life as a Jain monk, and in him was born complete aversion to the world, the companion of the attainment of final emancipation.

252 Valkalacīrin passed beyond righteous meditation into pure meditation. While in the second state, he gained brilliant omniscience.

253 As soon as Somacandra's son gained omniscience, he gave his father and his brother instruction in the Jain religion; it was like nectar.

254 Then Somacandra and Prasannacandra bowed before Valkalacīrin, whom a god had presented with the insignia of a Jain monk, and they became enlightened.
255 One day, your majesty, in the course of my wanderings I halted in a garden near Potana; its name is Lovely.
256 And there Valkalacīrin, the self-enlightened, entrusted his father to me.
257 King Prasannacandra returned to Potana. Because of Valkalacīrin's preaching, he remained constant in his aversion to the world.
258 Then Prasannacandra placed his son in charge of the kingdom, even though he was a child, and was initiated as a Jain monk by me.'

259 As the supreme Lord Mahāvīra finished speaking, the king of Magadha saw the gods assemble in the sky.
260 Śreṇika bowed once more to the Lord of the Universe, and asked, 'Why is the sky being illuminated by this assembly of the gods?'
261 The Lord replied, 'The ascetic Prasannacandra has just gained omniscience, and the gods have gathered to glorify him.'
262 The king of Magadha once more asked the Lord Jina, 'Reverend sir, who will be the last to gain omniscience?'
263 The Lord replied, 'Look, there is the god Vidyunmālin, accompanied by his four wives. He holds the rank of king of the Brahma heaven.
264 On the seventh day after this, he will fall from heaven, and be born in your city as Jambū, the son of the merchant Ṛṣabhadatta. He will be the last omniscient one.'
265 The king asked, 'If this god is about to fall from heaven, then should not the splendour of his appearance be diminished?' The Teacher of the Universe replied:
266 'Your majesty, at the time when gods are about to descend from heaven for their final existence, no signs of their fall, such as diminution in the splendour of their appearance, become apparent.'

267 At that moment, the god called Anādṛta, the lord of Rose-apple Tree Island, joyfully shouted in an extremely loud voice, 'Hurrah for the excellence of my family!'

268 Then Śreṇika respectfully folded his hands together, and asked Mahāvīra, 'why is that god praising his family like that?'

269 The omniscient one related: 'Your majesty, here in this city there once lived a wealthy merchant named Guptamitra, famous the world over.

270 In course of time, two sons were born to him. The elder was called Ṛṣabhadatta, the younger Jinadāsa.

271 The elder was always virtuous in his conduct; the younger was addicted to gambling and other vices. They were like the visible embodiments of the first and last ages of the world.*

272 Ṛṣabhadatta was sensible. Because Jinadāsa's conduct was bad, he renounced him, making his whole family witnesses.

273 The elder son of the merchant declared: "I have become brotherless." He forbade his younger brother to enter the house, as if he were a dog.

274 One day, Jinadāsa was gambling with another gambler. Suddenly a gamblers' quarrel broke out, and Jinadāsa was wounded by a sword.

275 As he rolled on the ground like a beggar, Jinadāsa realized that the blow of the weapon was the fruit of the poisonous tree of gambling.

276 Ṛṣabhadatta's family said to him, "Prominent Jain layman, save your younger brother's life with the compassion that is common to all living beings.

277 That kinsman or that leader is worthy of brilliant fame who rescues his relative or his follower from the chasm of disaster."

278 Sent by his family, Ṛṣabhadatta arrived at that place, and said to his younger brother, "Be of good heart, dear brother. I shall heal you with this medicine."

279 Jinadāsa said, "Forgive my bad conduct. Perform my funeral rites; I have no wish to live.

280 I have now embarked on the path to the next world. Give me instruction in the Jain religion; taken with religious fasting, it will be provender for my journey."

281 Ṛṣabhadatta instructed his brother, "Be selfless. With a clear mind recite the salutation to the beings in the five highest stages."*

282 Thus Ṛṣabhadatta himself instructed his brother, leading him in worship and fasting.

283 Then Jinadāsa died, and, because of the instruction he had received on his deathbed, was reborn as this very prosperous god, the lord of Rose-apple Tree Island.

284 He heard what I was saying, that the last omniscient one Jambū, the son of Ṛṣabhadatta, would be born in Rājagṛha.

285 Because he heard that the holy birth of an omniscient one would take place in his family, that's why this god is praising his family so highly.'

286 Then the king asked, 'Reverend sir, why is this god Vidyunmālin so splendid among gods, as the sun is among planets?'

287 The Lord said, 'In the country called Magadha in the Bharata of the Rose-apple Tree Island, is a village named Sugrāma.

288 In it lived a district officer named Āryavat. His wife was named Revatī, and his two sons were Bhavadatta and Bhavadeva.

289 While still a young man, Bhavadatta received from the Teacher Susthita initiation, a safe boat for crossing the ocean of existence.

290 He reached the far shore of the ocean of religious learning, and kept his vow like a sword held before his face. Bhavadatta wandered with his Teacher, as if he were the Teacher's second body.

291 In that group of monks was one who one day asked the Teacher, "Please give me permission to go where my family lives.

292 I have a younger brother who is very fond of me. If he sees me, he will become a Jain monk. He is noble in his disposition."

293 The learned Teacher gave his approval to the monk, for a Teacher delights in a pupil who is keen to help others to cross to the far shore.

294 The monk departed. As soon as he arrived at his father's house, he found that his brother's marriage festivities, the longed-for fount of the wishing-tree of passion, had begun.

295 The monk's younger brother was so excited about the marriage festivities, that he was oblivious to all other business. There was no use in discussing it.

296 He did not even greet his elder brother, as if unaware that he had arrived in time for the marriage ceremony. What point was there in talking to him about taking the vows?

297 Disappointed, the monk returned once more to the presence of

his Teacher. Having considered the matter, he related everything that had passed with his brother.

298 Thereupon, Bhavadatta said, "Oh, your brother was hard-hearted to treat with disrespect his elder brother, a monk who was visiting him at home!

299 Devotion to a respected elder is preferable to excitement over a wedding. Why didn't he abandon the wedding and joyfully follow his elder brother?"

300 One of the monks said, "You'll really be clever, Bhavadatta, if you can get your own younger brother to take the vow."

301 Bhavadatta said, "If the Teacher leads us to the country of Magadha, then you'll see something surprising."

302 One day, the Teacher led the monks to Magadha. Like the wind, monks do not remain in one place.

303 Bhavadatta bowed to the Teacher's feet, and said, "By your leave, I would like to visit my family, who live near here."

304 The Teacher gave Bhavadatta permission to go there alone; it is permissible for a monk who has mastered his passions to travel alone.

305 So Bhavadatta went to his family's home, in order to benefit his younger brother, by inducing him to become a Jain monk.

306 At that time, Bhavadeva, Bhavadatta's younger brother, was about to marry the daughter of Nāgadatta and Vāsukī.

307 Bhavadatta was joyfully welcomed by his relatives who had gathered to celebrate the marriage; they thought that he had come for the marriage festivities.

308 Straightaway, they washed his feet with filtered water, then worshipped the water which had washed his feet, considering it superior to water from a holy river crossing.

309 Wanting to cling to him through their fear of being sunk in the ocean of existence, his relatives embraced his feet and bowed before him.

310 The monk said, "Carry on with the wedding, good people. I'm going somewhere else. May the gain of righteousness be yours, sinless ones."

311 Delightedly, all his relatives begged the monk to accept food and filtered drink which was fit for a monk to accept.

312 At that time, Bhavadeva, according to the custom of his family, was assisting the bride's friends in helping her to dress.

313 He anointed his beloved's body with fine sandalwood water, like the essence of moonlight drawn down from the disc of the moon.

314 He bound her head in a braid wreathed with flowers; it rivalled the beauty of Rāhu when he has swallowed the moon.*

315 On her cheeks he drew decorative patterns in musk, like hymns of praise to the god of love.

316 The groom had begun to decorate her breasts when he heard that Bhavadatta the monk had arrived.

317 In his eagerness to see his brother, he suddenly leapt up like a winning gambler, leaving his beloved with her breasts half-decorated.

318 As if deaf, he did not heed his wife's lady friends, who exclaimed, "It is not right for you to go and leave your beloved half-decorated!"

319 They obdurately tried to prevent him from leaving, but he replied, "I'll pay my respects to my venerable brother, then I'll come back, girls."

320 Bhavadeva sprang from that place like a monkey. When he came to the place where Bhavadatta was, he bowed before him.

321 As soon as his younger brother rose from paying his respects, the monk handed his butter bowl to him, as if it were a promise to donate asceticism.

322 Bhavadatta, the crest-jewel of the homeless, the abode of wisdom, left the house, casting a quick glance at his brother.

323 Holding his clarified-butter bowl, Bhavadeva followed the monk, a bee for the lotus of his feet.

324 The other men and women, in the same way as Bhavadeva, also followed Bhavadatta; they were like lakes of joy billowing over the monk.

325 The monk did not dismiss any of them, for that is the practice with monks; people whom monks have not dismissed do not turn back.

326 When they had gone some distance, disheartened, of their own accord, first the women, then the men, humbly bowed to the great monk and turned back.

327 But Bhavadeva was true-hearted. He thought, "Those people left without being dismissed, but they are not his brothers or sisters.

328 But I am his brother, and we are very dear to each other, so unless I am dismissed by him, it is not right for me to leave.

329 Surely my elder brother was tired by the amount of food and drink he had taken, so he kindly gave me his butter bowl to carry.

330 I can't abandon my elder brother, who is tired from his long journey, and leave him in this place."

331 The great monk Bhavadatta told stories of their home life in order to distract his younger brother's mind lest he turn back:

332 "There are the trees on the outskirts of the village, those orchards for wayfarers, the very ones in which we brothers would play unhindered like a pair of monkeys.

333 There are the ponds where in our childhood we would make lovely necklaces from the stalks of lotuses for each other's necks.

334 There, at the edge of the village, are those sandpits where, in the rainy season, we would play at building temples in the sand."

335 In this way Bhavadatta amused his younger brother on the journey until he came to the village which was purified by the lotus-feet of the Teacher.

336 When the junior monks saw Bhavadatta the monk arrive at the door of the dwelling place accompanied by his younger brother, they said to each other, smiling wryly:

337 "The monk must have brought his brother, who is wearing fine clothes, to initiate him and fulfil his promise."

338 The Teacher asked, "Bhavadatta, who is this young man who has come with you?" Bhavadatta replied, "He is my younger brother. He wants to become a Jain monk."

339 The Teacher asked Bhavadeva, "Do you want to become a Jain monk?", and Bhavadeva, not wishing to make his brother appear a liar, said that he did.

340 The Teacher immediately initiated Bhavadeva, then commanded him to wander elsewhere in the company of two other monks.

341 Bhavadeva's family, worried because he had never returned, came and questioned Bhavadatta, saying:

342 "Bhavadeva followed you, leaving his beloved half-decorated. It's a pleasure for him, but when he did not come back, we suffered a living death.

343 His young wife grieves over her separation like a female 'cakra'-

cawing bird.* Like a stream of water, tears never cease to fall from her eyes.

344 That Bhavadeva should go anywhere without taking his leave of us is inconceivable even in a dream! Now that he's actually gone somewhere else—can this be?

345 Not seeing Bhavadeva, we have lost all interest in ourselves. So kindly tell us, monk, where your younger brother is."

346 Desiring the reward of religion for his brother, the monk said falsely, "As soon as he arrived, he turned back. We don't know which way he went."

347 Murmuring, "Did he go by some other way?", they immediately left, their faces downcast, as if they had been plundered by robbers.

348 Bhavadeva kept the memory of his young bride in his heart. Only affection for his brother led him to keep his painful vow.

349 In course of time, Bhavadatta the great monk grew old. He abstained from food and drink, died, and became a god in the Saudharma heaven.

350 Then Bhavadeva thought. "Nāgilā is my wife and I am her husband, but we have been separated.

351 I kept my vow for so long because I was detained by my brother. But now my brother has gone to heaven. What do I want with this vow which is the cause of trouble and fatigue?

352 But I am not as distressed by this troublesome and difficult vow as I am by my separation from her. How will she be faring now?

353 Like a female elephant fallen in a corral, like a bed of lotuses covered by the winter snow, like a flamingo in a desert, like a creeper withered by the heat of summer,

354 like a doe that has strayed from its herd, like a myanah bird tied by a cord, I suppose she feels miserable, an object of pity for the world.

355 If I find my wide-eyed wife alive, from that time on I'll enjoy the pleasures of love with her in a state of domestic bliss."

356 Fastening himself in the web of such thoughts, he became like a spider. Bhavadeva left without taking leave of his old Teacher.

357 The district officer's son hastily travelled to the village called Sugrāma, and hid by the door of his home.

358 Then his wife, bedecked in perfumed garlands, arrived,

accompanied by a Brahmin lady. Thinking that he was some monk, she greeted him respectfully.

359 Bhavadeva asked her, "Good lady, are the district officer Āryavat and his wife Revatī still alive or not?"

360 She told him that Āryavat and Revatī had died a long time before.

361 Then the monk asked, "That newly married wife who was abandoned by Bhavadeva, Revatī's son—is she still alive or not?"

362 She thought, "This is Bhavadeva! He must have been initiated by his elder brother. Should I detain him? He has come here free from sin."

363 Having considered the matter, she said, "You yourself are Bhavadeva, the son of Āryavat and Revatī. Why have you come here, you who are rich in asceticism?"

364 Bhavadeva replied, "Well done! You've recognized me. I am indeed Bhavadeva, the lord of Nāgilā's life.

365 I departed at that time, abandoning her, because I was detained by my elder brother. Then he initiated me into the hard life of a Jain monk, although I was most unwilling.

366 My brother died recently, so I was off the hook. I wondered how Nāgilā was faring, so I came here, hoping to see her."

367 Nāgilā thought, "He has not seen me for such a long time that he no longer recognizes me, now that my youthful beauty has perished.

368 I shall make myself known to him." Nāgilā said, "I am Nāgilā, alas!, that young bride whom you abandoned.

369 In so much time, my youth has passed by. See how much beauty I possess now, worthy ascetic!

370 Don't give up the three jewels* which give the reward of heaven or final emancipation, and take me, who am worth as little as a cowrie shell, great ascetic.

371 We are on the verge of falling into a terrible hell. Don't break your vow to abstain from sensual pleasures, those arrows of Love.

372 Your brother made you take the vow by a trick, although you were unwilling. Even if you cannot keep the vow, don't remain in love with me, a mine of sinfulness.

373 You should leave right now, and hasten to the feet of your Teacher. In his presence, confess your sin of feeling lust for me."

374 As Nāgilā was earnestly advising Bhavadeva to follow this course of conduct, the Brahmin lady's little boy came up to them, having just drunk his milk.

375 He said, "I've just drunk my milk; it was as sweet as nectar. I'm going to vomit it, so give me a bowl, mother.

376 I've been invited to go somewhere where I'll be given the food offering for Brahmins. If I don't vomit my mother's milk, I shan't be able to eat it.

377 As soon as I've eaten the food offering, I'll come back and drink my vomited milk. There's no shame in eating one's own leftovers."

378 The Brahmin lady said, "If you eat what you've vomited, you'll be disgusting. That's enough of this disgusting action, my child!"

379 When he heard this, Bhavadeva said, "Hey, Brahmin child, if you eat what you've vomited, you'll be lower than a dog."

380 Thereupon Nāgilā said to the ascetic, "If you mean what you say, then why, having vomited me, do you want to enjoy me once more?

381 I am the lowest of the low, full of flesh, blood, bone, excrement, and urine. Having been vomited, I too am disgusting. Don't you feel ashamed to want me?

382 You can see a fire blazing on a mountain but you are unable to see one under your own feet, for you teach another but you do not teach yourself.

383 What respect is there for those who are clever at teaching others? Those who are able to teach themselves are the ones who are respected."

384 Bhavadeva said, "You have taught me an excellent lesson, sinless one. I was like a man blind from birth, travelling on the wrong road, but I've now been placed on the right track.

385 As soon as I've visited my relatives, I'll return to the presence of my Teacher. I'll confess the transgression of my vow, and perform harsh asceticism."

386 But Nāgilā said, "What are your relatives to you? Since they are embodied, you will find them obstacles to your Teacher's instruction.

387 So go quickly to the presence of the Teacher. Subdue yourself, and practise your vow. I myself shall receive initiation in the presence of the Jain nuns."

388 Thereupon, Bhavadeva paid his devoted respects to the images of the Worthies. Then he went to his Teacher and confessed his sin.

389 Bhavadeva lived a life of religious austerity. Eventually he died, and became the god Śakra in the first paradise heaven.*

390–1 Eventually Bhavadatta's soul fell from heaven, and, in the town of Puṇḍarīkiṇī in the province of Puṣkalāvatī, the crest-jewel of Videha, descended into the womb of Yaśodharā, queen of King Vajradatta.

392 Since he had become a flamingo for the lake of her womb, the queen had a pregnancy-longing to dive into the ocean.

393 So the king had the queen frolic in a river which flowed into the ocean, and thus satisfied her pregnancy-longing.

394 Queen Yaśodharā, her pregnancy-longing satisfied, like a creeper, grew ever more beautiful.

395 When her time was due, the king's queen produced an excellent son, like the Ganges producing a golden lotus.

396 On an auspicious day, the king named him Sāgaradatta, after the fulfilment of Yaśodharā's pregnancy-longing.*

397 His nurses nourished him with draughts of milk, and in course of time the prince began to flourish like a tree.

398 As soon as he was proficient in speaking, the prince tried to teach the parrots and myanah birds to speak, eagerly lifting the golden creeper-perch.

399 When he had grown into a boy whose ruby earrings were dancing on the stage of his broad shoulders, he played with jewelled balls along with his friends.

400 Eventually, the king entrusted him to a teacher. He drank the teacher's knowledge, like a traveller drinking from a well.

401 Like the moon, he delighted the night-lotuses of the eyes of everyone as he grew into a young man.

402 He was married by his parents to maidens who had come to choose him as their husband; for maidens come to a suitable groom like rivers to the sea.

403 Like a bull with its cows, like an elephant with its wives, like the moon with its stars, he made love with them.

404 One day, he was enjoying himself with his wives like the god of love, when he saw a cloud in the sky with a mark like Mount Meru.*

405 He thought, "The shape of the cloud is just like the description of Mount Meru in the holy teachings. Oh, what loveliness!"

406 As he looked at the cloud like Mount Meru, his gaze never dropped, as if it were stuck to it.

407 The prince looked upwards and watched as the cloud vanished like a bubble of water and went elsewhere.

408 The prince thought, "This body is as ephemeral as that cloud; what then can one say of worldly prosperity?

409 What is seen in the morning is not seen at noon. What is seen at noon is not seen at night. In this existence impermanence is the characteristic of human life.

410 So I shall take the vow which is the fruit borne by the tree of human life when it has been sprinkled by the waters of right discrimination; its essence is the destruction of karma."

411 Sāgaradatta was intelligent. He became totally averse to worldly pleasures. He put his hands together in respectful supplication, and asked his parents for permission to become a Jain monk.

412 His parents said, "Dear child, your desire to become a monk in your youth is like reciting a textbook when a lute is playing.

413 At present you are a prince and you will become a king. When you have ruled the kingdom for a long time, that will be the right time for you to become a monk."

414 Sāgaradatta said, "I have rejected the worship of rank and prosperity, so why won't you allow me to become a monk?"

415 In this way he intelligently cut the bonds of their affection with the axe of obstinacy, and his parents gave their permission for him to become a monk.

416 Sāgaradatta, accompanied by many other princes, took the vow as sweet as an ocean of nectar, in the presence of the Teacher.

417 Keeping the various vows of asceticism, his chief object the service of his Teacher, Sāgaradatta eventually reached the far shore of the ocean of religious knowledge.

418 There is nothing better than asceticism for producing firm conviction. Sāgaradatta's asceticism produced in him knowledge of things that lie beyond the normal range of the senses.

419 When its time was up, Bhavadeva's soul fell from heaven into that very same district, in Vītaśoka, that crest-jewel of cities.

420 He was born the son of Queen Vanamālā and the very prosperous King Padmaratha. He was named Śiva.

421 He was protected as carefully as a wish-granting tree that had sprung up. In time, he grew into a young man, wearing sidelocks of hair on his temples.*

422 His tutor, a crest-jewel of learning, became a mere witness as he and the arts encountered each other, as if by mutual agreement.

423 In his youth, he was married to princesses of good birth. Surrounded by them, he was as beautiful as a tree surrounded by creepers.

424 One day he was in the palace with his wives, when Sāgaradatta the monk came to preach in a park on the outskirts of the city.

425 And there a wealthy merchant named Kāmasamṛddha, devotedly provided that great monk with hospitality, at the end of his month-long fast.

426 Through the potency of giving to a worthy recipient, a stream of wealth fell from the sky into Kāmasamṛddha's house. What does not come from giving to a worthy recipient!

427 Śiva heard about this miracle, and went to pay his respects to the monk. He sat like a swan before his lotus-feet.

428 Sāgaradatta was a mine of knowledge of the fourteen Original Collections of Teachings. He preached the Jain religion to Śiva and his entourage.

429 Śiva was intelligent. His mind expanded like an opening lotus flower as the monk gave him a detailed explanation of the worthlessness of worldly existence.

430 Śiva asked the monk, "What was our condition in our former lives? I feel affection when I look at you, and my joy grows stronger and stronger."

431 The monk knew the answer because of his powers of extrasensory perception. He said, "In your former life you were my younger brother, dearer to me than life.

432 I had become a monk, and by a trick I made you become a monk too, although you were unwilling, because I wanted you to go to heaven.

433 We became a pair of supremely fortunate gods in the Saudharma heaven. Even there we were as dear to each other as moons are to night-lotuses.

434 I am just as free from attachment as in my former life, but even now, because of your feelings of attachment, you still have the affection of your former life for me."

435 Śiva said, "Previously my taking the vow led me to become a god. So now, in this existence, give me initiation as in my former life.
436 Have pity for me, and stay right here, respected sir, while I go seek my parents' permission to become a monk."
437 Prince Śiva went to his parents, and told them, "I heard Sāgaradatta the monk preaching today.
438 Thanks to him, I have realized the worthlessness of existence, so I have become as averse to it as a porter is to his shoulder-yoke.
439 So please, by all means, give me your permission to become a Jain monk. Today Sāgaradatta is my refuge, dawn from the darkness of delusion."
440 His parents said, "Dear child, don't become a monk in your youth. Our pleasure in watching your games is not yet sated.
441 How did you manage to become suddenly so very selfless, honourable son, that you wish to mock us as if we were unknown to you?
442 If you have become a devotee, and if you want to take your leave of us and go away, then the sole use of our tongues will be to say no!"
443 Forbidden by his parents, Śiva was unable to go. At that point, through his restraint of anything blameworthy, he became a monk in internal conviction.
444 Remaining fixed in his resolution that he was the monk Sāgaradatta's pupil, he devoted himself to an ascetic way of life. An ascetic way of life wins every goal.
445 Even when compelled to sit down to a meal, he did not eat any food. He just repeated, "Nothing agrees with me."
446 The king was alarmed by Śiva's seeking final emancipation in this way. He summoned a merchant's son named Dṛḍhadharma, and ordered him:
447 "My child, my son Śiva was prevented from leaving to become a monk, but he is now leading the life of an ascetic. His heart is as hard as stone.
448 Like a leopard that is unable to pounce, like an elephant in its rutting season, not even by a hundred entreaties can he be induced to eat anything.
449 My boy, since you know my son Śiva, you know how to make

him eat. If you accomplish this, I'll give you any reward you want.

450 Magnanimous one, restrain my soul, which is eager to fly like a bird from the nest of my body, with the fetter of hope."

451 Dṛḍhadharma assented to the king's command, and, an ocean of the waters of intelligence, visited Prince Śiva.

452 Dṛḍhadharma was intelligent and he knew the rules. He entered Śiva's presence having first attracted his attention in the prescribed manner, and recited the formula for making atonement for inadvertently treading on any living organisms.*

453 He bowed twelve times and sat down, having first brushed the ground. Then he asked in an earnest voice, "Instruct me!"

454 Śiva said, "Merchant, I have seen this formality being observed among monks around Sāgaradatta. Why should it be applied to me?"

455 The merchant's son replied, "Wherever a person who has the same sentiment as those who have the right views is encountered, he is entitled to every respect, sir.

456 He whose heart is pervaded with the same sentiment as theirs is worthy of respect. There is no suspicion of fault in this, sir.

457 But prince, I came here to ask you something: have you given up food because of stomach sickness?"

458 Śiva said, "My parents would not let me leave to become a monk. So I decided to remain here, while leading the life of an ascetic. I have given up the life of a householder.

459 Since my parents were frightened to let me become a monk, though that was my desire, I have stopped taking food."

460 The merchant said, "If that is so, then you should eat, sir. Doing one's duty depends on one's body, and the origin of the body is food.

461 Ascetics accept food that is free from fault. But when the body lacks food, it is hard to destroy karma."

462 The prince said, "Merchant's son, here I am not being supplied with food that is free from fault. Therefore, it is better for me not to eat."

463 The merchant said, "You shall be my teacher, and I shall be your pupil. From now on, I shall supply you with all the faultless food you need."

464 The prince said, "My friend, as soon as it is the sixth hour of the day, I shall break my fast with rice-gruel and curds."

465 The merchant's son, knowing the proper observances, began to pay his respects to Śiva, who continued to live the life of an ascetic.

466 Śiva lived as an ascetic for twelve years, but his parents, through their ignorance, never allowed him to return to the Teacher.

467 When he died, Prince Śiva became a god in the Brahma heaven, that god called Vidyunmālin who holds the rank of king.

468 This is the splendour of that soul who is about to fall from heaven to be reborn as a human being, since he formerly had the splendour of the rank of king of the Brahma heaven.

469 On the seventh day after this, he will fall from heaven, and become the son of Ṛṣabhadatta, Jambū, the last omniscient one.'

470 As Vidyunmālin approached to pay his respects to Prasannacandra, his four wives asked the great monk:

471 'Henceforth, we shall be separated from the god Vidyunmālin. Will we be reunited with him somewhere, or not?'

472 The monk said, 'In this very city are four wealthy merchants: Samudra, Priyasamudra, Kubera and Sāgara.

473 You will become their four daughters. When Vidyunmālin becomes a mortal, you will be reunited with him here.'

474 Then holy Mahāvīra, his lotus-feet attended by gods and demigods, an ocean of compassion, a sun for the lotus flowers of those who are capable of enlightenment, a receptacle for the treasure of superhuman qualities, left to wander elsewhere.

Here finishes the first canto of the scholar-monk Hemacandra's epic poem, the Appendix, or Lives of the Jain Elders. In it were related the former lives of Lord Jambū.

CANTO TWO

In Canto Two the events surrounding the conception, birth, and marriage of Jambū are related, together with a remarkable series of stories which Jambū and his wives told each other on their wedding night. The history of Jambū is continued in Canto Three.

1–55 In Rājagṛha lived a merchant named Ṛṣabhadatta, one of King Śreṇika's councillors, and his wife Dhāriṇī, who was depressed because she was childless. One day, Ṛṣabhadatta took Dhāriṇī to a park on Mount Vaibhāra to cheer her up. There, they met a friend of Ṛṣabhadatta, a Jain layman named Yaśomitra, who informed them that Sudharman, the Supporter of the Flock, was preaching nearby. The three listened to Sudharman's sermon, after which Sudharman described the Rose-apple tree (*jambū*) after which the Rose-apple Tree Island is named. (The Rose-apple Tree Island and the other continents of the Middle World are described in the Appendix on the Jain Universe.) Then Yaśomitra prophesied that Dhāriṇī would give birth to a son named Jambū. The three then returned to the town.

56–91 As foretold by Mahāvīra in Canto One, the god Vidyunmālin fell from heaven and his soul entered Dhāriṇī's womb. In due course she gave birth to a son, whom his parents named Jambū. He thrived, and when he became of marriageable age, his parents betrothed him to eight maidens, the daughters of wealthy merchants. Their names were Samudraśrī, Padmaśrī, Padmasenā, Kanakasenā, Nabhaḥsenā, Kanakaśrī, Kamalavatī, and Jayaśrī; the first four had been Vidyunmālin's wives in their previous lives.

92–165 Meanwhile, Sudharman, the Supporter of the Flock, had returned to Rājagṛha. Jambū was converted by his preaching. He took a vow of chastity and decided to become a monk. His parents reluctantly gave their permission, and conferred with the parents of the eight maidens. The girls themselves insisted that the marriage should go ahead, even though Jambū was to become a monk on the day after the marriage ceremony. The marriage was performed with great festivity, and the house was filled with costly gifts.

166–88 After Jambū and his eight wives had retired to their marriage chamber, a robber named Prabhava, the exiled son of the king of the Vindhya mountains, and his gang broke into the house and began to steal the valuables. However, Jambū paralysed the thieves in the act of stealing by his speech which was full of the power of religious merit. Prabhava offered to give Jambū spells to open locks and to put people to sleep in return for the power to paralyse. Jambū replied that he had no need of spells, since he was going to abandon his wives and his possessions to become a monk in the following morning. Prabhava urged Jambū to enjoy sensual pleasures with his wives before taking the vows of a monk, but Jambū remained firm in his chastity. Then Jambū and his wives began to tell each other stories, the moral of the wives' stories being that Jambū should enjoy sexual pleasures while he had the chance, while the moral of Jambū's stories was that chastity was preferable, since the result of sexual pleasures enjoyed with women was rebirth in hell.

189–221	Jambū told: The Story of the Man and the Honey-drops
222–313	Jambū told: The Story of Kuberadatta
314–54	Jambū told: The Story of Maheśvaradatta
355–78	Samudraśrī told: The Story of the Farmer
379–405	Jambū told: The Story of the Crow
406–30	Padmaśrī told: The Story of the Pair of Monkeys
431–43	Jambū told: The Story of the Charcoal Burner
444–641	Padmasenā told: The Story of Nūpurapaṇḍitā and the Jackal
642–92	Jambū told: The Story of Vidyunmālin
693–718	Kanakasenā told: The Story of the Conch-blower
719–45	Jambū told: The Story of the Bitumen Monkey

1 After that, in the city of Rājagṛha, Śreṇika, the crest-jewel of kings, continued to rule the kingdom. He was like Indra, the king of the gods, in the bounty of his prosperity.

2 The ornament of his council was a merchant, distinguished for his good works, called Ṛṣabhadatta, among bull-men the one who bore the yoke.

3 Day and night Ṛṣabhadatta recited in prayer 'The Worthy is a god, the monk is a respected teacher', as if the syllables were of a spell fulfilling every wish.

4 The water of his mind was always clear, the impurity of bad

thoughts having been made to settle as dust by applying the purifying powder of the kataka plant* which was the doctrine of his teachers.

5 His wealth was like the water of an excellent lake and like the fruit of a tree at the wayside. To whom was it not of benefit?

6 Following righteousness in her thoughts, resembling a swan in her gait, his virtuous wife was called Dhāriṇī.

7 Endowed with excellent virtues such as depth of character, she bestowed great effort on her moral conduct; women of good family are characterized by virtue.

8 A virtuous lady, all her body was covered. She was resplendent in her veil, as if unable to bear the touch of the sun's rays.

9 Possessed of exceedingly pure virtues, morality and propriety of conduct, and so on, she was settled in her husband's heart, as the Ganges in the middle of the ocean.

10 Like nail and flesh, they were ever joined together. Their love was unbroken. Two bodies, they were of one mind.

11 Dhāriṇī was childless. One day she thought, 'Like a barren tree, my childless life produces no fruit.

12 Lucky are the women in whose lap a male child plays, like nectar producing an intense coolness in the limbs.

13 Living in a house leads to sin; moreover living there childless! It's like eating bad and saltless food.'

14 Dhāriṇī's husband asked her, 'Why are you depressed?' She told him of the sorrow fixed in her heart.

15 Although she had shared with her husband her worry about a son, it did not lessen; on the contrary, it increased.

16 Dhāriṇī, her sorrow an arrow in her heart, wasted away daily, like the crescent of another moon.

17 One day, her husband, wishing to make her forget her sorrow, said to her in a voice which was like the current of a river of affection:

18 'Let's go to Mount Vaibhāra today, slim-bellied one. We'll be delighted by the beauty of the garden there: it's like Indra's paradise.'

19 Dhāriṇī assented to her husband's suggestion, thinking, 'What my husband says must be respected, and besides, it may help me forget my sorrow.'

20 So, as soon as Ṛṣabhadatta had prepared his carriage, in which the cotton was as soft as goose-down, they both climbed into it.

21 Having climbed into the big carriage, which was harnessed to fine horses, the couple set out for the mountain.

22 'Dear wife, see the great king Śreṇika's horse-track! The driven horses have flecked it with bubbles of foam.

23 See the trees on the outskirts of the city! Because their trunks have been stripped of bark by tying them up, this indicates that they are the posts to which the king's elephants are tied when they are in rut.

24 See, my dear, that herd of cattle is delighted by the sound of the tinkling ornaments worn around the feet of the bulls. The calves' ears prick up at the rattling of our speeding carriage.

25 See the young mango trees by the roadside, slim-bellied one! Their shoots are a tonic for the voices of female cuckoos.

26 See! The deer, startled by the sound of the carriage, seem to have mounted the wind, as if they wish to leave the earth, and mainly travel through the sky.

27 Fawn-eyed one, see the water scoops showering water onto the sugar cane groves, like a new kind of rain cloud, one which hugs the ground!'

28 In this way Ṛṣabhadatta amused his wife by showing her the sights along the way. Finally they arrived at Mount Vaibhāra, attended by their servants.

29 Then the couple steadily alighted from the carriage, their hearts leaping with the wish to see the gardens of Mount Vaibhāra.

30 As Dhāriṇī asked the name of each tree by the wayside, and sipped again and again the sweet cascading water,

31 and rested again and again under the thick shade of the trees, taking pleasure in the touch of the cool leaves of the banana trees,

32 and smiled at the chatter of the parrots, feeling affection for the young deer and longing envy for the female monkeys who were carrying their young on their hips,

33 Ṛṣabhadatta took her hand, and supporting her, gently helped her gradually climb the mountain.

34 And there Ṛṣabhadatta, pointing with his finger, showed Dhāriṇī the heart-captivating beauty of the mountain garden.

35 'Look at these citron trees stooping down with the burden of their fruit, and the pomegranate trees with their coppery blossoms, as if they had resting on them twilight clouds!

36 Even the sun's rays find it hard to penetrate these vine bowers! Here are palmyra trees whose leaves look like dancing peacocks' tails!

37 Here are flowering trees with creepers mutually perfuming each other! The noise of the bees proclaims their kinship!

38 Enveloped in the shade of the rose-apple trees, orange blossom trees, mango trees, pine trees, and other trees, the mountain seems to be wearing a bodice!'

39 Then Ṛṣabhadatta saw Yaśomitra, a magician's son, arrive in that place, as quickly as a bird. He was a Jain believer and was almost a kinsman to Ṛṣabhadatta.

40 Thereupon the merchant Ṛṣabhadatta said to the magician's son, 'You are my fellow believer, so tell me, where are you going to?'

41 He replied, 'Friend, the fifth pupil of the last Worthy is in this garden: Sudharman the Supporter of the Flock, who is holding a preaching assembly.

42 I'm going to pay my respects to him. If you want to worship him, then hurry too. I'm rushing to hear his sermon.'

43 Husband and wife said 'Om' in agreement, and set out with him. Then the three came to the place which was purified by the presence of reverend Sudharman.

44 As was proper, the three devotedly saluted reverend Sudharman by walking around him twelve times. Then they sat before him.

45 They folded their hands, and with cupped ears eagerly drank the supreme nectar of reverend Sudharman's religious instruction.

46 At an appropriate moment, the magician's son asked the excellent Supporter of the Flock, 'What is the rose-apple tree like after which Rose-apple Tree Island is named?'

47 The Supporter of the Flock explained that the tree was made of genuine jewels, and that it had no superior in its dimensions, majesty, or form.

48 And then Dhāriṇī seized the opportunity and asked the excellent Supporter of the Flock, 'Will I give birth to a son, or not?'

49 The magician's son said, 'You should not ask about anything

blameworthy. Although the great seers know, they will make no declaration concerning anything blameworthy.

50 By means of the instruction I have received at the feet of the Jina, I have become conversant with the knowledge of signs and omens. I myself will tell you, good lady. Hear it!

51 Since Sudharman the Supporter of the Flock, resolute in mind and courageous in body, while sitting in the lap of a rock,

52 has been asked by you about the birth of a son, so, good lady, in a dream you will see a lion in your lap, and then you will bear in your womb a lion of a son.

53 You will have a son named Jambū (rose-apple tree), endowed with jewel-like virtues, like the rose-apple tree he described. He will have divine qualities.'

54 Dhāriṇī said, 'O wise one, in accordance with the prophecy concerning Jambū's divine qualities, I shall fast on rice-water for one hundred and eight days.'

55 Having bowed to the feet of Sudharman, the three descended Mount Vaibhāra, and returned to the town.

56 Thereafter, Ṛṣabhadatta and Dhāriṇī performed the duties of householders, and lived in hope of the promise made by the magician's son.

57 One night, Dhāriṇī saw a white lion in a dream. Like a deep lake full of bounteous joy, she told her husband.

58 Ṛṣabhadatta said, 'Lovely browed one, the prediction of the magician's son has been fulfilled. Consider it the truth; surely we believe it because of the dream.

59 A son named Jambū, of pure conduct, endowed with all the auspicious marks, will certainly be born to you, lady of great good fortune.'

60 Then the god Vidyunmālin fell from Brahma's heaven, and grew in Dhāriṇī's womb, like a pearl in a shell.

61 She had a pregnancy-longing to perform worship to the gods and teachers; the pregnancy-longings of women conform to the nature of the children they are carrying.

62 The merchant fulfilled her wish with copious expense. He spent his treasure on good works as if he too had a pregnancy-longing.

63 As her embryo grew, Dhāriṇī moved very slowly, as if attentive lest any harm should befall her baby.

64 In their surpassing whiteness, her cheeks were fellow students of the orb of the moon in the early morning.

65 And so when nine months and one week and a half had passed, Dhāriṇī gave birth to a son whose splendour diminished the sun.

66 Golden vessels, filled with unhusked grain, so pure as if it were made of powdered pearls, were deposited in Ṛṣabhadatta's house.

67 A grove of dūrvā grass grew on the ground around the merchant's seat from the shoots of dūrvā which had been scattered over him by women of good family.

68 Before the merchant's door, large bands of excellent wind instruments, suitable for all auspicious occasions, played the refrain of the dance of good fortune.

69 Little girls of good family, their hair tied into funnel-shapes with clusters of saffron-blossoms, sang and danced at a fast tempo before the door of his house.

70 Extremely relieved, Ṛṣabhadatta performed elaborate acts of worship to the gods and teachers, and gave gifts to whoever asked for them.

71 On an auspicious day, the merchant Ṛṣabhadatta, his mind fully armed with joy, named his son Jambū, after the rose-apple tree.

72 Fondling him on their laps day and night, his parents became delirious with joy; they forgot about everything else.

73 And the baby Jambū was the ornament of his parents' laps. He gradually grew up, just like their hearts' desire.

74 In time the son of Ṛṣabhadatta reached the prime of life, and became of marriageable age. He was the tree to the creeper of his parents' hopes.

75 Now in the same city lived Padmāvatī, wife of that crest-jewel of the rich, named Samudrapriya.

76 Likewise, the wife of Samudradatta, who was like an ocean of riches, was called Kanakamālā; virtue was her garland.

77 Likewise, the wife of Sāgaradatta, most venerable in his prodigious wealth, was Vinayaśrī, who ever abounded in modesty.

78 Likewise, the wife of Kuberadatta, like Kubera, the god of wealth, in his prosperity, was called Dhanaśrī; she possessed a great wealth of moral conduct.

79 Now the daughters of these couples had been in their previous

lives the wives of the god Vidyunmālin. Their names were, in order, as follows:

80 Samudraśrī, Padmaśrī, Padmasenā, and Kanakasenā; through their beauty they appeared as in their former lives.

81 Likewise the wife of Kuberasena was Kanakavatī. Śramaṇadatta's wife was Śrīṣeṇā.

82 The wife of Vasuṣeṇa was Vīramatī, and the wife of Vasupālita was called Jayasenā.

83 The names of their daughters were, in order: Nabhaḥsenā, Kanakaśrī, Kamalavatī, and Jayaśrī.

84 One day, the fathers of these eight maidens humbly requested Jambū's father:

85 'We have eight virgin daughters. They have well-rounded forms and graces, they have seen the far shore of knowledge of the arts, and are mistresses of the virtues. They are like the water nymphs.

86 They have reached the time of youth which is propitious to the auspicious rite of marriage. We have seen that your son would be a suitable husband for them.

87 The virtues of a bridegroom, good family, morality, youth, good looks, and so on, are possessed by the youth Jambū. This is a husband to be gained by acts of merit.

88 So graciously allow the young man Jambū to be betrothed to our eight daughters, as the moon was to the daughters of Dakṣa.

89 You are prosperous and of good family. Our request will not embarrass you. Join with us in a marriage alliance, and by all means oblige us.'

90 Ṛṣabhadatta joyfully agreed to their request. He himself had been longing eagerly for his son's marriage, and now he had been asked by them!

91 Having learnt that they were betrothed to a most excellent husband called Jambū, the girls, thinking themselves very fortunate, were delighted.

92 Meanwhile, holy Sudharman continued to wander, enlightening beings who were capable of enlightenment. He came and held a preaching assembly in that very place.

93 Suddenly the young man Jambū's hair stood on end. He was like

a bulb sprinkled with the nectar of the good news of Sudharman's arrival.

94 Jambū went to pay his respects to the excellent Supporter of the Flock, the repository of the wealth of religion, who had come there. Jambū travelled in his carriage, as swift as the wind.

95 He bowed to Sudharman, and foremost of the laity, listened to the teaching which flowed like nectar from the lotus of his mouth.

96 And this teaching caused a transformation in his mind, and granted him indifference to the world, a state difficult for wretched mortals to obtain.

97 Jambū bowed to reverend Sudharman and humbly declared, 'I shall undertake the life of a religious mendicant, which cuts the bonds of worldly existence.

98 Supreme master, I'll go and take leave of my parents and come back again, while you observe the beauty of the tree of religion in this garden.'

99 Reverend Sudharman agreed, and Jambū got into his carriage and drove to the city gate.

100 But the city gate was blocked with such a crowd of elephants, horses, and carriages that there was not even room for a sesamum seed to fall to the ground.

101 Jambū thought, 'If I wait until I can enter by this city gate, then I'll run out of time.

102 Having made reverend Sudharman wait, I can't stay here, since I need to go back to that place.

103 So I'll hurry my carriage, and enter by another gate. A better road is preferable to waiting for one who is impatient to make haste.'

104 But when the son of Ṛṣabhadatta hastened to the other gate, he saw there a rampart with catapults fastened to it.

105 On the catapults which were fixed to the rampart he saw big stones, studded with iron spikes, looking just like balls of adamantine thunderbolts fallen from the sky.

106 He thought, 'This stratagem has been undertaken through fear of an enemy army. What's the good of this gate which is full of hazards?

107 If a stone should fall on me while I pass by this road, it will be the end of me, the carriage, the road, and the driver!

108 If I encounter death in this way while not practising restraint, I will get a bad rebirth. For a good rebirth for those beings who die a bad death is as impossible as a flower in the sky.

109 Let me not deviate from my intention, having proclaimed it aloud. I shall be devoted to the honey of the lotus of the feet of the reverend Sudharman.'

110 So Ṛṣabhadatta's son turned around his carriage, and like a planet in a retrograde orbit, rushed back to that place which was protected by the feet of the Supporter of the Flock.

111 Jambū bowed to reverend Sudharman, and humbly declared three times, 'I undertake a vow of chastity.'

112 The holy one granted his acceptance. Thrilled at having undertaken that restraint, the son of Ṛṣabhadatta went home, free from the bad effects of desire.

113 He told his parents, 'I have heard from the mouth of the Supporter of the Flock the holy law which was first expounded by the omniscient one, which is a herbal medicine for the destruction of karma.

114 I am impatient to lead the life of a Jain monk. Please permit me, honoured parents. This continual cycle of death and rebirth is just like a prison for living beings.'

115 His parents wept, their voices faltering, 'Don't without reason become a wind uprooting the tendrils of our hopes!

116 We thought that you would take a bride, and that we would see our grandson's face, a moon for the night-flowering lotus of our eyes.

117 This is not the right time to become a monk. You should enjoy sensual pleasure in your youth. Why don't you want its usual customs, even for a short while?

118 Even if you insist on becoming a monk, dear child, consider for a while. We are your parents, after all.

119 Dear child, there are eight maidens whom we have chosen for you. Accept their hands, and perform the marriage ceremony.

120 Once you've done this, young man, there's nothing to prevent you from becoming a monk. We too, our purpose fulfilled, will join with you in becoming religious mendicants.'

121 But the young man said, 'I shall follow your command, but I must not be prevented from becoming a monk, like a hungry man prevented from eating.'

122 His parents gave their assent, and soon regretfully informed the wealthy parents of the eight girls:

123 'Our son will become a monk as soon as he has married the girls, but out of regard for us he will perform the marriage ceremony.

124 But if you are going to have the sin of remorse, then cancel the wedding. We are not at fault, for we are telling you.'

125 The eight rich men, their wives and families, were distressed, and conferred together in order to determine what was to be done.

126 The girls overheard their conversation, and said, 'Respected elders, we have made up our minds, so listen to what we've decided.

127 We have been given to a man named Jambū, and he alone is our husband. We cannot be given to another. This is the custom of the world:

128 kings speak once and for all, monks speak once and for all, and maidens are bestowed once and for all. These three, once and once only.

129 Since we were betrothed to Ṛṣabhadatta's son by the honoured feet of our parents, he alone is our resource. Our lives are subject to his wish.

130 Whether or not he becomes a monk, whatever Jambū does, that will be fitting for us, devoted to our husband.'

131 The girls' fathers told Jambū's father, 'Get ready for the wedding. What was said first is the thing to go by.'

132 Then the wealthy men and Ṛṣabhadatta, directed by the astrologers, fixed the auspicious time for the wedding for the seventh day after that.

133 The rich men were like brothers, and although there were eight of them, they were of one mind. They gathered together and ordered a large marriage-pavilion to be built.

134 There stood a canopy made of multi-coloured textiles, which looked like a mass of evening clouds drawn down from the surface of the sky.

135 There strings of pearls were everywhere festooned on banners, as if the moon had deposited his entire property of moonbeams.

136 The boughs of the radiant decorations which formed the arches of the doorways kept swaying in the wind, so that the pavilion

looked as if it were proclaiming by gesture an invitation to the wedding.

137 On all sides the pavilion was decorated with svastikas of seed-pearls, like rows of seeds sown for the growth of lucky-trees.

138 At the auspicious moment, Jambū was placed in a painted circle. Wearing clothes dyed in safflower, he blazed like Aryaman, the rising sun.*

139 The girls too were placed in the circle, and did not move outside it, like the wives of kings, who are forbidden ever to look upon the sun.

140 Then, at an auspicious moment, the young man and the maidens, standing in their respective places, duly performed the auspicious bathing ceremony.

141 When Ṛṣabhadatta's son had bathed, drops trickled from his hair, as if it were frightened of its imminent uprooting.

142 Perfume-girls censed young Jambū's hair; the smoke from the camphor and fragrant aloe-wood seemed to form a wreath.

143 One of the perfume-girls bound around his head a braid of flowers, curved like the neck of a noble horse.

144 Dhāriṇī's son wore a pair of radiant pearl earrings, their light like a pair of swans resting on the edges of the lotus of his face.

145 Jambū wore a string of pearls which hung down to his navel; they looked like a row of foam-bubbles from the salty ocean.

146 His body anointed with saffron, all his limbs bedecked with pearls, he shone brightly, like the full moon wearing strings of stars.

147 Ṛṣabhadatta's son wore white upper and lower garments, fringed and free from blemish, to bestow good fortune on the wedding.

148 Then, shaded by a parasol of peacock feathers, mounted on a noble horse, attended by followers like himself in age and dress,

149 his face covered by a veil, lavishly blessed by songs, sprinkled with salt by two young ladies at his sides,

150 as drums were struck with auspicious beating, as auspicious texts were read to him, Ṛṣabhadatta's son hastened to the door of the auspicious marriage-hall.

151 There a young married lady who still lived with her father bestowed wealth on young Jambū through gifts of curd and other lucky substances.

152 At the door he broke with his foot a round bowl filled with fire, and then entered the house of the mother goddesses, the house of prosperity and riches.
153 There young Jambū sat with the eight young maidens and awaited the auspicious marriage ceremony.
154 Then, at an auspicious moment, Ṛṣabhadatta's son entered the courtyard and led them round the fire, with the blessing of their parents.
155 Thrilled at the conjunction of the stars, flurried at the marriage rites, delighted at the auspicious turning, smiling at the offering of milk and honey,
156 attentive at the presentation of the wedding gifts, bustling at the lifting of the veil, tearful at the salutation, extremely pleased at the taking on the lap,
157 thus Dhāriṇī attained happiness at the auspicious wedding of her son. May married women enjoy uninterrupted happiness at the weddings of their sons!
158 When the wedding was over, a mountain of gold could have been made from the gifts given to the husband and his wives.
159 Then, with an assembly of companions bearing lucky torches, as women of good family sang a melodious benediction,
160 as musicians went before, sounding a low musical note, accompanied by singing which made the three musical instruments sound delightful,
161 as his joyful elder and younger relatives walked alongside him, Jambū went to his home, surrounded by his wives.
162 First of all, the husband and his wives bowed before the image of their family deity, and then the band tied around their wrists was loosened.
163 At that moment, Dhāriṇī and Ṛṣabhadatta, thrilled, themselves adored the god, the lord of Rose-apple Tree Island.*
164 Then young Jambū, adorned with all his finery, entered the bedchamber of the house, accompanied by his wives.
165 Although he was there with his wives, he maintained his state of chastity: even when by the side of the cause of passion, the great-minded remain passionless.

166 Now in Bharata there is a city near the Vindhya mountains named Jayapura; its king was called Vindhya.

167 That king had two famous sons: the elder was named Prabhava, the younger Prabhu.
168 One day, for some reason or other, the Lord of Jayapura gave the kingdom to Prabhu, the younger, although the elder, Prabhava, was still alive.
169 Thereupon, Prabhava in his pride left the city, and stayed in a rugged part of the Vindhya mountains.
170 He lived upon the proceeds of house-breaking, taking people hostage, highway robbery, and other thievish practices.
171 His spies came and told him, 'Tomorrow, the wealth of the young man Jambū will mock that of the god of wealth.'
172 They reported that at his auspicious wedding would be gathered many rich men, like wealth-bestowing wishing-gems.
173 So, provided with two spells, one to subdue people by sleep, the other to undo bolts and locks, he immediately entered the house of Dhāriṇī's son.
174 By means of his sleeping spell, King Vindhya's son put to sleep all the people who were awake, except for Jambū.
175 That spell had no power over him, since he was highly devoted to religious merit; usually even the god Śakra is unable to cause distress to those who are rich in religious merit.
176 Then, while everyone was asleep, Prabhava and his gang began to steal all their ornaments and money and other possessions.
177 Although the robbers were plundering, the great-minded Jambū was not angry or disturbed, but said playfully:
178 'Gentlemen! Gentlemen! Don't touch those invited guests, who are sleeping unsuspectingly. I'm the one who stays awake, their night-watchman.'
179 This utterance, endowed with the power of Jambū's religious merit, immediately paralysed the thieves' bodies. They were like clay statues.
180 As Prabhava looked, he saw Dhāriṇī's son surrounded by his wives, like a bull elephant surrounded by his females.
181 He introduced himself. 'I am the son of King Vindhya. I am called the great Prabhava. Favour me with your friendship.
182 Dear friend, give me the spell to paralyse people and set them free again, and I shall give you two spells which put people to sleep and open bolts and locks.'

183 Jambū said, 'Although I have eight excellent newly married wives, I am going to forsake them and become a monk, devoid of egotism.

184 Since I have now taken on the life of an ascetic, friend Prabhava, the spell which puts people to sleep is of no use to me.

185 Tomorrow, Brother, I shall abandon these riches, as abundant as blades of grass. So what would I, whose body is without activity, do with a spell?'

186 Prabhava loosened the sleeping spell, bowed to Dhāriṇī's son, and said, placing his hands together in salutation:

187 'Friend, enjoy sensual pleasure in your early manhood, and have compassion on these newly married wives of yours. You are intelligent.

188 Reap the fruit of sexual pleasure with these lovely-browed maidens. Your renunciation will be splendid, if undertaken immediately after that.'

The Story of the Man and the Honey-drops

189 The young man Jambū said, 'Even a very little pleasure which originates in sexual enjoyment entails a lot of pain; so why do I need the cause of sorrow?

190 Even though the pleasure in sexual intercourse is much smaller than a grain of mustard, the soul's pain is very great, like the man and the honey-drops:

191 Once upon a time a certain man who was travelling with a caravan came to a forest which was full of mighty streams, crocodiles, and thieves.

192 Robbers, fierce as tigers, charged towards the caravan in order to plunder it, and the caravan-travellers fled like deer.

193 Abandoned by the caravan, the man entered the great forest, his heart in his mouth, like rising water in a hollow.

194 A wild elephant, like a huge mountain, oozing a waterfall of rut-sap, its trunk uplifted, as if to pull down the clouds from the sky,

195 making the earth sink with the blows from its feet, as if it were riddled with holes, its jaws as red as heated copper, roaring mightily like a thundercloud,

196 like Yama, the god of death in person, wild with fury, charged towards the man, who ran away.

197 As if shouting, "Run, run! I'm going to kill you!", the elephant kept hitting his back with water sprayed from its trunk.

198 The man, jumping up and down in fear like a wooden ball, had almost been caught by the elephant, when he came to a well, covered over with grass.

199 Thinking, "The elephant will surely take my life; perhaps I shall survive in the well", he jumped into it. The hope of life is indeed hard to abandon.

200 By the rim of the well grew a fig-tree; one of its long roots hung down into the middle of the well, like a coiling serpent.

201 As the man fell into the well, he came to the root inside it. He grabbed it, and remained dangling, like a bucket hanging on a rope.

202 The elephant inserted its trunk into the well and touched the man's head, but was unable to grasp him, just as a sick man cannot grasp a healing-plant.

203 Deprived of its booty, it looked down over the side of the well, and saw a huge boa constrictor within it.

204 The boa constrictor saw the man as he fell, and opened its mouth with the intention of swallowing him; it was like another well within the well.

205 On the four sides of the hole he saw four cobras, arrows of the life-taking brother* of Kālindī.

206 Wishing to bite him, the malevolent cobras spread their hoods. They hissed, puffed, and blew.

207 Two mice, one white, one black, were intent on sawing the root of the fig-tree with their teeth, in order to cut through it.

208 And the mad rutting elephant, unable to reach the man, beat the trunk of the fig-tree, as if trying to uproot it.

209 As the root of the fig-tree swung, the man clung to it firmly with his hands and feet, as if he were wrestling with it.

210 As the elephant struck the root with its foot, spear-faced honey bees abandoned their honeycomb and soared upwards.

211 The bees bit the man with the iron pincers of their jaws; their bites penetrated to his bones, as if intent on dragging out his soul.

212 The man's limbs were covered by bees with upturned wings; he looked as if he had himself grown wings. He heartily longed to get out of the well.

213 Now and again, drops of honey from the honeycomb in the fig-tree fell onto his forehead, like drops of water from a water jar.
214 A drop of honey rolled from his brow and entered his mouth. And when the man tasted it, he experienced a blissful pleasure.
215 Now Prabhava, listen to and understand the moral of the story. The man is, of course, wandering in existence, and the forest is the cycle of death and rebirth.
216 Now the elephant is death, and the hole is birth as a human being. The boa constrictor is hell, and the four cobras, they are anger, pride, deceit, and greed.
217 The fig-tree root is the duration of life, and the two mice, the white one and the black one, are the light and the dark halves of the month, whose object is to cut away the length of life.
218 The bees are ailments, and the drops of honey, they, my friend, represent sexual pleasure; what wise man would delight in it?
219 Now if a god or a master of magic* could lift him out of the well, do you think the man, ruined by fate, would desire that or not?'
220 Prabhava said, 'Who indeed, when sinking into a sea of misfortune, would not wish for someone intent on helping him, to be like a raft?'
221 Jambū said, 'Why should I drown in the boundless sea of existence, when there is a Supporter of the Flock who is indeed a divine raft?'

The Story of Kuberadatta

222 Prabhava said, 'Brother, how can you be so cruel as to abandon your affectionate parents and your loving wives?'
223 Jambū replied, 'Who, although he is without relatives, remains attached to relatives, as a consequence of which he is bound by karma, like Kuberadatta?
224 Once upon a time, in the city of Mathurā lived a very fine prostitute named Kuberasenā; she was like the weapon of the god of love.
225 During her first pregnancy, she felt great distress. Her mother took her to the doctor, for a healer is a remedy for pain.
226 From the beat of her pulse and other symptoms the doctor knew that she was healthy. He said, "She is not sick, so what is the reason for this pain of hers?

227 A pair of twins has been conceived in her womb. They are very difficult for her to carry. That is the cause of her distress; it will last until she gives birth."

228 Her mother told her, "I shall abort your foetuses. Why bring about your death by preserving them?"

229 The prostitute said, "Blessings on my foetuses! A sow repeatedly gives birth to a large litter, and yet she survives."

230 So she endured the pain, and in due course gave birth to twins, a boy and a girl.

231 Her mother said to the prostitute, "These twins are your enemies; while they were in your womb, they brought you to death's door.

232 Breast-feeding these twins will take away your youth, and the youth of prostitutes is their livelihood; protect your youth, as your life!

233 Child, this pair of twins is like a turd fallen from your womb. Throw it out! This is our custom, after all."

234 The prostitute said, "Although that is the case, please be patient, mother. I shall nourish the twins for ten days."

235 In the end, the prostitute was given permission by her mother, and she nourished the babies, suckling them day and night.

236 And as she thus looked after the children day and night, the eleventh day dawned, looking like a night of death.

237 She had two rings made and engraved with the names Kuberadatta and Kuberadattā, and put them on their fingers.

238 With breaking heart, she made a wooden chest, filled it with jewels, and placed the two babies in it.

239 She herself let the chest float away in the current of the river Yamunā, and it travelled free from harm, floating like a duck.

240 Then Kuberasenā turned and went home, having given a libation to her children with the tears from her eyes.

241 The chest arrived at the gate of the city Śaurya which faced onto the River Yamunā. Two sons of wealthy merchants saw and grabbed it.

242 And when they saw the baby boy and the baby girl inside it, one took the boy, and the other took the girl.

243 And by inspecting the writing on the rings on the babies' fingers, they discovered that they were called Kuberadatta and Kuberadattā.

244 They both grew up in the houses of the two rich men, and were protected by them as carefully as a deposit entrusted by a powerful man.

245 In time, the two children became learned in the arts, and they attained their first youth, the purifier of beauty.

246 The two rich men realized that they were really suitable for each other, and with great joy prepared the festival in which they would take each other's hand.

247 As young people anointed them, a wise religious teacher placed in the couple's laps the image of the god of love, the guider of man and wife.

248 On the following day, the newly wed couple began playing at dice. They were like oceans whose flowing streams revealed their mutual love.

249 Somehow Kuberadatta's ring fell from his hand into the hand of his wife Kuberadattā.

250 Kuberadattā examined the ring in her hand, as if it were a coin to be tested, turning it again and again.

251 Kuberadattā thought, "This ring was fashioned with great care in a foreign country, and it seems, from the model of another ring."

252 Then, looking at her own ring again and again, with body trembling from her concentration on her idea, she became convinced:

253 "Made in one country by one craftsman, of equal weight, with names in the same writing, the two rings are like siblings.

254 Kuberadatta and I are like the two rings. Very similar in appearance, there is no doubt that we are twin brother and sister.

255 Alike in our bodies, we are certainly twins. Alas that fate has made us perform such a forbidden marriage!

256 The two rings were certainly made the same by our father or mother, with the same affection for us both.

257 Because we are twins, I should never have thought of him as a husband, and he should never have thought of me as a wife."

258 Kuberadattā, having thought this over, was certain that it was true. She placed the two rings in Kuberadatta's hand.

259 Then Kuberadatta examined the two rings in the same way, and became sunk in thought. Then he became very depressed.

260 Then he returned Kuberadattā's ring, and wisely went to his mother. He placed her under oath, and asked:

261 "Am I your legitimate son, or was I found, given or adopted, or am I another kind of son of yours? For even sons are of various kinds, no doubt about it."
262 And his mother yielded to his obstinate questioning, and told him the whole story of the discovery of the chest.
263 Kuberadatta said, "Mother, why has this sin been committed, marrying us, although we were known to be twins?
264 She was the better mother, the mother who, unable to nourish us, made a vessel for her fortune, and abandoned us in the current of a river.
265 The river current should have led to death, not to the committing of sin. Death is preferable to life. Committing sin is not life."
266 His mother replied, "We fools were deluded by the extremely captivating beauty of the two of you, so very suitable to each other.
267 Except for her, no girl seemed suitable for you; except for you, no man seemed suitable for her.
268 Today, you have only performed the ceremony of the taking of hands, but no sinful actions arising from the union of man and woman.
269 Even now you are still a youth, and, likewise, she is still a pure maiden. Farewell to her! Tell her that you are brother and sister, and let her go.
270 Son, you should go on a long business trip. May you travel safely and come back quickly, with our blessings.
271 When you come back safely, my son, I shall marry you with great festivity to another girl."
272 Thereupon Kuberadatta, who was right-minded, said "Very well", and went and told Kuberadattā what had been decided.
273 He said, "Go to your parents' house, my dear. You are my sister. You are intelligent and wise, so you should do the right thing.
274 What can we do, sister, thus deceived by our parents? Yet it is not their fault; it is our destiny.
275 In the way that parents sell or abandon their children, or order them to commit sins, in that way they incur bad karma for themselves."
276 Having spoken to her in this manner, Kuberadatta dismissed

her. Then he took up his trader's merchandise and went to the town of Mathurā.

277 And there he became very rich by trading in his merchandise, and he stayed there a long time, delighting in the customary pleasures of youth.

278 One day he gave money to the prostitute Kuberasenā, who was possessed of elegance and beauty of form, and made love with her.

279 And from his enjoyment of sensual pleasure with Kuberasenā, a son was born. Such is the drama of fate.

280 Meanwhile, Kuberadattā had gone home and questioned her mother, and her mother told her about the discovery of the chest.

281 Through hearing this, her own story, Kuberadattā became indifferent to the world. She became a Jain nun, and performed austerities, difficult to be endured.

282 But on becoming a nun, she hid the ring and abandoned it. Practising forbearance, she confessed to the nun who initiated her.

283 Her unbroken austerities, in which she had been instructed by the nun who had initiated her, produced a blossom on the tree of asceticism: the knowledge of things which lie beyond the normal range of the senses.

284 She wondered how Kuberadatta was faring, and saw that he had a son by his union with Kuberasenā.

285 And she, who was without sin, lamented, "Alas, my brother is like a boar, wallowing in the mire of sin!"

286 In order to enlighten him, she, an ocean of the water of compassion, went to Mathurā, accompanied by her fellow nuns.

287 And the venerable Kuberadattā, a harbinger of the attainment of righteousness, sought refuge with Kuberasenā.

288 Kuberasenā bowed to her and said, "Venerable lady, I'm a prostitute, but at present I'm living with one man, like a respectable woman.

289 Because I'm living with a respectable man, I wear these clothes of a respectable woman, and because of my respectable behaviour, I'm certainly worthy of your blessing.

290 So accept refuge in my home, and be close to me, like an ever-longed-for goddess."

291 Thereafter, Kuberadattā, attended by her retinue, a milk-cow of auspicious wishes for Kuberasenā, lived happily in the room assigned to her.

292 Kuberasenā used to go there day and night and let her little boy roll on the ground before the lotus-feet of the venerable nun.

293 Thinking, "As one has been enlightened one's self, so should one enlighten the soul of a child", the venerable nun spoke to the little boy, in order to enlighten him:

294 "Child, you are my brother, you are my son, you are my husband's younger brother, you are my paternal nephew, you are my paternal uncle, and you are my grandson.

295 Child, the man who is your father is my brother, father, grandfather, husband, son, and father-in-law also.

296 Child, the lady who is your mother is my mother, grandmother, sister-in-law, daughter-in-law, mother-in-law, and co-wife, alas!"

297 Kuberadatta heard this and cried, "What does this mean, venerable nun? What you say is self-contradictory. I am astounded!"

298 The venerable nun said, "This child is my brother, because we have the same mother. I say that he is my son, because he is my husband's son.

299 Because he is my husband's brother, he is my brother-in-law too, and because he is my brother's son, I declare that he is my nephew.

300 And he is my paternal uncle, because he is the brother of my mother's husband. I called him grandson, because he is the son of my co-wife's son.

301 His father is my brother, since we both have the same mother, and his father is my father, since he was my mother's husband.

302 Him I declare to be my grandfather, since he is my paternal uncle's father, and because he married me, he is my husband.

303 This is my son, because he was born from the womb of my co-wife, and because he is the father of my brother-in-law, he is my father-in-law also.

304 And the lady who is his mother is my mother as well, since she gave birth to me, and because she is the mother of my paternal uncle, she is my grandmother.

305 She is also my sister-in-law, because she is the wife of my brother, and because she is the wife of the son of my co-wife, she is my daughter-in-law.

306 Because she is the mother of my husband, she is my mother-in-law, no doubt about it, and because she is my husband's second wife, she has become my co-wife too."

307 She finished speaking, and showed her ring to Kuberadatta. He saw it and understood the entire calamity of his family connections.

308 Thereupon, Kuberadatta, having become desirous of emancipation, became a Jain monk. He practised austerities, and when he died, he became a guest of the women of heaven.

309 Kuberasenā became a Jain laywoman, and the venerable nun returned once more to the presence of her superior.

310 Thus one is bound by one's karma, alas. Like an oyster in a shell, the family relationships of foolish people are bound in it.

311 He who is himself situated in worldly bondage but who frees others from worldly bondage, that patient Jain monk is a relative; the others are relatives in name only.'

312 Prabhava spoke again, 'Young man, at least beget yourself a son to prevent your forefathers from falling into hell.

313 Fathers who are deprived of descendants certainly go to hell, so if you do not beget a son, you will not be freed from the fathers.'

The Story of Maheśvaradatta

314 Jambū said, 'This is an error, this belief that the father is saved by the son. Sir, the merchant Maheśvaradatta provides an example:

315 Once upon a time, in a town called Tāmaliptī, lived a rich merchant named Maheśvaradatta.

316 His father was a well-known man named Samudra, as greedy for wealth as is the ocean for water.

317 Abounding in various kinds of trickery, his mothers was named Bahulā; there was no limit to the extent of her miserliness.

318 When his father, a hole for the sweepings of greed, addicted to the hoarding of wealth, died, he was reborn as a buffalo in the same town.

319 His mother became like a moth to the fire of her thoughts of distress at her husband's death; she died and was born a bitch in the same place.

320 Maheśvara's wife was named Gaṅgilā; she was the source of his domestic bliss, as Gaurī is for the god Śiva.

321 Bereft of her in-laws, she lived on her own in the house, pleasing herself, like a doe in a forest.

322 Deceiving her husband, she had an affair with another man. How long lasts the fidelity of independent women?

323 The god whose emblem is a sea-monster* sees women who live alone in seclusion and, like one without fear, violently excites them.

324 One day, while she was making unrestrained love with her paramour, her husband suddenly stepped through the door and entered the house.

325 When the hussy and her paramour saw him, their hair dishevelled, fearful and tired from making love, their knees shaking, their eyes rolling,

326 grabbing their clothes which had been turned inside-out when they took them off, their feet stumbling, they ran away.

327 But Maheśvara grabbed the paramour by the hair, like a hunter grabbing a monkey, and slapped him, as a magician slaps someone tormented by ghosts.

328 He pounded him with blows from his feet, like a potter pounding a ball of clay, and he beat him with a club, as if he were a dog that had entered a house.

329 Why say more? Maheśvara half-killed him. But wise men feel anger towards neither thieves nor paramours.

330 The paramour, half-killed by Maheśvara, who was angry because of actions in his former lives, somehow managed to escape.

331 Gaṅgilā's paramour went a little way then fell. As his vital spirits ascended to his throat he thought:

332 "Alas! Alas! I'm going to die! I've performed a blameworthy action, which was like a wish-granting bathing place, auspicious for my death."

333 Thinking thus, he died, and in his very own semen in the womb of Gaṅgilā, whom he had just before enjoyed, he was conceived as a male embryo.

334 In due course, Gaṅgilā gave birth to a son. Although he was another man's son, Maheśvara regarded him as his own son and cherished him.

335 Because of his affection for his son, Maheśvara forgot about the sin of adultery committed by Gaṅgilā, who had given birth to him.

336 Filled with joy, Maheśvara was not ashamed to perform the duties of a nurse for his cuckolder's soul, which was embodied in his son.

337 As the boy grew and began to sprout a beard, Maheśvara always gave him the first place in his heart, just as a miser does his money.

338 One day, on the first anniversary of his father's death, Maheśvara bought the buffalo in which his dead father's soul was embodied, because he wanted its flesh.

339 He killed the buffalo as the sacrifice for the anniversary of his father's death, the hair of his body bristling for unbounded joy, himself Samudra's son!

340 Then Maheśvara, full of delight, ate the buffalo meat and fed it to the boy, who was lying in his lap.

341 Then his mother, who was the bitch, crept in, greedy for the meat. He threw down for her broken bones with scraps of meat on them.

342 She swallowed the bones in which her husband had been embodied, wagging her tail: it was like the plume of a column of smoke, wafted by the wind.

343 And while Samudra's son was thus eating his father's flesh, a Jain monk, who had completed a month-long fast, came by to seek a food offering.

344 The monk had gained supernatural knowledge, and so knew clearly all that had befallen Maheśvara.

345 And he thought, "Oh! Alas for the ignorance of this wretched man: he's eating his father's flesh and dandling his enemy on his lap!

346 And this bitch is eating with unbounded pleasure her husband's flesh-bearing bones! Alas, such is the cycle of death and rebirth!"

347 Comprehending the true situation, the monk passed by Maheśvara's house. But Maheśvara ran after him, and bowed and said:

348 "Reverend Sir, why have you turned from my house without accepting food? I'm by no means unreligious, I haven't treated you with contempt, and what's more, I'm in a good mood!"

349 The monk replied, "I never stop in the house of a meat-eater,

so I didn't accept a food offering. Besides, I was extremely disgusted."

350 When the merchant asked him why, the monk told him the whole story of the buffalo and the bitch.

351 And when Maheśvara asked, "What proof is there?", the monk said, "Oh, ask the bitch where something has been previously buried."

352 So he asked the bitch, and with her paw she scraped the earth where their savings were buried, as if making a place to rest, in the manner of her kind.

353 Maheśvara was convinced. He became disgusted with the world. He gave away his fortune to worthy people, and became a Jain monk.

354 So, good Prabhava, what have you got to say now about the opinion of those who believe that sons enable their parents to cross the waters of hell?'

The Story of the Farmer

355 Straightaway, Samudraśrī said to Jambū, 'Husband, don't be regretful later on, like the farmer:

356 Once upon a time in a village called Susīma, famous the world over, lived a farmer named Baka. He was prosperous in property and grain.

357 When the right season of the year arrived, with great diligence he sowed millet and kodrava* seeds in his ploughed and harrowed fields.

358 Dark coloured shoots of grain sprang up in the field; they looked like masses of thick hair tied in braids.

359 When he saw that the grove of millet and kodrava was flourishing, he was delighted, and went to a certain distant village as the guest of his kinsfolk.

360 His kinsmen fed him on syruped wheatcakes. He was exceedingly pleased with this food, which was quite new to him.

361 Gratified, he said to his kinsfolk, "Ah, life is good for you who have this beautiful food. It is as sweet as nectar!

362 Not even in a dream have I seen such food as this! Alas for us hog-men whose bowels are parched by millet and kodrava!"

363 Then, since he did not know what the treacled wheatcakes were,

he asked his kinsmen, "What are the ingredients of this dish, and where do they come from?"

364 They told him, "Oh, wheat is sown in the same way as other grains, when the fields have been sprinkled with water from a waterscoop.

365 When it is ripe, it is reaped and ground by a millstone, then cooked in an iron vessel heated by a fire: wheatcakes!

366 Sugar cane is planted in the same way. When it has grown, it is pressed; syrup is made from the juice which comes from it."

367 Thus the farmer learnt how to make syruped wheatcakes. He returned to his own village, taking seeds of wheat and sugar cane.

368 Then Baka, who only had a mother's education, went to his field and frantically started mowing down his crop-bearing millet and kodrava.

369 His sons asked him, "Father, why are you mowing down the half-grown crop, as if it were just grass?"

370 Baka replied, "Hey sons, away with this kodrava and stuff! I'm going to sow sugar cane and wheat here. We'll live on syruped wheatcakes!"

371 His sons replied, "In a few days this grain will be ripe. Reap it, Father, and you may sow as much sugar cane and wheat as you like.

372 This crop is ripe; there is uncertainty about the wheat and the sugar cane. Why build up hopes for a child in the womb, when there's one being carried on the hip?"

373 Although his sons opposed him in this way, Baka cut down the grove of kodrava and millet; for there he was the master.

374 When he had mown down the corn, that simple Baka made the ground of the field fit for playing a ball game on it.

375 Then he dug a well alongside. But no water came from it, just as milk does not come from a breast bound in bands.

376 Baka tirelessly dug his well, hole upon hole; it looked like the pit of hell. But not even mud came out of it.

377 So then he had not even millet or kodrava, never mind sugar cane and wheat, and afterwards he regretted it very much.

378 In renouncing the pleasures of wealth and women in this world, while hoping for the pleasures of the other world, don't be like

him and build your hopes upon a doubtful matter, and then be deprived of both!'

The Story of the Crow

379 But great-hearted Jambū replied with a smile, 'Hey, Samudraśrī, I'm not stupid, like the crow!

380 Once upon a time, on the bank of the river Narmadā in the Vindhya forest, lived a huge elephant, the leader of the herd; he was like the heir-apparent of the Vindhya mountain.

381 Roaming freely in the Vindhya forest, he passed away his youth; he reached old age, the far shore of the river of life.

382 His strength gone, no longer able to bite on trees, no longer producing ichor, like a mountain whose cascading torrents are dried up by the summer heat,

383 having abandoned breaking groves of sallakī, karnikā, and other kinds of tree, too frightened to climb up and down, from high to low and from low to high,

384 eating scantily because his teeth had fallen out, suffering stomach pains because of his desire to eat, his body looking like a bag of bones, the elephant was in his dotage.

385 One day, the elephant trapped his foot while crossing a dry mountain stream; he fell like the peak of a mountain.

386 The old elephant was not able to rise. He remained in that place, just as if he were protecting a tree from approach.

387 In that position he died. Dogs, jackals, mongooses, and other animals devoured the flesh from the buttocks of the corpse.

388 The carcass of this huge being, the cleft of its buttocks looking like a valley in a mountain, became the abode of beasts of prey.

389 Crows repeatedly flew in and out of the anus, which was a place of refuge, sating themselves on the food. They were like Brahmins.

390 One crow was still very hungry after eating the flesh. He remained there inside the anus; it was as if an excrement-worm had appeared.

391 Relishing the best parts in the interior of the body, he entered deeper and deeper inside, like an insect in a piece of wood.

392 His body performing a forcible entrance into another's body, the crow was like an extraordinary magician.

393 Steadily devouring the raw flesh of the elephant's body, like an ant, not discriminating between the front and rear portions, he reached the very middle.

394 But the anus of the elephant's body was touched by a ray of sun. It closed, just as before when it had discharged excrement.

395 Thereupon the crow was shut in the elephant's body, the anus having closed, just like a snake in a wicker basket when its lid is shut.

396 When the rainy season came, the elephant's body was drawn away by the hands of the waves and carried by a swollen stream of rainwater to the river Narmadā.

397 Like a floating sailing ship, the elephant's corpse was carried by the river Narmadā to the ocean, as if it were a gift for its crocodiles.

398 The crow emerged from an opening formed in the corpse, which had been split by the billowing waters which had penetrated it.

399 The crow settled on its upper part; it was like an island. The crow sat and looked round in all directions.

400 In front, on both sides, and behind, he saw nothing but water. He thought, "I'll fly up and go to the ocean shore."

401 Again and again he flew up, but he did not come to the end of the ocean. Again and again he settled back on the same place on the body.

402 Seized on all sides by fish, sharks, and other creatures, the corpse suddenly sank, like an overloaded ship.

403 Lacking any support, the crow too sank in the ocean, and soon gave up the ghost, as if from fear of bathing in the water.

404 Now, women are like that fallen forest elephant, the cycle of death and rebirth is like the ocean, and men are like the crow.

405 I'm not going to become enamoured of you, who are like the elephant's corpse, and, like the crow, drown in the ocean of existence.'

The Story of the Pair of Monkeys

406 Then Padmaśrī said, 'If you set us aside, husband, you'll regret it very much later, like the monkey:

407 Once upon a time, in a certain forest lived a male monkey and a female monkey. They were passionately devoted to each other and always avoided being separated.

408 Side by side they fed each other, like a pair of talking birds. Side by side they climbed the trees, as if racing each other.

409 Side by side they ran, as if pulled together by a rope. Side by side they did everything, as if always of one mind.

410 One day, the two monkeys were playing among the reeds along the banks of the river Ganges. The male monkey failed to take care while jumping and fell to the ground.

411 Immediately, through the power of that holy place, the monkey turned into a young man. He looked like a young god; it was like magic.

412 Then the female monkey, having seen the male monkey attain the form of a man, desired the form of a woman. She abandoned her life in the same way as the male monkey.

413 Thereupon the female monkey immediately turned into a woman, as beautiful as a goddess. With renewed affection she embraced the male monkey.

414 The man and the woman played together as in their previous monkey-lives, and were ever inseparable, like the moon and the night.

415 One day the monkey who had become a man said to the woman, "Today we shall become gods, just as we previously became human beings."

416 The woman said, "My dear, don't be discontented; we already have human form. Let's enjoy sensual pleasures.

417 Let divinity be; our pleasure certainly surpasses divinity, that pleasure which we two enjoy, always unseparated, freely and without hindrance."

418 But although she tried in this manner to prevent him, the brave monkey-man jumped from the high reeds, just as he had done before.

419 By the power of that holy place, an animal who had become a human being and a human being who had become a god would turn back into their former shapes, if they fell again.

420 So when he jumped back into that same holy place, he became a monkey again, because he had been a monkey in his former life.

421 Now the woman's face was like a ray of the full moon at night; her neck was a spiral shell; her breasts were large, her belly slim; she had fine hips; her hands and feet were like lotuses.

422 The auspicious mark on her forehead looked like the ocean; her hair was bound with a creeper. She wore a chaplet of wild ketaka and a bracelet of tālikā leaves.

423 She wore a necklace of lotus stalks; her eyes were like those of a doe. One day some royal servants who were passing by saw her.

424 The men took her and handed her over to the king; for whatever has no owner belongs to the king.

425 He made her, whose beauty was divine, the crest-jewel of his harem; the signs of good fortune shown by a woman endowed with beauty are indeed honoured guests.

426 But the male monkey was captured by some men who had come to that place. They trained him, like a son, to perform various kinds of dances.

427 One day, the dancers came before the presence of that very king. As they danced, they exhibited the monkey to him.

428 The monkey began to cry when he saw his beloved sharing a seat with the king, as if he were showing his inner feelings by his falling tears.

429 The king said, "As is your fate, monkey, so you must endure it! You fell from the reeds, so don't feel regret for your present fallen state."

430 So don't you too, like that monkey, feel sorrow and regret after you have abandoned the sensual pleasures which are here at hand.'

The Story of the Charcoal Burner

431 Jambū replied, 'I am not thirsty for sensual pleasures, Padmaśrī, like the charcoal burner:

432 Once upon a time, a certain charcoal burner went to a big forest to burn charcoal. He took a lot of water to drink when the heat should become oppressive.

433 While making his charcoal with a very hot fire, he became inflamed by the heat; his thirst was unquenchable.

434 Again and again the poor man drank and sprinkled his body with water, like a wild elephant; he used up all his water.

435 All the water did not assuage the charcoal burner's thirst, even in the slightest degree; it was like oil on a fire.

436 The charcoal burner set out for a lake to drink its water, but he was so blind with thirst that he fell down half-way there.

437 He happened to fall into the shade of a roadside tree; a pool of nectar, it was like the goddess of coolness.

438 Refreshed by the cooling shade at the foot of the tree, he gradually fell into a slumber, which was an ocean of sweet waters.

439 In a dream he dried up lakes, wells, ponds, every receptacle of water, like a brand of fire shot with a magic spell.

440 Still his thirst was not assuaged. As he wandered, tormented by his craving for water, he saw an old well, its water thick with mud.

441 Unable to drink its water with his hands, he lapped it with his tongue, but, like a man with a burning fever, he was not in the least satisfied.

442 So the soul is like the charcoal burner, dearest, and the pleasures of gods, demigods, and other deities are like the water in the lakes and the other receptacles.

443 How can the soul, which is not satisfied by the various heavens, be satisfied by human pleasures? Have no yearning for them!'

The Story of Nūpurapaṇḍitā and the Jackal

444 Then Padmasenā said, 'The vital parts of our bodies are subject to decay, so enjoy sensual pleasures!

445 There are many parables of encouragement and discouragement: the story of Nūpurapaṇḍitā and the jackal, for instance.

446 Once upon a time, in the city of Rājagṛha, lived a goldsmith named Devadatta and his son Devadinna.

447 Devadinna's wife was named Durgilā; foremost of cunning women, she was an ocean of beauty.

448 One day, she went to the river to bathe. She stirred the senses of the young men with her sidelong glances, arrows of amorous passion.

449 Wearing golden bangles on every limb, resplendent in her radiant garments, she ornamented the river bank. She was like the river goddess personified.

450 The big-bosomed woman slowly removed her blouse, revealing both her breasts; they were like citadels of the god of love.

451 The slim-bodied lady handed her blouse and upper garment to her maid. Then she wrapped her breasts with her folded scarf.

452 Inflamed by the knowing chatter of her lady friends, her sexual

passion alive, she slowly passed from bank to bank like a flamingo.

453 The river reached up from below his billowing hands, and embraced her entire body, as if she were a girlfriend seen after a long absence.

454 Her eyes were like those of a startled dappled antelope. Eager to play with the water, like a ship she cleft the river with the oars of her hands.

455 As she slowly bathed, splattering the river in fun, her hands and feet shone like dancing water lotuses.

456 Her one garment untied, her hair unbound, her lips gleaming, engrossed in playing in the water, she looked as if she had been made for love.

457 As she played in the middle of the river, like a goddess in the middle of the ocean, a certain dissolute young-man-about-town happened to stroll by and see her.

458 She was covered only with a single garment which was thin and damp with water; he could clearly see her entire body. He burst out excitedly:

459 "The river wishes you a pleasant bath; so do the trees, and I too, as I fall before the lotus of your feet."

460 She replied, "A blessing on the river; may the trees long be joyful. I shall satisfy the desire of those who wish me a pleasant bath."

461 When he heard her reply, which was like a sprinkling of nectar for the bud of the creeper of love, he still held himself back, as if at the command of a king.

462 And while this man was wondering who she was, he saw some boys under a tree, their faces upturned as they waited for the fruit to fall.

463 Thereupon the young man threw clods of earth at the branches of the tree, and with a rat-tat! he made the fruit fall to the ground.

464 The boys were delighted because he had got them as much fruit as they wanted. He asked them, "Who is that lady bathing in the river? Where does she live?"

465 The boys replied, "Sir, she is the daughter-in-law of a goldsmith called Devadatta, and her home is over there."

466 Now Durgilā thought about that young man with single-minded

concentration. She ceased her playful bathing and went straight home.

467 Day and night, they both wondered, "On what night, on what day, in what place, and at what moment, shall we two meet together?"

468 Distressed by their separation, hoping for a secret union, the couple remained apart, like a pair of long-devoted "cakra"-cawing birds.*

469 The next day he won over, with offerings of food and other things, a Jain nun who was like a family goddess for loose women, and begged her:

470 "Devadatta's daughter-in-law and I are in love with each other. Be like the goddess of our destiny made manifest, and quick, bring about our union!

471 Herself the go-between, I have already spoken with the lovely-browed lady. A meeting has been promised me. Your job is easy."

472 Saying "I'll do it easily", the shrewd nun straightaway went to Devadatta's house, pretending to beg for food.

473 She saw the goldsmith's daughter-in-law busy cleaning her pots and pans. She quickly said to her,

474 "There is a young man, an image of the god of love, who wants to enjoy sexual pleasure. By my mouth he begs you, 'Oh big eyes, please don't disappoint me!'

475 Meet this young man who is your equal in beauty, youth, intelligence, shrewdness, and other qualities, and fulfil his wishes!

476 Since he saw you bathing in the river, dear, he's been mad with singing your praises; he pays no regard to other women."

477 But Durgilā was clever. To conceal the feelings of her heart she scolded the nun with harsh words:

478 "Have you been on the booze, baldhead,* that you speak among people of good breeding what is not fit for those of low breeding? You worthless creature, are you a procuress?

479 Ugh! Go away! Get out of my sight, you whose very appearance is lustful! Your appearance is bad enough, how can one describe your wicked talk!"

480 As the scolded nun turned to go, Durgilā slapped her on the back with her hand, which was black with grime, as if on a whitened wall.

481 Then the nun, not understanding Durgilā's mind, was annoyed.* She went to the dissolute young man and said roughly:

482 "Hey!, you were wrong when you said, 'She's in love with me'. She's proud of her unbroken wifely virtue. She scolded me as if I were a bitch.

483 My errand to this virtuous lady was in vain, you simpleton. Even a skilful painting needs a wall to be spread upon.

484 She was busy with her housework, she angrily slapped me on my back with her open hand; it was black with grime."

485 With these words the nun showed this eminent rogue her back, which was marked with the smears of grime placed there by Durgilā.

486 But he realized that the five fingers of the hand placed on the nun's back signified that she had agreed to meet him on the fifth night of the dark fortnight:

487 "How clever of her to let me know the time of the meeting in this roundabout way! Courage, my heart!

488 She did not name the place of the meeting for some reason. Alas! even now there is an unhappy obstacle to union with her."

489 Again he spoke to the nun, "You don't know her mind; she's certainly in love with me. Go and ask her again.

490 By all means, don't despair about my plan, mother. Go once more! Confidence is the first root of the creeper of good fortune."

491 She replied, "That well-bred lady cannot stand your very name. What you want is as difficult as making water rise up a mound.

492 There is uncertainty about the accomplishment of your plan, but I'm certain about the abuse! Nevertheless, I'll set aside despair and go right now."

493 Having said this, the nun hurried to the goldsmith's daughter-in-law and spoke to her once more with words like flowing nectar:

494 "Come, make love with that young man who is like yourself in beauty! Pluck the fruit of youth! That is right for youth, surely."

495 Durgilā, pretending to be angry, grabbed her by the throat, and with vehement abuse pushed her through the door back into a grove of Aśoka trees.

496 Although she was bald-headed, she covered her face for shame

in her drawn-over veil. Full of distress, she quickly hurried back to the man and said:

497 "She abused me just as before. Then she grabbed me by the throat and pushed me through the door back into a grove of Aśoka trees nearby."

498 The clever man realized, "She has surely given me a signal that I should come to the nearby grove of Aśoka trees."

499 And he said to her, "I must endure this humiliation which she has given me. She is certainly a bad woman. Speak to her no more after this."

500 Then, on the evening of the fifth night of the dark fortnight, the young man went by a back way to the nearby grove of Aśoka trees.

501 Although a long way off, he saw her glancing* along the path. She saw him too. Brilliant was the conjunction of their unwavering eyes.

502 Like their eyes, their arms stretched out towards each other, and as they ran together, all the hair on their bodies bristled with excitement.

503 Before, they were of one mind; now, their bodies became one. They embraced as tightly as an ocean and a river.

504 With talk of love, and with continually renewed acts of love, sunk in an ocean of sexual pleasure, they spent two watches of the night.

505 Then, exhausted by sexual pleasure, as they rested their cheeks upon their arms, sleep came upon them, a starry night for the lotuses of their eyes.

506 But then Devadatta got up to see to his bodily functions. He entered the Aśoka grove and saw them lying together.

507 He thought, "How shameful! This wicked daughter-in-law of mine is sound asleep, tired out from making love with another man."

508 To find out whether the man was indeed a paramour, the old man went home and saw his son sleeping. He came back and thought:

509 "I shall gently remove her anklet from her foot so that my son will believe me when I tell him that she is untrue."

510 At once, Devadatta, like a thief, removed her anklet and went home by the same way.

511 At the removal of her anklet the goldsmith's daughter-in-law immediately woke up. As if through fear, the sleep of those who sleep in fearful situations is usually light.

512 She knew that her father-in-law had removed her anklet from her foot. She awoke her lover and, quaking with fear, said:

513 "Quick! Go away! My wicked father-in-law has seen us! Please try to help in this disaster which has befallen me."

514 He agreed to do what she asked, and half-dressed ran away in fright. The adulteress quickly went and lay by the side of her husband.

515 Foremost of clever women, she pretended to be randy and roused her husband, embracing him tightly.

516 She said, "Husband, the heat is oppressing me, so come to the Aśoka grove; its blossoms waft a cool breeze."

517 Devadinna, who was sincerely devoted to his wife, got up and went to the Aśoka grove; she clung to his neck.

518 She went to the very same place where her father-in-law had seen her lying with her lover; she lay down and embraced her husband tightly.

519 And there too her husband, whose disposition was innocent, fell asleep; for sleep usually comes easy to the pure of heart.

520 Then, the crafty woman, her facial expression guarded like an actress, said to her husband, "What is this custom in your family which no one can give a name to?

521 After I had made love with you, as I was sleeping with my breasts uncovered, my father-in-law removed the anklet from my foot and took it away.

522 Daughters-in-law should not be touched by their fathers-in-law at all, let alone when they are lying with their husbands in the chamber of love!"

523 Devadinna replied, "My good wife, I'll rebuke my father about this first thing in the morning, while you watch."

524 She said, "You should ask your father to explain himself right now. In the morning he will certainly declare that I was sleeping with another man."

525 He said, "With you right by my side, I shall accuse my father, saying, 'You took the anklet while I was asleep.'"

526 And the clever woman made him promise firmly: "At daybreak he'll be spoken to, just as you say now, dear."

527 So in the morning Devadinna angrily asked his father, "Why did you remove your daughter-in-law's anklet?"

528 The old man replied, "My son, this here daughter-in-law has loose morals, no doubt about it. Last night I saw her lying with another man in the Aśoka grove.

529 To give you firm proof that she is a loose woman, I removed the anklet from my daughter-in-law's foot and brought it away."

530 His son said, "I was the one who was sleeping; it wasn't another man. Father, why have you, shameless, shamed me so?

531 Return the anklet, which you removed while I was sleeping, to your daughter-in-law. Don't you, my father, accuse her. She is an exceedingly virtuous wife indeed."

532 The old man said, "When I removed the anklet, I returned and saw you sleeping in the house."

533 Durgilā said, "I am not able to endure the imputation of false accusations to myself. I shall convince my father-in-law by performing a holy deed.

534 A mere word such as this is a stain on me, a woman of good breeding. A black speck on a newly washed white garment has a bad appearance.

535 I shall now pass between the legs of the Yakṣa Śobhana;* for no impure person is able to pass between his legs."

536 The vow of this ocean of audacity was approved by the father, who doubted her, and by the son, who believed her.

537 She bathed, and, wearing a clean white garment and bearing incense, flowers, and food, went to worship the Yakṣa in the presence of all her kinsfolk.

538 But as she was worshipping the Yakṣa, her lover, by previous arrangement, like a man possessed, clung to her neck, just as the 'k' sound sticks in the throat.

539 The people, thinking he was mad, grabbed him by the throat and bound him. She bathed again, worshipped the Yakṣa, and declared:

540 "I have never touched another man except my husband and this madman who clung to my neck before everyone's eyes.

541 No other man besides my husband and this madman has embraced my body. So give me back my good name; I am virtuous and you favour the virtuous!"

542 And while the perplexed Yakṣa was wondering what to do, she quickly passed between his legs.

543 Immediately the tumultuous people shouted, "She is pure! She is pure!" The royal official threw a garland round her neck.

544 A trumpet sounded as her joyful kinsmen thronged around her. Welcomed by Devadinna, she returned to her father-in-law's house.

545 Because she had refuted the stain of dishonour which had come about through the removal of the anklet (nūpura), people called her Nūpurapaṇḍitā (Clever Nūpurā).

546 From that time on, Devadatta, who had been outwitted by his clever daughter-in-law, could not sleep for worry, like an elephant tied to a post.

547 When the king found out that he was as sleepless as a magician, he granted his request to be made watchman of the royal women's quarters.

548 One night, one of the queens kept looking again and again at the watchman to see whether or not he was asleep.

559 He thought, "I don't know why she keeps getting up and watching me again and again."

550 To find out what she would do if he were asleep, the watchman lay down, pretending to be asleep. Then she came out again.

551 Thinking he was sound asleep, she became overjoyed. She went over to the window, as softly as a thief.

552 Below the window, the king's favourite elephant was tied. Always in rut, he was like the younger brother of the elephant god.

553 She was passionately in love with the keeper of that elephant. She opened the movable window-shutter and went outside.

554 The elephant, well trained by the regular occurrence, grasped her by his trunk and set her on the ground. But when the elephant-driver saw her, he became angry.

555 He gave her a harsh look and said, "Why have you come so late?" He struck the queen with the elephant chain, as if she were a slave.

556 She cried, "Don't strike me! The king has set a new watchman over the royal women's quarters; he always stays awake. He held me back."

557 She explained, "At last, when I saw that he was sound asleep, I came. Don't be angry, Sundara."

558 When this was explained to him, the elephant keeper set aside his anger and began to make love with her, fearlessly, in just the way he wanted.

559 But in the last watch of the night, this great ocean of audacity was lifted by the elephant's upraised trunk and returned to her bedchamber.

560 Then the goldsmith thought, "Oh, who is able to understand the behaviour of women! They are like neighing horses.

561 Even the virtue of queens, who never look upon the sun, is corrupted! What shall one say about other women!

562 How long preserved is the morality of common housewives who go to town for food and drink and things?"

563 Thus he abandoned his unbearable thoughts about his daughter-in-law's bad morals. And there he slept soundly, like a man who was weighed down by debt but whose debt has now been paid.

564 But in the morning the old goldsmith did not awake, and the servants told the king about the state he was in.

565 The king said, "There is some reason for this occurrence. When he awakes, bring him to our presence."

566 Thus commanded, the servants went. But the goldsmith slept sweet and sound for seven nights long.

567 At the end of the seventh night he awoke, and the servants brought him before the king. The king asked him:

568 "Sleep never comes to you, like a beloved woman to an unfortunate man. So why have you slept for seven nights? Speak! Don't be afraid!"

569 So then he told the king about the nocturnal doings of the queen, the elephant keeper, and the elephant, just as he had seen them.

570 The king pardoned him and dismissed him. He returned to his own home. Thinking, "When sorrow has wasted away, happiness remains", the man attained a state of fortitude.

571 In order to find out which one was the immoral queen, the king ordered an elephant to be made out of bamboo. He commanded all the queens:

572 "I saw in a dream that you should, wearing no clothes, climb this imitation elephant made from bamboo, as I watch."

573 All the queens did this, as the king looked on. But then that particular queen cried, "I'm frightened of that imitation elephant!"

574 In anger the king hit her with the stalk of a blue lotus. Pretending to swoon, she fell to the ground.

575 The king had deliberately found out that she was that very same unchaste, wicked woman whom the old man had told him about.

576 And when he saw that her back was bruised from the blows of the chain, he clicked his fingernails and said with a sneer:

577 "You sport with a rutting elephant, yet you are frightened of an elephant made of bamboo! You delight in the blows of a chain, yet you swoon at the blow of a lotus!"

578 A mass of blazing anger, he went to Mount Vaibhāra, and summoned the elephant keeper, mounted on the elephant.

579 He made the elephant keeper's girlfriend, the queen, mount the elephant also. The king, who was severe in punishment, ordered that vile elephant keeper:

580 "Make the elephant climb this rugged mountain side; then make it jump down. Let your punishment come from its fall."

581 The elephant keeper made the elephant climb to the summit of the mountain. Then he made it stand firm on three feet, with one foot raised.

582 The people exclaimed "Ah! Ah!" in astonishment, and said, "Excellent king, it is not right that this animal which performs its orders, this excellent elephant, should die."

583 But the king did not listen and just said, "Make it jump!" Whereupon the elephant keeper made the elephant stand on two feet.

584 Again the people cried, "Ah! Ah! Don't kill the elephant!", but the king remained silent. Then the elephant keeper made the elephant stand on one leg.

585 The people could not bear to see the death of this excellent elephant. Exclaiming "Ah! Ah!", with upraised arms, they shouted to the king:

586 "Lord of the Earth, there can be no other elephant like this well-trained royal elephant. It is as hard to come by as a conch shell which spirals from left to right.

587 You are the king; you don't depend on another. You do what you

want. Disgrace might freely come upon you for your lack of judgement.

588 The master must decide for himself what he should or should not do. Make your decision, protect this excellent elephant, and grant us your favour."

589 The king said, "So be it. All of you call to the elephant keeper in my name to save the elephant."

590 The people said, "Chief of elephant drivers, can you bring the elephant back to the ground?"

591 He replied, "I shall bring down this elephant in safety, if the king grants us both safety for today."

592 The people reported this to the king, and he granted the couple their safety. The elephant keeper carefully brought the elephant down.

593 The king ordered them, "Leave my kingdom!", and the elephant keeper and the queen climbed down from the elephant's back and ran away.

594 They continued to run. At the end of the day they came to a village. They slept together in a deserted temple.

595 Then, at midnight, a robber ran from the village, fleeing the police. He went into the temple.

596 But the village police surrounded the temple, declaring confidently that they would capture the thief in the morning.

597 The thief investigated the temple with his hands, like a blind man. He gradually came to the place where those two were sleeping.

598 Although the robber touched him, the elephant keeper did not wake up, for sleep sticks like cement to a person in the sleep of exhaustion.

599 But at the light touch of his hand, the queen awoke, and at his touch she fell in love with him. She asked, "Who are you?"

600 She spoke to him quietly and he replied quietly, "I'm a robber. The police are chasing me, and I came in here to save my life."

601 Her passion aroused, she, an unchaste wife in deed if not in name, said to the thief, "I'll save you, no doubt about it, my dear, if you desire me."

602 The thief said, "I have got gold and perfume, if you become my wife and save my life.

603 But first let me ask you, beautiful, how will you save me? Tell me and cheer me up, you clever woman."

604 She said, "My dear, when the men of the village come, I'll say that you are my husband." He agreed to this.

605 And in the morning the village guards entered. Frowning fearfully, brandishing their swords, they asked the three, "Which is the robber?"

606 The cunning woman, truly the embodiment of deception, pointed to the robber and said to the village guards, "This is my husband."

607 She put together her hands in greeting and continued, "Brothers, we two are travelling to another village. When evening came, we spent the night in this abode of the gods."

608 The villagers gathered together and deliberated, saying, "Such a worthy woman couldn't possibly be found in a thief's house.

609 She must be the wife of a Brahmin, a merchant, a cavalryman, or some other. She is an image of purity. A thief could not possibly be her husband.

610 Adorned with brilliant garments, she is as beautiful as the goddess of Prosperity. How could the one who has this lady for his wife live by theft?"

611 Therefore, they accused the elephant driver, saying "This one is the thief!", and immediately impaled him on a stake.

612 Impaled upon the stake, he cried out in distress to whomever he saw coming along the road, "Give me water! Give me water!"

613 But through fear of the king, no one gave him water; for everyone obeys the law of self-preservation.

614 He saw a Jain layman named Jinadāsa travelling along the road and begged him for water. He replied:

615 "I shall relieve your thirst. But follow my advice: you should call out 'Reverence to the Worthies' while I'm bringing the water."

616 Thirsting for water, the elephant keeper began to shout this. The Jain layman brought the water with the permission of the royal ministers.

617 When the elephant keeper saw him bringing water, he took heart, although he was in distress. Loudly reciting "Reverence to the Worthies", he gave up the ghost.

618 Although he was uninstructed in morality and had not renounced sensual pleasure, he became an Interstitial god.*

619 The adulteress had set out along the way with the thief. They came to a river; its waters were swollen and it was impossible for her to cross.

620 The thief said to the adulteress, "My dear, I can't get you across in one go, laden down with your clothes and ornaments.

621 Give me all your clothes and ornaments, beautiful. I'll take them across first, then you. It will be easy.

622 Hide yourself in the reed thickets while I'm away. Don't worry about being alone. I'll be back soon.

623 I'll cross with you on my back and, like a boat on the sea, take you to the other side. Don't worry. Do what I say."

624 The adulteress obeyed and went into the reed thicket. But when he had reached the other side with her clothes and ornaments, he thought:

625 "This woman who caused her husband's death because she was in love with me is like turmeric; she becomes red with passion in an instant. She might cause my destruction."

626 The thief stole her clothes and ornaments. He turned his head to look at her, and ran like an antelope.

627 Like a female elephant, she raised her hands,* as naked as she was born. As she saw him go, she shouted, "Why are you running away and leaving me?"

628 The thief replied, "Seeing you standing naked and alone in the reed thicket like a demon, I'm afraid of you for what you've done."

629 As he spoke, he disappeared from view like a soaring bird. The unchaste woman, the murderess of her husband, remained in the same place.

630 But the soul of the elephant keeper who had become a god was aware of things which lie beyond the normal range of the senses. He saw the distressed state in which she was in.

631 In order to enlighten the woman with whom he had lived in his former life, he turned himself into a jackal which was holding a scrap of meat in its mouth.

632 He ran to eat a fish which had leapt from the water to the bank of the river, and released the scrap of meat.

633 Then the fish leapt back into the river. The god turned into a vulture and carried off the scrap of meat.

634 And although she was in distress sitting naked in the reed thicket

by the bank of the river, her interest was stimulated by what she had seen, and she said to the jackal:

635 "You fool, you abandoned the scrap of meat because you wanted the fish. What are you going to do now you've lost both the meat and the fish, jackal?"

636 The jackal replied, "You abandoned your wedded husband because you wanted a lover. What are you going to do now you've lost both your husband and your lover, naked woman?'

637 Hearing this, she was very frightened. The Interstitial god revealed to her his own perfect supernatural form and said:

638 "Although you have indulged in sin, sinful woman, you should resort to the Jain religion. It is a boat for the muddy sea of sin.

639 Foolish woman, I am that elephant driver whose death you caused. Through the power of the Jain religion I've become a god. Look at me!"

640 She decided to resort to the Jain religion. He took her to a nun and encouraged her to take initiation.

641 So pay no heed to these parables of persuasion and dissuasion. They're unsuitable for people like us. Enjoy sensual pleasure!'

The Story of Vidyunmālin

642 Jambū said, 'I'm not amorous like Vidyunmālin the master of magic.* Listen to what happened to him.

643 In this land of Bharata there is a mountain called Vaitāḍhya, from which the two halves of Bharata spread, like wings from a bird.

644 On it there is a capital city called Dear-to-the-Sky; it is very dear to the gods.

645 In it lived two affectionate young master of magic brothers named Megharatha and Vidyunmālin.

646 Together they discussed how they might gain magic power: "Let's go to the earth. We'll certainly gain those powers there.

647 This is the way to gain magic power: one should live for a year with a girl of very low caste, but preserve one's chastity."

648 Thereupon they took leave of their elders and went to the city of Vasantapura in the southern half of Bharata.

649 Then the two, who were rich in wisdom, disguised themselves as untouchables and went to the untouchables' quarter. They offered their respects to the untouchables.

650 The untouchables whom they had greeted said, "Why have you come here? Tell us, how long have you been here?"

651 Concealing their true identities they replied, "We've come from the town of Abiding-in-the-Earth.

652 Because our parents threw us out of the house, we left in anger, and our wanderings brought us here."

653 The untouchables replied, "Since you have sought refuge among us, remain here. We'll bestow two of our girls on you, if you like.

654 But if you marry two of our maidens, will you perform all the customs of our caste?"

655 They agreed, and the untouchables gave them two girls to marry. They were one-eyed and buck-teethed.

656 But Vidyunmālin fell passionately in love with his untouchable girl, although she was deformed, and neglected to gain magic knowledge.

657 Eventually Vidyunmālin's wife became pregnant. But when the year had passed, Megharatha gained magic power.

658 Then Megharatha joyfully said to Vidyunmālin, "Brother! We have gained magic power. Let's leave this community of untouchables.

659 We are capable of enjoying the blessed pleasure of the delights of Mount Vaitāḍhya. Abandon your untouchable wife; we have free choice of beautiful goddesses."

660 Vidyunmālin hung his head in shame and said, "Go to Vaitāḍhya, virtuous one. By doing your duty, you have gained magic power.

661 The tree of self-restraint has been shattered by my low character; from where will I get its produce, the fruit of magic power?

662 I lack the moral worth to abandon this pregnant, low-caste woman, and, sinless one, lacking magic power, I'm ashamed to go with you, since you have gained magic power.

663 Go, now you have gained magic power! May all go well with you! But how can I show my face before my relatives without having gained magic power?

664 I have caused myself to go astray through this lustfulness of mine. Now I shall strive to gain magic power.

665 Bear your brother in your heart, and please come back when a

year has passed. Then, since I'll have gained magic power, I'll come back with you."

666 Megharatha was unable to take his brother, who was bound in the snare of his love for an untouchable woman. He returned alone to Mount Vaitāḍhya.

667 His relatives asked him, "Why have you returned alone? Where's your brother?", so he told them what had befallen Vidyunmālin.

668 Vidyunmālin's deformed untouchable wife gave birth to a son; he was as happy as if he had gained magic power.

669 Because of his excessive devotion to his untouchable wife, and particularly because of his affection for his son, the fool forgot about heavenly pleasures, as if they were a bad dream.

670 The one-eyed, buck-teethed untouchable woman made love with Vidyunmālin to her heart's delight and became pregnant again.

671 Then Megharatha, possessed of magic power, came back to that place, having passed the year with difficulty, pained by his separation from his brother.

672 "I am surrounded by the women of the masters of magic, who almost resemble the women of heaven, while he lives in hell with a one-eyed, buck-teethed untouchable woman for his wife.

673 I live in a seven-storied palace, beautified by gardens; he lives in an untouchable's hovel, strewn with bones from the cremation ground.

674 All my needs are satisfied by various kinds of magic power; he dresses in worn-out rags and lives on bad food."

675 With these thoughts of concern for his brother, Megharatha returned to the city of Vasantapura.

676 He said to his brother, "Brother, why don't you come to Mount Vaitāḍhya and enjoy all the choice things which are to be obtained among the pleasures of the masters of magic?"

677 But Vidyunmālin gave an embarrassed laugh and said. "My wife here has a baby boy and she's become pregnant again.

678 She has no other support, she's devoted, she has a baby boy and she's pregnant. I do not have a heart of diamond like you, and I'm not able to abandon her.

679 So, Brother, go, and let me see you at the end of a year. I'll spend this year here. Don't cry."

680 Megharatha kept trying to put him right, but in the end he left once again, feeling very depressed. What can a well-wisher do in the case of a person who is very stupid?

681 A second son was born to Vidyunmālin. In his excessive joy he preferred his untouchable family to heaven.

682 Although he was in a bad situation for clothes, food, and everything, he did not feel sorrow. He playfully fondled the two baby boys born to the untouchable woman.

683 Now and then they pissed as he was holding them in his lap; in his opinion being bathed in piss was like being bathed in perfumed water.

684 His untouchable wife, thinking she was well off, scolded him at every step. Although he had become a slave to his untouchable family, nevertheless, he still clung to her.

685 In his affection for his brother, Megharatha came back again. He embraced Vidyunmālin and sobbed:

686 "You are of good family; don't stay among an untouchable family. Does a swan, born in Lake Mānasa,* frolic in a house-drain?

687 So don't defile the family in which you were born, like smoke from a fire defiling a house."

688 Despite being exhorted like this, he still did not want to go. Megharatha said, "I shan't come back again" and went away.

689 For a long time thereafter Megharatha ruled his paternal kingdom. Eventually he handed it all over in its entirety to his son, like a pledged deposit.

690 Rich in thoughts of religion, he took initiation as a Jain monk in the presence of the wandering ascetic Susthita. He practised austerity and became a god.

691 Thus Megharatha obtained blessing after blessing, whereas Vidyunmālin wandered in the sea of existence.

692 So, Padmasenā, I'll not become blinded by passion, lusting for ever increasing pleasures like Vidyunmālin.'

The Story of the Conch-blower

693 Then Kanakasenā said, 'Pay attention to me for a little while, husband. Don't overdo things, like the conch-blower.

694 Once upon a time in Śāligrāma lived a certain farmer. He always watched over his field from dusk to dawn.

695 He used to stand on a platform, which was like a ship on the ocean of his field, and whenever animals began to creep up, even though they were a long way off, he frightened them away with blasts from his conch shell.

696 One night, some robbers who had stolen a herd of cattle came by his field. They heard the blaring of the conch shell and thought:

697 "Ah! This sounding of the conch shell nearby means that the men of the village, intent on recovering their property, have managed to get in front of us."

698 The robbers abandoned the herd of cattle and fled. They scattered in all directions, like birds in the morning flying from a tree.

699 The cattle, which were hungry, grazed at leisure. By daybreak they had reached the farmer's field.

700 The farmer ran towards the herd. When he saw that there were no men with it, he thought:

701 "The robbers heard the sound of my conch shell and abandoned the herd. Surely bad men will always be alarmed by the fright they receive here!"

702 He drove the herd into the village and confidently gave them to the villagers, saying "A god gave them to me. Help yourselves, good people."

703 The village, which by his means had become rich in cattle, treated him with intense devotion, as if he were the village Yakṣa in bodily form; for he who gives is a god.

704 Thus he gained affectionate applause. In the following year he entered his field and began to blow his conch in the night.

705 One night, the very same robbers came by his field, having stolen a herd of cattle from another village in the dead of night.

706 They heard that conch-blower's loud conch blaring, and, rightly relying on their intelligence, said to each other:

707 "In this place, here in this same field, we previously heard the sound of a conch, and we can hear the same sound now. There are the holes and there are the posts.

708 Surely this is a person watching over his fields and blowing his conch in order to protect his fields from animals. Damn! We were fooled last time!"

709 Rubbing their hands, as if rolling a cotton lamp-wick, pressing and gnawing their lips, like calves at cow's udders,

710 raising their clubs, like elephants raising their trunks, making the corn vibrate, like bulls in a field,

711 those unmitigated thieves followed the sound of the conch and saw the conch-blower standing on the platform.

712 They shook the poles of the platform, and made it fall to the ground. The man fell with it. There was nothing left to collapse.

713 The robbers beat him with their clubs, as if he were a sheaf of corn, while the man clasped his hands to his face, as if he were eating.

714 Then they tied his hands together with a bone-tight bond. With his hands joined together in greeting, he looked as if he wanted to welcome the thieves.

715 The thieves stole his property, from his cows to his clothes; the field watchman became a naked field watchman.*

716 The thieves left him there in that place and went away. In the morning, when the cowherds questioned him, he said this:

717 "One should blow, one should blow, but one should not blow too much. Too much blowing turns out badly. What I gained through blowing has been lost by blowing too much."

718 So, husband, it isn't right for you to overdo things. You should not disregard us, as hard as stone.'

The Story of the Bitumen Monkey

719 Then Jambū said, in a voice like cool water, 'I know about bondage; I'm not like the bitumen monkey.

720 Now, there is a mountain called Vindhya, fruitful with the wealth of the forest. In it lived a monkey, the king of a large tribe of monkeys.

721 Like the prince of the Vindhya mountain, he frolicked in the mountain thickets, driving away the other male monkeys belonging to his tribe.

722 He was very strong and he alone made love with the female monkeys, enjoying manifold sensual pleasures in his country of many females.

723 One day, a certain young monkey, who was excited by lust and in heat, approached the female monkeys, paying no heed to the male monkey.

724 He kissed one on her tawny mouth, in which were little shoots of white teeth; it looked like a ripe pomegranate which had gone red and burst open.

725 He powdered another's face with dust from the ketakī tree; he placed a necklace of guñja berries around another's neck.

726 To another he fed pān,* which he kept preparing from the leaves of the wood-apple tree; another he embraced tightly and placed in a hanging swing.

727 Thus he made love to the female monkeys without any fear. It was as if his excessive pride in the strength of his arms led him to disregard the king of the tribe.

728 As his tail was being scratched by one female monkey with the blades of her fingernails, and the streaks of hair on his body were being stroked by another,

729 and as he was being fanned with a banana leaf by another, as another made him a garland of lotus stalks,

730 while seated on a high peak, that old leader of the tribe saw the young monkey. Full of anger, he swiftly charged forward.

731 Waving his tail in anger, the cow-tailed monkey who was lord of the tribe struck the young cow-tailed monkey with a round stone.

732 Struck by the stone, the powerful young monkey roared fearfully, like a lion, and rushed towards him.

733 They clasped each other's bodies limb to limb, and the two, although they were enemies, became united, like friends who have met after a long time.

734 Crinch crunch! they used the edges of their teeth, crick crack! they used their fingernails, while they fought each other, body to body.

735 Covered in blood from the gashes rent by their nails and teeth, they were soon as red as if they had put on red jackets.

736 At one moment they wrestled, at another they boxed. As they fought with their fists, they looked like a couple of dice players.

737 His bones shattered by a punch from the young monkey, the old monkey quickly backed away while the other advanced deliberately.

738 As the old monkey retreated, the young monkey hit him with the stone and split his head open.

739 Overcome by the pain of this blow, the old monkey fled, running into the distance, just as a bird when freed flies for a long way.

740 Oppressed by the pain of his wounds and tormented by thirst, he wandered until he saw some bitumen oozing from a rock.

741 The monkey thought that it was water and put his face in it, but it remained stuck to that spot, as if it had grown from the ground.

742 The monkey, who was not very bright, decided to drag his face out, and put both his arms in the bitumen. They too remained stuck to that spot.

743 He put his feet in, and they stuck just as his face and hands had done. Thus he met his death, just like a man impaled through five parts of his body.

744 If the monkey had managed to extricate his face without getting his hands and feet stuck, then he would surely have been freed from the pool of bitumen, no doubt about it.

745 Thus an embodied soul, at first only greedy for the pleasures of the tongue, may go astray, and sinking with all five senses in women, who are like bitumen, be utterly lost.'

Here finishes the second canto of the scholar-monk Hemacandra's epic poem, the Appendix, or Lives of the Jain Elders. In it were related Jambū's marriage, the story of the man and the honey-drops, the story of Kuberadatta, the story of Maheśvaradatta, the story of the farmer, the story of the crow, the story of the pair of monkeys, the story of the charcoal burner, the story of Nūpurapaṇḍitā and the jackal, the story of Vidyunmālin, the story of the conch-blower, and the story of the bitumen monkey.

CANTO THREE

Jambū and his wives continued to relate stories:

1–43	Nabhaḥsenā told: The Story of Siddhi and Buddhi
44–106	Jambū told: The Story of the Thoroughbred Horse
107–21	Kanakaśrī told: The Story of the Village Headman's Son
122–40	Jambū told: The Story of Sollaka
141–7	Kamalavatī told: The Story of the Don't-Be-Foolhardy Bird
148–84	Jambū told: The Story of the Three Friends
185–213	Jayaśrī told: The Story of Nāgaśrī, the Brahmin's Daughter
214–75	Jambū told: The Story of Lalitāṅga

276–92 Finally, Jambū's wives became convinced of the truth of the Jain religion, and they, together with Jambū, Prabhava, and Jambū's parents and relatives, decided to become Jain ascetics. When morning came, Jambū and his followers were initiated by Sudharman, as was Prabhava on the following day. Prabhava became Jambū's pupil.

The Story of Siddhi and Buddhi

1 Then Nabhaḥsenā put her hands together in salutation and said to the son of Ṛṣabhadatta, 'Don't you be like the old woman in the story.

2 In a certain village lived two old women. Their names were Buddhi and Siddhi. They were friends with each other and were always extremely badly off.

3 Outside that village was the shrine of the ever famous Yakṣa named Bholaka; he was a granter of wishes.

4 Every day the old woman named Buddhi, who was a garden for the tree of poverty, worshipped the Yakṣa in due form.

5 At dawn, noon, and dusk she cleaned his shrine and always offered him food and a high degree of reverence.

6 One day the gratified Yakṣa asked, "How shall I reward you?"; for even a statue is gratified when it is constantly worshipped.

7 The old lady said, "If you are pleased with me, my god, then give me enough to live on happily and contentedly."

8 The Yakṣa replied, "Be prosperous, old Buddhi! Every day you'll find a gold dinar at my feet."

9 From then on she received a gold dinar every day, and the old lady became much richer than her relatives and neighbours.

10 She who had not seen such ornaments even in a dream now like a queen continually kept putting on a new array of heavenly ornaments.

11 She whose hunger had not been satisfied even by boiled rice-water now had milk-cows with full udders in their thousands.

12 She who had lived from birth in an old straw hut now lived in a stuccoed mansion adorned with verandas and pinnacles.

13 She who had lived by distributing cow-dung to others' homes was now served by slave girls who were fastened to posts like puppets.

14 She who had always been depressed with worry about getting enough to eat was now made cheerful by the wealth given to her by the Yakṣa.

15 Siddhi noticed Buddhi's prosperity and became jealous. She wondered where her wealth had come from:

16 "Right, I've always shared the confidences of her friendship. I'll speak very nicely to her and ask her about it."

17 So clever Siddhi went to Buddhi's house. Buddhi welcomed her as an old friend, treating her with great respect. Siddhi asked:

18 "Where has this unexpected wealth of yours come from, sister? From its magnificence, one might suppose you'd found a wishing-gem!

19 Has the king favoured you? Is a god pleased with you? Have you found treasure? Have you prepared a magic elixir?

20 My friend, your wealth has made me wealthy. Now I have cast a funeral libation upon my wretched poverty!

21 I am you, and you are me. We are never gladly separated. We have no secrets from each other. So tell me, where has this wealth come from?"

22 Buddhi was not wise, so she told her friend all about her prosperity, how she had worshipped the Yakṣa and how he had given her wealth.

23 When she heard this Siddhi thought, "Excellent! Excellent! This will be an infallible way for me to get rich.
24 I'll worship the Yakṣa with greater devotion than her, so that greater wealth comes to me."
25 Now that Buddhi had shown her the way to riches, Siddhi began to worship the Yakṣa day and night.
26 She devotedly decorated the row of steps to the Yakṣa's temple with lines of chalk in a variety of patterns.
27 Everyday she decorated the Yakṣa's courtyard with rows of auspicious svastikas, as if reckoning that her means of devotion should be auspicious like him.
28 Every morning she herself fetched water and she herself bathed the Yakṣa; she had made a vow of devoted service.
29 At dawn, noon, and dusk she presented the Yakṣa with oleander leaves, basil, and roses which she had gathered herself.
30 Totally engrossed in eating once a day only, fasting, and other acts of abstinence, she remained day and night in the Yakṣa's temple. She was like an Interstitial goddess in constant attendance on a Yakṣa.
31 Continually worshipped in this way, the Yakṣa said to Siddhi, "I'm pleased with you, good lady. Ask for whatever you want."
32 She told the Yakṣa, "That inexhaustible wealth you gave to my friend—give me twice as much!"
33 The simple Yakṣa declared, "It will be so!" and disappeared. Siddhi, for her part, soon became much richer than Buddhi.
34 When Buddhi saw that her friend had become the richer, she went and worshipped the Yakṣa again, and every day he gave her twice as much money as he was giving to Siddhi.
35 Siddhi was envious of her and went to worship the Yakṣa once more. When the Yakṣa was gratified, this extremely evil-minded woman thought to herself:
36 "Whatever I ask the Yakṣa for when he is gratified, Buddhi will go and worship him and ask for twice as much.
37 Therefore, I'll ask for something which will harm Buddhi when she asks for twice as much. Then I'll be the clever one!"
38 She asked the Yakṣa, "Blind me in one eye!" And when the Yakṣa said, "So be it!", she immediately became blind in one eye.
39 But Buddhi, thinking that the Yakṣa had once again given her

something more, worshipped him asking for twice as much as that.

40 So when the Yakṣa was pleased, she asked him, "The very same thing you've given to Siddhi, give me twice as much!"

41 The Yakṣa declared, "It is so!", and disappeared. But she instantly became blind; a divine utterance is never false.

42 So thus the old woman Buddhi took no pleasure in the wealth she had previously acquired and through her excessive greed destroyed herself.

43 You have gained human prosperity; if you still wish for further prosperity, you will become like that blind old woman!'

The Story of the Thoroughbred Horse

44 But Jambū replied, 'Simple-minded one, like the thoroughbred horse, I shall not go along the wrong path. Listen to his story:

45 In the city of Vasantapura lived a king called Jitaśatru, whose enemies had been conquered by his might. He ruled in remarkable splendour.

46 The sharer of that king's confidence was a merchant named Jinadāsa, foremost of the wise and wealthy.

47 One day, horse-breeders showed the king colts with auspicious body marks; they were like the sons of Revanta.*

48 So then the king ordered men who were knowledgeable about the bodily marks of horses to say which horses were endowed with which auspicious marks.

49 They told the king that one colt only was marked with all the auspicious marks which are described in books:

50 "He has a round hoof and a firm joint between the ankle and the knee; he is lean in his knee, shank, and jaws;

51 his breath has the fragrance of lotus flowers; his coat is sleek; his voice is like a cuckoo's; his eyes are flecked with white; his ears are quick to prick up; his mane is long.

52 He has the five lucky marks; his spine is not visible; he is broad in the seven places, the shoulders, and so on; he is adorned with backward-turning locks of hair on his chest and on other places;

53 he is devoid of unlucky locks of hair on the rump and other places; his teeth are smooth: this is a colt which will increase the prosperity of his master."

54 When the king, who was himself discerning, learnt that the horse was of such a kind, with his own hands he decorated the horse's whole body with water mixed with saffron flowers.

55 Then the king offered the horse flowers and garments and, among other ceremonies, made him fetch salt.

56 He thought, "Who will be a fit person to look after this horse? In this world valuable things are the most likely to perish, as a rule.

57 However, there's the Jain layman, Jinadāsa. He's devoted to me and always shares my confidence. He's well known for having undertaken the vows of a Jain layman.

58 He's intelligent, devoted to his master, and he's not careless. He's the very person to be a worthy receptacle for such a jewel!"

59 So he summoned Jinadāsa and graciously told him, "You must look after this colt as if he were your very soul."

60 Jinadāsa agreed to undertake the king's command and led the horse, which was escorted by footmen, to his home.

61 He made the colt's stable pleasant to live in by spreading soft sand; it was like the sandy bank of the Ganges.

62 He himself led the horse to graze on leafy, dust-free, sweet green foliage.

63 Grasping the reins, he himself rode the horse in the royal grounds, on sandy soil free from clods and thorns.

64 At the time he took his bath, he himself would bathe the horse in perfumed and fragrant lukewarm water.

65 In order to find out whether the horse was well or not, several times a day he himself examined the horse's eyes and eyelashes.

66 Every morning he himself mounted the horse and at a gentle trot led it to a lake to drink its water.

67 Between Jinadāsa's home and the lake was a Jain temple, like an island in the ocean of existence. He never left it unvisited.

68 The pious man knew that one should not ignore the house of a Worthy, so every day, on his way out and on his return, while mounted on the horse, he rode around the temple from left to right three times in veneration.

69 While seated on the horse, he worshipped the deity, since he understood the true nature of divinity. In order not to show disrespect to the deity, he would dismount, but he never entered the temple.

70 Thus Jinadāsa taught the horse to go nowhere except to the lake, the house, and the temple.

71 As the colt gradually increased in size, so the riches in the king's palace increased as well.

72 And through the power of that colt, the king became superior to the other kings. His power was like that of Śakra, the king of the gods.

73 The vassal kings were fearful of the cause of the king's power and thought, "We must steal or kill that horse by whose power we have been vanquished."

74 The vassal kings tried but were unable to harm the horse. One of the kings had a minister whose pride in his intelligence was like a mountain. He said:

75 "I'll steal the horse by some subterfuge. What is too difficult for a subterfuge? The power of a subterfuge is immeasurable."

76 The king ordered him to do so, thereupon the minister, who was an ocean of cunning, disguised himself as a Jain layman and went to the city of Vasantapura.

77 There, after he had venerated the Jain temples and the well-provided Jain monks, he went to Jinadāsa's home and worshipped at his house-shrine.

78 He greeted Jinadāsa with the greeting of Jain laypeople, and, like a cunning bird disguised as a peacock, displayed the signs of Jain laymanship.

79 Jinadāsa was unsuspicious and was friendly to those of the same religion as himself. He stood up and welcomed the man, asking where he had come from.

80 The bogus Jain layman said, "I am free from attachment to existence. Before long I shall become a Jain monk. I have finished with the life of a householder.

81 When I have finished my pilgrimage, I shall make religion my kinsman, and in the presence of a holy teacher I shall take a vow to lead a very pure life."

82 Jinadāsa replied, "You are welcome, saintly man. Our characters are alike, so I hope we'll have pleasant conversations about religion."

83 The bogus Jain layman concurred. Jinadāsa loved to be kind to his fellow believers, so he kindly bathed the man as if he was his own kinsman.

84 He carefully shampooed and cleansed his hair; then he darkened it with musk unguent.

85 Around the minister's head Jinadāsa plaited a braid of hair entwined with a chaplet of flowers; it looked like a painting.

86 Jinadāsa spread over the man's body the finest fragrant sandalwood ointment; its cooling effect was like moonlight.

87 Piously he clothed his feigned fellow believer in garments pervaded by the incense of aloes, camphor, and musk.

88 Then Jinadāsa quickly prepared a meal for him: there were savoury dainties, pickles, drinks, soups, and sweet dishes.

89 Jinadāsa sat him on a cushion stuffed with swans' feathers, then the man ate the various delicacies, stirring and blowing on them.

90 After the meal saintly Jinadāsa began to talk about religion to that wicked, bogus Jain layman.

91 Then a relative of Jinadāsa happened to come by. He said, "Kinsman, come to my house tomorrow for an auspicious ceremony.

92 You can stay there all day and night. You know all about auspicious matters; what could be auspicious without you?"

93 Jinadāsa agreed and bid farewell to his kinsman. Then that honest man, with a pleasing voice, guilelessly said to the bogus Jain layman:

94 "I must go to my kinsman's house. My home is your home; look after it while I'm away."

95 The bogus Jain layman agreed with a smile. Jinadāsa set off, fully trusting in that bad man.

96 That day a big full moon festival was being celebrated in the town with a performance in which the citizens' wives sang and danced.

97 At night, while the people were intoxicated with joy at the full moon feast, the bogus Jain layman took the horse and stole it away.

98 But the horse rode three times in veneration around the Worthy's temple, and, although his rider tried to prevent him, refused to go anywhere except to the lake.

99 Each time the horse returned from the lake, he went to the temple. Then the horse went to his home; he would not go anywhere else.

100 Finally, while the minister of the bad vassal king was still trying to make the horse go in a different direction, dawn appeared.
101 The villain fled. The sun rose, and Jinadāsa started to return home.
102 While on his way, the people told Jinadāsa that someone had been riding his horse throughout the night of the full-moon festival.
103 Jinadāsa was completely perplexed about this. He returned home and saw that his horse was tired, wasted, and stained with sweat.
104 "Thank heaven! There is the horse! I've been deceived by the pretence of religion!" he thought, filled with joy and grief.
105 From that time on, Jinadāsa protected the horse with great care, and it was even dearer to him because it had not followed the wrong path.
106 I'm like that horse; no one is able to lead me along the wrong path. I will not forsake the path which leads to the blessings of the other world.'

The Story of the Village Headman's Son

107 Then Kanakaśrī said with a lovely smile of affection, 'Husband, don't you be stupid, like the village headman's son.
108 Once upon a time, in a certain village, lived a village headman's son. He was the only son of his deceased father and of his mother, who lived in great need.
109 One day his mother said to him in tears, "You really are a lazy good-for-nothing. All day long you do nothing but chatter with the others.
110 Your father was a hard-working man; he lived by his hard work. Once he'd begun a job, he always finished it.
111 But you, my son, never begin a job, even though you are young. As for you completing a job you've begun, why, that's unheard of!
112 Your friends of the same age all support themselves by their work. Aren't you ashamed to wander around doing nothing, like the village idiot?
113 My poverty supports your belly, and you seem to think by filling your belly you're saving a treasure!"

114 Her son replied, "Very well, mother. From now on I'll change. I'll make money by working really hard.

115 What's more, mother, in order to make money, I'll cheerfully see the work through to the end, just like father did."

116 One day, as he was looking on in the village assembly, his sister's husband's donkey snapped the tether at its feet and broke loose.

117 The donkey sprang away. His sister's husband tried to chase it but he couldn't catch it. He raised his arms and shouted:

118 "Hey, village councillors! Hey, village youths! Can any of you catch my donkey?"

119 The village headman's son thought that he would earn money by doing this. He ran and grabbed the donkey by its tail, like a fruit by its stalk.

120 Although the people tried to prevent him, he did not let go of the donkey. Thereupon the donkey kicked out his teeth, and he fell to the ground.

121 So you too, husband, if you don't let go of what is out of control, and leave off not consummating your marriage,* who knows what result you will find!'

The Story of Sollaka

122 Then Jambū, with a smile upon his lips, said, 'I'm not going to act like a madman, as Sollaka did.

123 Once upon a time there was a victualler who had a very fine mare; he cherished and cared for her as if she was his own daughter.

124 He appointed a man named Sollaka, who was knowledgeable about horses to care for her and to give her clarified butter, sesamum oil, porridge, and other things.

125 Sollaka took the delicacies which were supposed to be eaten by the mare, but he only gave her a small amount and ate the remainder himself.

126 In time, Sollaka, because of his deception, acquired a karma which entailed hard service to the mare's soul.

127 After his death, the karma caused by his deceit caused him to wander for a long time in animal incarnations, as if lost on a forest track.

128 Eventually, Sollaka's soul was reborn in the city Kṣitipratiṣṭha as the son of the Brahmin Somadatta and his wife Somaśrī.

129 Meanwhile, the mare died, and, wandering through existence, was born in the same lovely city, as the daughter of the prostitute Kāmapatākā.

130 The boy was raised by his parents. Eventually, he became a youth. He lived by begging for grain.

131 Held like a string of pearls in the foremost part of her nurses' hearts, in time the prostitute's daughter also attained youth.

132 Her body, graced by youth and beauty, was equally an adornment and a thing to be adorned.

133 The rich young men of the city vied with each other over her, and attached themselves to her in clusters, like bees on a jasmine bloom.

134 The Brahmin's son was also attached to her. He used to lie before her door every day; love stimulates everyone.

135 Sporting amorously with the rich young sons of royal ministers and wealthy merchants, she despised him. He lived just to glimpse her.

136 She did not even favour him with a glance, for he was poor. Such is the character of prostitutes, to love the rich, not the poor.

137 The young Brahmin, rent by the god of love's arrows, made it his life's work to serve her; he was unable to leave her presence.

138 He ploughed her fields, drove her coach, drew her water, and ground her grain. He left none of her tasks undone.

139 Although she turned him out of doors, he did not leave her house. He patiently endured thirst, hunger, humiliation, even blows.

140 So I shall not, among you, my dear wives, who are like that mare, incur karma which entails hard servitude, as Sollaka did. Enough of your clever arguments!'

The Story of the Don't-Be-Foolhardy Bird

141 Then Kamalavatī said, 'Hey, my lotus-faced husband, don't you be like the don't-be-foolhardy bird!

142 Once upon a time there was a man who was oppressed by hunger. He left his family, joined a big caravan, and set out for foreign parts.

143 When the caravan halted in a big forest, the man went off on his own to fetch grass, wood, and other provisions.

144 Suddenly, in the forest glade, a bird stole from the jaws of a

sleeping tiger some pieces of meat which were sticking to its teeth and settled on the branch of a tree.

145 As it ate the flesh, the bird repeated, "Don't be foolhardy, don't be foolhardy!" The man replied in astonishment:

146 "You're shouting 'Don't be foolhardy!', yet you're eating meat taken from a tiger's jaws! You look stupid, saying one thing while doing the other."

147 In your desire to undertake austerities and to abandon the visible pleasures of this existence, because you want the pleasures of something which is invisible, you're just like the don't-be-foolhardy bird.'

The Story of the Three Friends

148 Jambū replied with a smile, 'I shan't let your voice delude me. I will not deviate from my purpose; I know the story of the three friends.

149 In the city of Kṣitpratiṣṭha lived a king named Jitaśatru. He had a Brahmin chaplain called Somadatta, to whom he delegated authority on every matter.

150 The chaplain had a friend named Constantfriend. They constantly met to eat and drink together; there was harmony between them.

151 He had a second friend named Festivalfriend, whom he treated with honour on festival days, but not at other times.

152 He had a third friend named Greetingfriend, to whom he would just give a friendly greeting, whenever he happened to see him.*

153 One day the king, whose punishments were cruel, became angry about some fault committed by his chaplain and decided to punish him.

154 The chaplain learnt of the king's intention and on that very night went, full of anxiety, to his friend Constantfriend's house.

155 The chaplain told him that the king had become angry with him and said, "Friend, I'll spend this time of adversity at your house.

156 Dear friend, one finds out who one's friends are in times of need. Protect me in your home, and prove our friendship by your actions."

157 But Constantfriend replied, "Our friendship is now over. There can be no friendship between us as long as there's danger from the king.

158 You'll be my ruin, if you stay in my house while the king is angry with you. No one would throw a brand of burning wool onto a blanket in his own home.

159 I will not place my own family in need for the sake of you alone. Go somewhere else! Goodbye."

160 After being rejected by Constantfriend in this manner, Somadatta hastened to the home of his friend Festivalfriend.

161 The chaplain told Festivalfriend about the king's disfavour, hoping that he would be given refuge.

162 Festivalfriend wanted to repay Somadatta for his friendship on festival days. He greeted him with great respect and said:

163 "By your friendly conversation and other marks of respect at many festivals, my friend, you have bought a firm claim to my life.

164 My brother, if I fail to share in your misfortune, then the good name of my family will be exposed to contempt.

165 However, I'm unable to do anything to help you. I could bear any hardship myself, but to place my family in hardship is unbearable.

166 My family is dear to me, yet you too are dear to me, my friend. What shall I do? I'm in a dilemma: on one side there's a tiger, on the other, a precipice.

167 My little children are as many as the worms in a piece of rotting flesh. Have pity on them. Farewell to you; please go somewhere else."

168 Although he treated the chaplain with respect, he rejected him. When one's fate is bad, even one's own son behaves badly.

169 Festivalfriend escorted him as far as the crossroads. The chaplain thought, "The waters of the sea of bad luck are difficult to repel.

170 I've been rejected by the two people I have honoured. To whom shall I turn now in my need?

171 Now should I go to my friend Greetingfriend, even though there's no hope in him, since I only speak to him in passing?

172 But away with hesitation! He's still an acquaintance. I'll go see him. Who else can I ask for help?"

173 So he went to his friend Greetingfriend's house. Almost as soon as he arrived, Greetingfriend stood up and placed his hands together in greeting.

174 Greetingfriend said, "Welcome! How are you? Tell me, what can I do for you?"

175 Thereupon the chaplain told him what had passed between himself and the king, saying, "I'll leave the king's jurisdiction. Please help me, my friend."

176 Greetingfriend said, "I'm in your debt for your friendly greetings, my friend. I shall repay you with my help.

177 Don't be afraid. I'll look after you now. As long as I live, no one will harm a hair of your head."

178 Greetingfriend placed his quiver on his shoulder and strung his bow. Fearlessly, he guarded the chaplain from behind.

179 In Greetingfriend's company the chaplain reached the place he wished to go to, and there he enjoyed the pleasures of the world without any fear.

180 Here's the explanation: the soul is like Somadatta and the body is like his friend Constantfriend.

181 At the time of death, which is represented by what the king did, the body, despite the good treatment it has received, will not go with the soul, even for a short distance.

182 Friends and relations are like Festivalfriend: they go as far as the cremation ground, that is represented by the crossroads, and then they all turn back.

183 Religion, which is the foundation of well-being, is like Greetingfriend. It accompanies the soul when the soul goes to another destination.

184 Therefore, my clever wife, I'll not be fooled by the pleasures of this world, and I'll not neglect religion in any respect; it is the cause of the pleasures of the other world.'

The Story of Nāgaśrī, the Brahmin's Daughter

185 Then Jayaśrī said, 'Husband, you have the gift of the gab, and you're deluding others with tricky stories, like those of Nāgaśrī.

186 Once upon a time in a city called Ramaṇīya lived a king who was very fond of stories. The citizens would take it in turn to tell him a story on each day.

187 In the same city lived a Brahmin who was racked by poverty. He gained his livelihood by wandering about the whole day long begging for grain.

188 One day it became the turn of this Brahmin, who was the crest-jewel of illiterates, to tell a story. He thought:

189 "Even when I say my name my tongue always stumbles as if it is falling. How can I tell a story?

190 If I say that I don't know how to tell a story, then I'll be taken to prison. What shall I do?"

191 The Brahmin had a young daughter. She saw that he was cast down with worry and asked what was troubling him. He told her the reason.

192 His daughter said, "Worry no more, Daddy. I'll go instead of you, and tell a story."

193 She bathed, put on a clean white dress and entered the presence of the king. She greeted him with a prayer for his victory, and said, "Listen to my story."

194 Now the king was struck by her remarkable self-possession, and became all ears to hear her story, like a deer attracted by a song.

195 She began her story: "In this city dwells a Brahmin named Nāgaśarma. He's a priest of the fire sacrifice, and he lives by begging for grain.

196 His wife is called Somaśrī, and I'm her daughter: my name is Nāgaśrī. In the course of time I've reached the age of puberty.

197 My parents have betrothed me to a Brahmin's son named Caṭṭa, for suitors usually choose women whose family status corresponds to their own.

198 One day my parents went to another village on some business to do with the wedding, and left me alone in the house.

199 And on the very day on which my parents had gone to the other village, the Brahmin Caṭṭa came to our house on a visit.

200 So, although my parents weren't at home, it accordance with custom I treated him with suitable hospitality. I prepared a bath and food for him.

201 At night I prepared our bed, the entire furniture of our home, for him to lie on.

202 Then I thought, 'Hooded snakes slither on the floor of our house. How can I sleep there?

203 I'm too frightened to sleep on the ground, so I'll sleep on his bed. No one will see me in the thick darkness of night.'

204 I lay down with him without feeling any excitement, but he touched my body and became sick with passion.

205 His shame, excitement, and the suppression of his lust caused a sudden ache in his stomach, and the pain of it killed him.

206 Then I thought, 'I'm frightened to see him lying dead. I'm a sinner; it's my fault he's died.

207 To whom can I explain what's happened? Who will help me? What shall I do? How can I remove him from the house?'

208 So I sliced his body into pieces like a cucumber. Then I dug a hole and placed him in it, as if burying a hoard of money.

209 Then I filled the hole. I carefully levelled the earth on top, cleansed it and smeared it over, so that no one would notice anything.

210 Finally I strewed the place with flowers, perfume, and incense, and soon after my parents returned from that other village."

211 Then the king asked, "This story you have told, young lady, is it all true?" The girl replied:

212 "Your majesty, if all the other stories you have heard are true, then mine is true as well, from beginning to end."

213 So, husband, just as Nāgaśrī beguiled the king, you are beguiling us. What's the point of these tricky stories?'

The Story of Lalitāṅga

214 Jambū said, 'I love you all, but I don't long for sexual pleasure, like Lalitāṅga. There's a city called Śrīvasantapura.

215 In it ruled a king named Śatāyuddha. The mighty obeyed him as if he were the god Vajrayuddha;* he was like the god Kusumāyuddha* in his bodily form.

216 Lalitā was his queen. Her figure was lovely; she was like a goddess. She was the single repository of every kind of beauty.

217 One day she climbed one of the palace turrets to divert herself with the view. She began to watch the people moving about below.

222b She saw a young man walking along the street.

218 His braid of hair was so thick, he looked as if he had two heads. His moustache was spread so thickly with musk, that he looked like an elephant in rut.

219 His shoulders were like those of a bull. His chest was broad, and

his hands and feet were like lotus flowers. On his neck, hands, and feet he wore ornaments of pure gold.

220 His mouth was perfumed with camphor-filled betel leaves, and his forehead was adorned by an ornamental mark which shone like the god of Love's victory banner.

221 The unguents applied to his body made him seem clothed in loveliness. His perfumed garments filled the streets with fragrance.

222a In his bodily beauty he looked like another son of the goddess of Prosperity.*

223 The queen's beautiful eyes became drunk from gazing at his beauty. Her mind became fixed upon him. She was as still as a wooden statue.

224 She thought, "If he makes love to me, our lovely bodies clasped together like creeping tendrils, then my life as a woman will have had its fulfilment.

225 If I had wings, I could act as my own go-between, fly quickly to that delightful young man, and make love with him."

226 At the queen's side stood a shrewd maidservant. She thought, "Surely my mistress is taking great delight in looking at that young man."

227 She said to the queen, "Mistress, your heart delights in that young man! No wonder! Whose eyes wouldn't delight in looking at him?"

228 Lalitā replied, "You're so clever! You read my mind extremely well. Unless I make love with that handsome young man, I can't go on living!

229 Find out who he is and let me know, so that you can bring us together and make an offering of my body to him."

230 The maidservant, who was the starring actress in the play of craftiness, withdrew to make enquiries. She hurried back quickly and told the queen:

231 "He lives in this very city, he's called Lalitāṅga, and he's the son of a wealthy merchant named Samudrapriya.

232 In beauty he's like the god of Love, he's a treasure of the seventy-two arts, and he's a young man of good family. Your heart has chosen wisely.

233 His character corresponds to his appearance, you may be sure of that. Everyone says that where there is physical beauty there also is good character.

234 Among women you are pre-eminent for good character, just as he is among men. Say the word, and I'll bring together you two people of good character."

235 The queen said, "Do it!", and handed the maidservant a letter which contained a verse which was a rain cloud for the seedlings of the plant of love.

236 The maidservant understood the business of a love-messenger like no other. She went at once, and gave Lalitāṅga the message sent by Lalitā.

237 First she let the message arouse Lalitāṅga's lust, then she gave him the letter, to win over his mind.

238 As soon as he read the letter, the declaration of love, Lalitāṅga's bodily hair bristled with delight; he looked like a blossoming kadamba tree. The letter said:

239 "Ever since I first saw you, handsome, I've been wretched. You are my whole world. Favour me with your union."

240 When he finished reading the letter, he said, "Come, clever one, what can she, a lady of the palace, and I, a mere trader, have to do with each other?

241 My heart can't bear it—or if it could bear it, my tongue can't speak it—that I shall make love with a wife of the king!

242 It's easier to touch the moon's disc while standing on the earth, than for another man to make love with the king's wife!"

243 The maidservant said, "Everything is difficult for one who lacks someone to help. I'll help you. Don't worry!

244 My intelligence will enable you to walk about unseen in the royal ladies' quarters, as if you were in the middle of a bunch of flowers. Have no fear!"

245 Lalitāṅga told her to call him when the time was right. The maidservant quickly returned and told the queen, whose brow lifted with joy.

246 One day, while Lalitā was looking forward to her union with Lalitāṅga, there was a delightful full moon holiday in the city.

247 The king went hunting in the country, where the fields gleam with corn and the water is as pure as milk.

248 Then, when the palace was all deserted, Lalitā told the maidservant to fetch Lalitāṅga.

249 In order to please the queen, the maidservant had him brought into the royal ladies' quarters disguised as a new Yakṣa statue.
250 Lalitā and Lalitāṅga made love together for a long time, embracing each other tightly; they were like a branch and a creeper.
251 But the guards of the royal ladies' quarters were shrewd. Various signs led them to think, "Surely some man has entered the ladies' apartment."
252 As they stood there thinking, "We've been tricked!", the king returned from his hunting trip.
253 The guards told the king that they were sure that another man had entered the royal ladies' quarters.
254 The king removed his clattering hunting boots and stepped into the ladies' quarters, as quietly as a thief.
255 But the maidservant was clever. She kept her glance fixed upon the door and saw the king coming while he was still far away. She warned the queen.
256 The queen and the maidservant lifted up the paramour, carried him upstairs, and hastily threw him out, as if throwing a heap of garbage from a house.
257 He fell into a large cesspit which was situated behind the palace, and remained lodged in it, like on owl in its lair.
258 While he was stuck in that dirty, stinking hole, like a being in hell, he recollected his former pleasure.
259 He thought, "If I can somehow get out of this hole, I'll have nothing more to do with the pleasures which bring such future consequences."
260 The queen and the maidservant felt pity for him, so every day they threw into the hole the remains of their meals, on which he lived like a dog.
261 In the rainy season the hole was filled with water flowing from the palace gutters, just as a bad man is filled with wickedness.
262 With a rushing torrent the water carried him through a small drain, and dumped him in the moat outside.
263 Then the stream of water lifted him up and spat him onto the bank of the moat, like a pip from a pumpkin. Gripped tightly by the water, he lost consciousness.

264 His old nurse happened to be standing at that very spot. She saw him and took him back to her own home.

265 Her family looked after him. They massaged him with ointment, bathed, and fed him. His vigour was renewed, like a tree which flourishes after its branches have been pruned.

266 Now here's the explanation of the story: embodied souls are like Lalitāṅga; they have no abhorrence of sensual pleasures.

267 Just like sexual pleasure with that queen, sensual pleasures are momentarily sweet but have very bitter consequences.

268 The time spent in the hole represents the time spent by the foetus in the womb, and the man's recuperation by being given food and drink represents the mother's nourishment of the foetus with food and drink.

269 The man's exit from the hole when it had been filled with rain water represents the exit from the womb through the vagina, when the foetus has fully grown.

270 The fall from the hole into the moat outside represents the baby's birth from the womb into its mother's room.

271 The swooning on the bank of the moat which was full of water represents the baby's swooning when it is freed from its protective membrane of skin and blood.

272 The nurse who helped save his life—understand that she represents the continual ripening of karma.

273 Now if the queen, beguiled by Lalitāṅga's good looks, were to send her maidservant to bring him into the royal women's quarters once again, would he go?'

274 Jambū's wives replied, 'Even if he's not very bright, how could he return once more, if he remembered the unpleasantness which followed on the first occasion, the fall into the cesspit?'

275 Jambū replied, 'Led by his ignorance, he may perhaps return once more. But I, for my part, will not follow a course of action which will cause me to enter a womb.'

276 Thereupon Jambū's wives became convinced that he would remain firm in what he had undertaken, and they attained enlightenment. Asking forgiveness, they said:

277 'Save us too, just as you are saving yourself. Holy ascetics don't delight in filling their own bellies.'

278 Jambū's parents, in-laws, and relatives said, 'You've spoken very

well about religion, so we also shall become Jain monks and nuns.'

279 And Prabhava said, 'I'll quickly go and ask my parents, then I'll certainly become a monk along with you, my friend.'

280 The young man Jambū said to Prabhava, 'My friend, may you neither meet with any hindrance nor cause any obstruction.'

281 At break of day great-minded Jambū eagerly prepared for his ceremony of initiation as a Jain monk.

282 He bathed, anointed his body with fragrant unguents, and bedecked his limbs with golden ornaments studded with jewels; he knew that was the rule.

283 Jambū looked like a newly discovered god. He ascended a palanquin which was carried by a thousand men.

284 The people praised Jambū of the Kāśyapa clan, and he, like a wish-fulfilling tree, distributed gifts to everyone,

285 on his way to that place in the forest, the abode of blessings and good fortune, which was purified by the lotus-feet of the holy Sudharman, the Supporter of the Flock.

286 When he arrived at the entrance of the park which was ornamented by the presence of the Supporter of the Flock, Jambū, who had no thoughts of self, stepped down from the palanquin, as if from the cycle of death and rebirth.

287 Jambū bowed before Sudharman's feet, boats for the crossing of the ocean of misfortune, touching the earth with his head, hands, and feet. He said:

288 'Supreme master, receive me and my family into the life of religious mendicants, that conveyance over the sea of existence. Have pity on me.'

289 Requested in this way, the fifth holy Supporter of the Flock initiated Jambū and his followers, as was fitting.

290 On the next day, Prabhava, having asked his parents, returned, and, like Jambū, was initiated as a Jain monk.

291 Sudharman entrusted Prabhava to Jambū to be his pupil, and Prabhava became a duckling at the lotus-feet of holy Jambū.

292 Jambū was like a bee serving the lotus-feet of holy Sudharman. He patiently wandered the earth, counting as nothing hardships that were extremely difficult to bear.

Here finishes the third canto of the scholar-monk Hemacandra's epic poem, the Appendix, or Lives of the Jain Elders. In it were related the story of Siddhi and Buddhi, the story of the noble steed, the story of the village headman's son, the story of Sollaka, the story of the don't-be-foolhardy bird, the story of Nāgaśrī, the Brahmin's daughter, the story of Lalitāṅga, the renunciation of Jambū and his followers, and the renunciation of Prabhava.

CANTO FOUR

The themes of this short Canto are Jambū's gaining of omniscience, and his and Sudharman's final emancipation.

1–55 King Kūṇika* of Campā went to hear Sudharman preach. Sudharman told him about Jambū, whom he declared to be the last to gain omniscience.

56–61 After Mahāvīra's final liberation, Sudharman became the head of the monastic order. After Sudharman passed away, aged 100, Jambū became his successor. In turn, Prabhava became head of the monastic order after Jambū passed away, sixty-four years after Mahāvīra's final liberation.

1 One day, while the holy Supporter of the Flock Sudharman was wandering the earth with Jambū and his disciples, he came to the city of Campā.

2 The supreme lord, the Supporter of the Flock, began to preach in a park on the outskirts of the city. He was like a wish-fulfilling tree for the promotion of religion.

3 The townspeople came to bow in devotion before holy Sudharman's lotus-feet, their minds feeling great excitement.

4 Certain townswomen who had been unable to conceive children came. Their braided hair was loosened, their anklets tinkling as they walked.

5 Other townswomen climbed into their carriages, urging their husbands to drive at top speed.

6 Some, whose karma was different, Jain laywomen, left their homes and came bearing their children on their hips; the children looked like monkeys clinging to trees.

7 Certain rich men with dangling earrings came, mounted on white horses. Their white parasols made the sky look as if it was filled with white lotus flowers.

8 The surface of the road was indented by the pearls which fell from the necklaces of the wealthy ladies who repeatedly bumped into each other as they hurried along.

9 Then Kūṇika, the king of the city, saw the people rushing like that. He asked his doorkeeper:

12b 'Why are all the people rushing in this manner?
10 Is a pilgrimage in honour of some goddess taking place near the city today, or is this a festival to celebrate some wealthy man's safe return from a journey?
11 Perhaps it's a big full moon festival or some other holiday, or is a special act of worship taking place by the holy tree in the park?
12a Or is it because some holy Jain monk is preaching there?'
13 The doorkeeper went to investigate. He informed the king, 'The excellent Supporter of the Flock Sudharman is preaching in assembly.
14 All the townspeople are hurrying to pay their respects to him. Your kingdom prospers, ruled in accordance with the teachings of the Jain religion.'
15 The king replied, 'See how happy the townsfolk are, the ones hurrying to pay their respects to holy Sudharman.
16 Although seeming awake, I would be fast asleep, if I didn't visit the holy Supporter of the Flock today.
17 So I too shall hurry and pay my respects to the Supporter of the Flock's feet, for they're like the wind; they don't stay fixed in one place!'
18 The king rose from his throne, his eyes gleaming like blue lotuses. He put on a white garment that looked as if it had been woven with moonbeams.
19 On his ears he fixed a pair of pearl earrings; they were like bowls of milk filled with heaps of shining pearls.
20 On his chest he hung a necklace of white pearls: it looked like a string of salt-sea foam lying on a beach.
21 On his limbs he placed various jewelled ornaments; he looked like an unparalleled wishing-tree.
22 Then he put on a jacket, as white as crystal. As if dancing, its fringes fluttered in the breeze.
23 He tied a braid of hair around his head with a chaplet of fragrant flowers. His hair was as dark as lamp-black; it was like the night sky in the rainy season when the moon does not shine.
24 The king, the obstructor of his enemies, was like a lion. Raised by its trunk, he mounted his elephant; the sire of other elephants, it was as big as a mountain.
25 With his hands the king brandished the elephant-goad; it danced

like a flash of lightning in the sky. With his feet he urged on the elephant.

26 Thinking, 'I hope my mighty footsteps don't shatter the earth,' the elephant proceeded very slowly, as if from pity.

27 The people gazed at the elephant. It trumpeted loudly, and rut juice rained continually from its temples; the elephant was like a rain cloud which had descended to the earth.

28 Leaping horses, mounted by cavalrymen, thronged the elephant in hundreds of thousands. As they pranced, their knees touched the tips of their noses; they looked as if they were dancing.

29 In the front skilled musicians played a rhythmic victory march on their instruments.

30 The resounding echo of the instruments created a mighty noise in the heavens; it sounded superhuman.

31 The king and his retinue approached the place in the park which was the abode of the lotus-feet of the Supporter of the Flock Sudharman.

32 The king halted the elephant with a tap of the goad on its forehead. He grasped its girdle and climbed down.

33 The long-armed king removed his shoes, set aside his parasol and fly whisk, and laid down his mace.

34 When he saw the reverential Jain laypeople, the king thrilled with delight. He meditated with devotion, in the same way as the people.

35 As soon as he saw holy Sudharman from afar, he repeatedly put his hands together in respectful greeting.

36 When he arrived, the king sat down in front of Sudharman, and gazed intently on his face, as if he were his most junior pupil.

37 Then the divine Supporter of the Flock Sudharman gave religious instruction, a spring of nectar for the ears of those who heard it.

38 When the sermon was over, the king began to look at the Supporter of the Flock's disciples. He noticed holy Jambū, and asked Sudharman, the supreme master:

39 'What a remarkably handsome appearance, your reverence! What remarkable grace! His dignified bearing is remarkable too! Everything about that holy saint is remarkable!

40 His hair is as black as the stream of the waveless river Yamunā.

His eyes rest on the corners of his ears, as if supported by a pair of bending props.

41 His ears are like oyster shell resting on the shore of the ocean of his eyes. His neck is like a spiral conch shell. His chest is like the door-leaf to his mighty abdomen.

42 His staff-like arms are long and straight; they extend to his knees. His waist can be encircled by one hand. His thighs are like the posts to which elephants are tethered.

43 His shanks are like those of a deer. His hands and feet are like lotus flowers. But why say more about his beautiful appearance?: he's like me!

44 My heart delights not in praising but in looking at that blessed person's beauty: he could be my kinsman!

45 His splendid appearance indicates that he must be some great ascetic. Such is his beauty that it is unable to be viewed properly.

46 Not to be looked upon and unapproachable is the splendour of that great ascetic. Have the rays of the sun been brought down and gathered in one place?

47 How can one describe the mass of splendour of that ocean of asceticism? Beams flash from his toe-nails; they look like maid-servants at his feet!'

48 Then excellent Supporter of the Flock related the history of Jambū's former lives, just as the holy scion of the Jñātṛ clan had previously related it to King Śreṇika.*

49 When he had finished, he said, 'Your majesty, this great-souled ascetic is endowed with such splendour of beauty and form because of the ascetism he practised in his former lives.

50 This is his final embodiment, and in this birth be will become the final omniscient one.' Thus declared the supreme lord.

51 And the holy one went on to declare, 'After Jambū passes away, no one will attain the knowledge of the thoughts of others or the highest kind of the knowledge of things which lie beyond the normal range of the senses.*

52 No other person fasts like he does. He eats shrivelled husks of grain or not at all! He's a tonic for the monastic order.

53 And in the future, wherever the threefold restraint* is no longer practised, there prosperity will continually diminish.'

54 When the king had finished listening to what the reverend

Teacher Sudharman had to say, he bowed to the Supporter of the Flock's lotus-feet, and returned to the city of Campā.

55 Then Sudharman, accompanied by his followers, left the park and lived in the presence of Lord Mahāvīra, in like manner as he.

56 Holy Sudharman took the fivefold vow at the age of fifty; after that he was the disciple of the final Worthy Mahāvīra for thirty years.

57 After Mahāvīra passed away and gained final liberation, the excellent Supporter of the Flock guided the affairs of the monastic order for twelve years, as a monk without omniscience.

58 Then, at the end of his ninety-second year, Sudharman gained omniscience. He dwelt on earth for eight more years, enlightening beings capable of enlightenment.

59 Sudharman died and gained final liberation when he was a hundred years old. Then Jambū became head of the monastic order.

60 Holy Jambū practised harsh austerities, and gained omniscience. Full of compassion, he enlightened the righteous who were capable of enlightenment.

61 Jambū passed away sixty-four years after holy Mahāvīra attained final liberation. He appointed Prabhava, the descendant of Katī, to be his successor, whom Jambū taught to be his rival in the destruction of karma.

Here finishes the fourth canto of the scholar-monk Hemacandra's epic poem, the Appendix, or Lives of the Jain Elders, which contains the description of holy Jambū's attainment of final liberation.

CANTO FIVE

Canto Five articulates the Jain attitude to the Vedas, the revealed sacred texts of the Brahmins, and to the Brahminical sacrifice at which they are recited: the Vedas are untrue and the sacrifice an imposture. The Canto also provides a rationale for the composition of the Jain canonical text, the Ten Evening Chapters,* which provides a concise code of conduct for monastic behaviour.

1–37 Prabhava wandered the earth preaching the Jain religion. One night he wondered who he should appoint as his successor. He used his supernatural mental powers to survey all the Jain ascetics, but he could discern no one with the right qualities, so he then surveyed the followers of other religions, and at length discerned in Rājagṛha a Brahmin named Śayyambhava who, with his fellow Brahmins, was about to perform an animal sacrifice. Śayyambhava had the right qualities. Prabhava sent two monks to convert him to the Jain religion. The monks stimulated doubts in Śayyambhava's mind. To find out the truth, Śayyambhava threatened his Brahmin teacher, who confessed that the sacrifice was an imposture, performed solely to gain a living for Brahmins, and that the Brahmins were able to carry out the sacrifice only because the statue of a Worthy had been buried beneath the sacrificial post.

38–54 Śayyambhava was initiated by Prabhava, and in time learnt the fourteen Original Collections of Teachings. Prabhava died, having appointed Śayyambhava his successor.

55–105 Shortly after her husband had left to become a monk, Śayyambhava's wife had given birth to a son, who was named Maṇaka. When he was eight years old, the boy learnt that his father had become a Jain monk, and left home to seek him. Śayyambhava recognized his son as he approached in the distance. He took Maṇaka to a Jain monastery where he initiated him, without revealing his true relationship to his son or to the other monks. Realizing that Maṇaka had only a short time to live, Śayyambhava prepared for him an epitome of the fourteen Original Collections of Teachings called the Ten Evening Chapters. After Maṇaka's death six months later, Śayyambhava wanted to suppress the epitome, but was prevailed upon to change his mind by the other monks.

106–7 Śayyambhava died, having appointed Yaśobhadra to be his successor.

1 From that time on holy Prabhava, the descendant of Kati, purified the surface of the earth, by travelling and preaching the Jain religion.

2 One night, when the other monks were asleep, worn out by performing religious duties, Prabhava was in a meditation-sleep.* He wondered:

3 'Who will succeed me as leader of the monastic order, to be a sun for the day-lotus of the religion of the Worthies and a boat for the crossing of the sea of the cycle of death and rebirth?'

4 Gnawed by this worry, he used his powers of cognition to survey his own group of monks as well as the entire monastic order to see if there was anyone suitable.

5 He spread the light of his cognitive powers, but did not see anyone who had the qualities to enable him to cope with the task without respite.

6 Then, still seeking such a person, he used his powers of cognition to survey the followers of other religions; for a mud-lotus grows in mud.

7 And in the city of Rājagṛha he saw a Brahmin, Śayyambhava of the Vatsa clan, who was performing a sacrifice. That man had the right qualities.

8 Thinking, 'Trusty Jain ascetics must go and convert him!', holy Prabhava went to that excellent city.

9 He ordered two Jain monks, 'Go to that sacrificial grove and beg for alms. Pray that the Brahmins there may accept the Jain religion.

10 And if the Brahmins in the sacrificial grove refuse to give you anything, say this, as they send you away:

11 Alas, alas! They don't know the truth! Alas, alas! They don't know the truth!'

14b When it was time for them to beg for alms, the two monks went to the sacrificial grove, as commanded by their superior.

12 The gateway was festooned with swathes of leaves. A banner flew upon a pole. By the open gate stood a pail of purifying libation water. Men were busy preparing the sacrificial fuel.

13 A goat was tethered to the wooden ring on the tip of the

sacrificial post. The holy fire blazed in the centre of the altar. There were countless vessels bearing sacrificial oblations, and a large number of Brahmin priests.

14a The Brahmin whose task it was was intent on placing the kindling for the sacrifice.

15 The two Jain monks were sent away by the Brahmins, who did not wish to give them anything. Very loudly, they shouted what their superior had ordered: 'Alas, alas! They don't know the truth!'

16 The Brahmin named Śayyambhava was officiating at the sacrifice. As he stood by the gateway of the sacrificial grove, he heard what the two monks said.

17 He thought, 'These Jain monks have peace of mind as their chief object. Because they never speak vainly, my mind has doubts about the truth.'

18 His mind wavering with doubt, this most pious of men asked his teacher, 'What is the truth?'

19 His teacher said, 'The Vedas are the truth. They lead to heaven and to the final emancipation of the soul. Those who know the truth declare that there is no truth other than the Vedas.'

20 Śayyambhava replied, 'Surely you're deceiving people like me because of your greed for sacrificial fees, when you say that the Vedas are the truth.

21 These holy monks are free from hatred, free from passion, and free from thoughts of themselves. They have no possessions. They are tranquil. They don't say anything untrue.

22 You're not a teacher, you've lied about this all your life! On the contrary, you're very much in need of teaching. You're intentions are bad!

23 Come, tell me the real truth, even if it is as they say it is. If you don't, I'll cut off your head; punishing a villain is not murder.'

24 Śayyambhava drew his knife from its sheaf. To his Brahmin teacher it looked like his death warrant.

25 The teacher thought, 'He's going to kill me! The time has come for me to tell the real truth.

26 I must tell the real truth about our continually memorizing and reciting the Vedas, otherwise my head will be cut off.

27 So I'll quickly tell him the real truth, so that I can continue to live. When he's alive, a man sees good things.'

28 So considering his own well-being, the teacher said, 'The statue of a Worthy has been deposited below the sacrificial post.
29 Hidden in its place down below, the image of the Worthy receives clandestine worship. Through its power our sacrificial ceremonies are unimpeded.
30 If the statue of the Worthy is not there, the great ascetic Nārada, a magician's son, always prevents the sacrifice.'
31 Then the teacher pulled out the sacrificial pole from its position, and showed Śayyambhava the lustrous image of the Worthy, saying:
32 'This is a statue of the divine Worthy. The religion he preaches is the truth. Sacrifices and suchlike are an imposture.
33 The religion taught by the holy Worthy has compassion towards living beings. What good is a religion which slaughters animals in the sacrifice?
34 We know the truth but, alas!, we live by means of a huge deception. Release me, and become a supreme Worthy.
35 I deceived you for so long in order to perform the meritorious duty of filling my belly. No longer will I be your teacher. Farewell to you, sinless one.'
36 But Śayyambhava bowed to the teacher of sacrificial rites, and said, 'You're still my teacher because you showed me the real truth.'
37 Śayyambhava was absolutely delighted, and gave the teacher his gold and copper vessels, his paraphernalia for the sacrifice.

38 Then Śayyambhava hurried off, searching for the two holy Jain monks. In their company, he eventually came to the presence of holy Prabhava.
39 As he entered, he bowed respectfully to holy Prabhava and to all the monks. He was welcomed by them with an expression of hope that he would embrace the Jain religion.
40 Placing his hands together in salutation, Śayyambhava humbly requested Prabhava, the spiritual leader, 'Venerable one, instruct me in the true religion which leads to final emancipation.'
41 Prabhava said, 'The supreme principal is not-harming. One's thoughts for others must be as well intentioned as the thoughts one has for one's self.
42 One should speak pleasantly, truthfully, and briefly, using words

that do not cause pain to others, even though they may be true.

43 One should not take what has not been given. One should be content with one's own possessions. The man who enjoys contentment with his lot seems to partake of the pleasures of final emancipation.

44 The wise man should be chaste, and renounce sexual activity completely; sexual activity is the sprout of the poisonous tree of the cycle of death and rebirth.

45 Abandoning all possessions, free from bodily desires, the wise man should cherish his soul, if he desires final emancipation.

46 By these five vows—not harming, true and kindly speech, not stealing, chastity, and renunciation of possessions—he will free his soul from existence.'

47 As soon as he understood the truth, Śayyambhava became disgusted with worldly existence. He bowed before holy Prabhava's feet and said:

48 'Because I was taught falsehood by my teacher, for a long time I held the truth as untruth; to a drunk man a clod of earth looks like gold.

49 So now that I know the truth, please grant me initiation as a Jain monk; it will be like a helping hand to me as I sink into the well of existence.'

50 Thereupon holy Prabhava initiated the great Brahmin Śayyambhava, who was frightened of the enemy existence.

51 For his part, noble Śayyambhava, who was not covetous because he was rich in forbearance, became excited, thinking, 'Thank heaven! I'm destroying karma!' He practised religious austerities.

52 He performed many acts of austerity, difficult to be performed. Like the sun, he shone with the heat generated by his austerities.

53 Performing austerities at his master's feet, Śayyambhava listened to his teaching. In time he memorized the fourteen Original Collections of Teachings; he was extremely intelligent.

54 Prabhava passed away and went to heaven, having appointed as his successor Śayyambhava, who, because of his scriptural knowledge and learning, was equal to himself in character and morality.

55 When Śayyambhava took initiation as a Jain monk, many people felt sorry for his young wife. They said to her:
56 'Ah! Śayyambhava is a learned monk, but he's crueller than cruel people to abandon his young wife, even though her character is good.
57 Women without husbands live in hopes of their sons, but she doesn't even have a son. How will she survive?'
58 The people asked her, 'Is there any possibility that you might be carrying a foetus in your womb?'
59 She replied, 'Maṇayam' in the local dialect, which is 'manāk' in Sanskrit; it means 'a little'. And at that time she was indeed carrying a little embryo.
60 Gradually the embryo grew, just like her confidence, and in time she gave birth to a son, a moon for the ocean of her mind.
61 Then, because the Brahmin lady had previously given the reply 'Maṇayam', her son was given the name Maṇaka.
62 Cared for by his own Brahmin mother, who nursed him herself, the child gradually learned how to toddle about on his feet.
63 When he was eight years old, the boy asked his mother, 'Where is my father? You don't wear a widow's clothes, Mother.'
64 His mother told him, 'Your father became a Jain monk while you were still in my womb. I brought you up myself, my child.
65 Just as you have never seen your father, so your father has never seen you.
66 Your father's name is Śayyambhava. He used to devote himself to performing sacrifices, but some crafty Jain monks converted him, and made him follow the life of a religious mendicant.'
67 But the boy wished to see his father, the monk Śayyambhava. Unknown to his mother, he left home.
68 At that time the Teacher Śayyambhava was staying at Campā, and the boy arrived at that very place, guided by his auspicious wish.
69 By means of his bodily, mental, and superhuman cognition, the learned monk saw and recognized his lotus-eyed son while he was still approaching in the distance.
70 When Śayyambhava beheld his son, like a boat on a lake, his emotions of joy and deep affection struggled to outdo each other.
71 As soon as the little boy saw the beaming monk in the distance,

his face became wreathed in smiles; it looked like a bunch of white water lilies.

72 The Teacher, filled with joy, asked the boy, 'Who are you? Where have you come from? Whose son and grandson are you?'

73 The boy replied, 'I've come here from Rājagṛha. I'm the son of Śayyambhava, a Brahmin of the Vatsa clan.

74 While I was still in my mother's womb, my father became a Jain monk. I'm travelling from town to town, trying to find him.

75 If your reverence knows my father Śayyambhava, please would you be so kind as to tell me where he is.

76 If I find my father, then in his presence I too will be ordained a Jain monk; his way of life will be the best way of life.'

77 The Teacher replied, 'I know your father. He's my friend. Believe me, he's alive and in good health, just like you.

78 You should be ordained by me, well-intentioned one. Please agree. What's the difference between a father and a father's brother?'

79 Realizing that the boy was intelligent, the Teacher took the boy to a Jain monastery.

80 The child's thoughts were not childish; they consisted of an aversion towards anything blameworthy. The Teacher made him acquainted with the vows.

81 The Teacher used his superhuman powers of cognition to find out how long the child's life would be. He immediately knew that the boy had only six more months to live.

82 The great monk Śayyambhava thought, 'This child's life will be extremely short. How will he learn the teachings?

83 The last Teacher who knows just ten of the fourteen Original Collections of Teachings is permitted to make an epitome of their doctrine, but for what reason may one who knows all fourteen?

84 The reason has arisen: it's to enlighten Maṇaka! I'll prepare a compilation of the topics of the Original Collections of Teachings.'

85 When the spiritual leader Śayyambhava had finished his compilation of the Teachings, he named it the Ten Evening Chapters.

86 The treatise is called the Ten Evening Chapters because he composed the ten chapters in an evening.

87 Holy Śayyambhava, the excellent Teacher, the leader of the monastic order, most eminent of the compassionate, recited the treatise to Maṇaka.

88 The learned Teacher himself ensured that Maṇaka performed all the necessary acts of devotion, but at the end of the six months' period Maṇaka died and went to heaven.

89 At Maṇaka's death, tears poured from the holy Teacher Śayyambhava's eyes, like water from the monsoon rain clouds.

90 The religious Teacher's pupils, Yaśobhadra and the others, were dismayed and distressed. They asked him, 'This behaviour is unworthy of you. What is the reason for it?'

91 Then the Teacher told his pupils that Maṇaka was his son, and related his story from his birth to the time of his death.

92 He said, 'Although he was just a boy whose life was extremely short, he lived a sinless life in accordance with his vows, and he died in meditation.

93 My tears fell through joy, because, although he was a child, his conduct was not childish. Affection for a son is indeed hard to abandon.'

94 Yaśobhadra and the other pupils bowed their heads and said, 'We should have treated your son with respect. Why didn't you tell us about this?

95–6 If, reverend Teacher, you had informed us that the junior monk Maṇaka was your son, saying, "Although he is little, you should treat your Teacher's son as you would your Teacher himself", then we would have obeyed out of respect for him.'

97 Full of joy, the Teacher replied, 'He had the blessings of good life among you, who are rich in religious asceticism. Religious asceticism is the supreme duty.

98 If you had known that the young monk Maṇaka was my son, you wouldn't have made him perform his religious duties, but now he is free from the bonds of existence.

99 Knowing that his life would be short, I made an epitome of the religious teachings called the Ten Evening Chapters, so that he could learn the holy teachings.

100 This treatise which I prepared for Maṇaka's sake caused him to gain emancipation from existence, but now I'll suppress it, in accordance with my original intention.'

101 Thereupon, Yaśobhadra and the others informed the monastic community that Śayyambhava intended to suppress the Ten Evening Chapters.

102 The monastic community joyfully requested the religious Teacher, 'Let this treatise which was prepared for Maṇaka, be of benefit to the whole world.

103 Then beings who have the capacity for enlightenment, even those of little understanding, will perform their religious duty. Let them enjoy the benefits of your kindness, in the same way as Maṇaka.

104 Like homeless bees, may they delight in continually resorting to the Ten Evening Chapters, the flower of the lotus plant of religious teaching.'

105 Thus the monastic congregation prevented the noble religious teacher Śayyambhava from suppressing the Ten Evening Chapters.

106 The holy religious Teacher Śayyambhava appointed as his successor the leading monk Yaśobhadra, who had reached the far shore of the ocean of religious learning.

107 Śayyambhava died in meditation and went to heaven. How can the deeds of one who is omniscient in the religious teachings and whose actions are the light of the universe miscarry?

Here finishes the fifth canto of the scholar-monk Hemacandra's epic poem, the Appendix, or Lives of the Jain Elders. In it were related the deeds of Prabhava and Śayyambhava.

CANTO SIX

Canto Six describes the founding of the city of Pāṭalīputra and the establishment of the Nanda dynasty. The historical background to these events is discussed in the Introduction.

1–4 Yaśobhadra died, having appointed Bhadrabāhu and Sambhūtavijaya to be his successors.

5–21 Four merchants were converted by Bhadrabāhu's preaching and became Jain monks. However, all four perished in an extremely cold winter.

22–40 Kūṇika, the son of Śreṇika died in Campā, and his son Udāyin became king. Overwhelmed by grief at the death of his father, Udāyin decided to transfer his capital to a new location, so he sent interpreters of omens to seek a suitable place. On the banks of the Ganges, the interpreters of omens came to a Pāṭala tree, in which nestled a blue jay, swallowing insects. They returned and informed the king of this omen, which signified that the place was suitable for founding a city.

41–92 Thereupon an old interpreter of omens related the story of Annikā's son and the Pāṭala tree:

Devadatta, a merchant from the north of Bharata visited the south, where he married the merchant's daughter Annikā. One day, a letter came from Devadatta's parents in the north, begging him to visit them, since they were now old and infirm. On Devadatta's journey home, his wife gave birth to a son, who was known by all as Annikā's son. The baby thrived, and when he reached middle age, he became a Jain monk.

93–145 In his old age, Annikā's son came to the city of Puṣpabhadrā on the banks of the Ganges. Puṣpacūla, its king, was married to his own sister, Puṣpacūlā, who was converted by Annikā's son and became a Jain nun.

146–75 Puṣpacūlā cared for Annikā's son in his infirm old age. One day, she gained omniscience. She foretold that Annikā's son would gain omniscience while crossing the Ganges. He boarded a ferry, and was thrown overboard by the other passengers. He gained omniscience while being impaled on a stake by a hostile goddess. He died and gained final liberation. Eventually, his skull was washed to the bank. The interpreter of omens concluded his story by saying that a Pāṭala seed settled in the skull, and grew into the tree that they had seen.

176–230 The city which was built in that location was named Pāṭalīputra after the Pāṭala tree, and there Udāyin ruled in great prosperity, until he was murdered by the son of a vassal-king whom he had deposed.

231–52 The royal insignia recognized Nanda, the son of a barber and a prostitute, as king. Nanda established himself on the throne of Magadha, ruling with great splendour.

1 After that, the holy religious Teacher Yaśobhadra wandered the Earth, his glory filling its four quarters. He fasted on the four holy days of the month and on other days.
2 He knew the fourteen Original Collections of Teachings, and refreshed the earth with the religious teachings of the Worthies, as a cloud refreshes the earth with its rain.
3 Two clever monks who had memorized the fourteen Original Collections of Teachings, Bhadrabāhu and Sambhūtavijaya, were his pupils.
4 The holy spiritual teacher appointed those two, who were oceans of scriptural knowledge, his successors, and departed for heaven.
5 Lord Bhadrabāhu, the creator of blessings for the world, while wandering the earth, illustrious with his congregation of ascetic monks, came to the city of Rājagṛha.
6 In that town lived four merchants of the same age; indeed they had grown up together, like trees in an orchard.
7 In the presence of Bhadrabāhu, they heard the religious teaching of the Worthies, which is water for the fire of sin, and attained enlightenment.
8 Self-conquering, together they turned their backs on their homes, and were immediately ordained Jain monks by holy Bhadrabāhu.
9 Practising fierce austerities, having learned a great deal of religious teaching, their glances fixed upon the ground, wandering over the face of the earth,
10 speaking pleasantly, truthfully and briefly, taking no provisions for travelling apart from their stomachs, free from desires,

without thoughts of self, in a state of equanimity, content with what they received without begging,

11 devoted to religious teaching, oceans full of the milk of compassion, they settled in their teacher's heart, like swans settling in a lake.

12 Their teacher ordered each of the four to wander alone for a period. They separated, but eventually they all returned to Rājagṛha.

15 Then came a severe winter; a wayfarer performing the wishes of Death; the warmth of whose sun is consumed by monkeys with upturned faces at the tops of trees;

13 the cause of the chattering teeth of needy children, the one who casts fiery frost on the clusters of lotuses in the lotus-beds;

14 the instigator of the embraces of young people pinched by the cold; the personified god of huddling around stoves.

16 At the third watch of the day, the four monks finished their begging round and turned back. They set off for Mount Vaibhāra.

17 By the fourth watch, one of them had reached a cave in the mountain, the second had reached the city park, the third was nearby the park, and the fourth was not far from the town.

18 Because they had finished and returned from their begging round in the third watch, in the fourth watch they ran out of time.

19 The one who was in the cave suffered from extremely cold weather, but the one who was staying in the garden suffered from a somewhat lesser cold.

20 The one who was staying nearby the garden felt a much milder cold, while the one who was near the town only felt a very slight chill because of the warmth coming from the city.

21 In succession, first, second, third, and fourth, they all died of cold and went to heaven.

22 After that, King Kūṇika, the son of Śreṇika, died in the city of Campā, and his son Udāyin became king.

23 Udāyin was overcome by grief at the death of his father, and, like the moon covered by a cloud, his majesty was dimmed, and he took no pleasure in his kingdom.

24 He said to his well-born ministers, 'My thoughts are disturbed

because in the whole city I see only places in which my father delighted.

25 Here is the same audience chamber in which my father would sit on his throne, never letting me go from his lap.

26 Here my father ate; here he played; here he made love; here he slept. I see him everywhere, like the moon reflected in water.

27 To bear the emblems of royalty, while gazing at my father's feet, as if they were standing before my glance, would be to break the rules of filial obedience.

28 I feel joy that my father remains in my heart while I am here, but I'm forever tormented by my grief; it's like a splinter in my flesh.'

29 His ministers were efficient, experienced, and well informed. Like monks practising restraint of speech, they spoke to him with words that removed the sting of sorrow:

30 'Who wouldn't feel sorrow to lose a loved one? But you must digest your grief like boiled rice, lest it cause you embarrassment.

31 But your majesty, if living here in this city distresses you, then you should move to some other city.

32 In the past, your father Kūṇika abandoned the city of Rājagṛha because of his grief for his father, and founded the city of Campā.'

33 Thereupon Udāyin summoned interpreters of omens, and told them to search for a place suitable for the founding of a city.

34 They searched high and low in every direction. Eventually they came to the lovely bank of the river Ganges, a rest house for the eyes.

35 On its bank they saw a pink-blossomed Pāṭala tree, its dense leaves providing so extensive a shade that it was like the river's parasol.

36 As they were expressing astonishment that such a luxuriant tree should be growing outside a park, they saw a blue jay sitting in it.

37 It was perched upon a branch, and every time it opened its mouth, insects spontaneously threw themselves into it, to be gobbled up.

38 The ministers thought, 'Just as insects come and continually

throw themselves of their own accord into the mouth of this bird here in the tree,
39 so success and prosperity will come of their own accord to our pure-souled king, if the city is founded in this excellent place.'
40 Having come to this conclusion, they went and informed the king that the place was suitable for founding a city, and described the omen given by the blue jay.

41 An old interpreter of omens, the chief authority on such matters said, 'It is related that that Pāṭala tree is no ordinary tree:
42 Now there are two cities called Mathurā, one in the North, and one in the South. Sharing the same beauty and virtuous qualities, they are like twin sisters.
43 In the northern Mathurā lived a merchant's son, Devadatta. He decided to go on a long pilgrimage to southern Mathurā.
44 In that city he became a friend of a merchant's son, Jayasiṃha; each made the other the sole depository of his secrets.
45 Jayasiṃha had a sister, a young maiden named Annikā. She was so beautiful she was like a heavenly goddess come down to the earth.
46 One day, Jayasiṃha told his sister Annikā, "Prepare a fine meal! I'm going to dine with my friend today."
47 Then Jayasiṃha invited Devadatta. When he arrived at Jayasiṃha's house, the two sat down for dinner.
48 Annikā, dressed in her finest clothes, served them sixteen different courses, beautiful dishes, savoured with the six flavours.*
49 Performing two objectives with one action, she shook her fan to refresh the two men with its breeze, and to drive away the bees.
50 As she shook the fan, the bracelets on her arms tinkled like a lute. As Devadatta gazed upon the moon-faced maiden, he fell in love with her.
51 As he looked at her, she seemed to him a lake full of the waters of beauty. His mind set on enjoying the pleasures of love with her, he was unable to taste his food.
52 His glance passed over her from head to foot; up and down it went, like a monkey on a creeper.
53 Not wishing to break the contact of his eyes with her, he ate like an elephant, with an ever more fixed expression.

54 On the following day, Devadatta sent messengers to Jayasiṃha, to ask on his behalf for Annikā's hand in marriage.

55 When they arrived, they said, "If you intend to marry her to any man at all, then marry her to Devadatta, since you know what kind of man he is."

56 Jayasiṃha replied, "He is of good family, well educated, intelligent, and young. Why say more? He has all the qualities of a good husband.

57 But I will only give my sister to a man who will never leave my house, and who will stay here while I myself keep an eye on him.

58 But it is likely that this handsome man will leave, one day or another. Don't you know? People who are staying in foreign parts usually depart eventually.

59 My sister is my very life. In my home she is like the goddess of Prosperity, so I shall not allow her to depart, not even to her husband's home.

60 Good sirs, if Devadatta is able to live on these conditions until the birth of his first son, then he may marry my sister Annikā."

61 On Devadatta's instructions, they agreed to this. So Devadatta married the maiden on an auspicious day.

62 While he was living in his brother-in-law's house, bound by the thread of his affection for Annikā, a letter came from his parents in northern Mathurā. It said:

63 "Our eyes have become blind, so we have only four senses left. Our limbs are infirm with old age. Soon we will be under the dominion of Yama, the god of Death.

64 You are healthy. If, like a son of a good family, you wish to see us while we are still alive, then come, so that you can dry our weeping eyes."

65 He read the letter, which was a moon for the ocean of his affection, and made it a vessel for the tears which incessantly flowed from his eyes.

66 He thought, "Alas, I am a wretch! I have neglected my parents. I remain sunk in pleasure, while they are in such a bad situation!

67 What shall I do? How can I go? My wife has not yet seen her child; I'm bound by the fetters of my oath. How can I find a way out of this?"

68 But Annikā wiped his eyes with her garment, and, pained by his distress, said to him in tears:

69 "Who has sent this letter which eclipses the moon, and makes tears flow from the moon-stones of your eyes?

70 Looking at your face, which lacks its radiance, like the moon in daytime, I am sure that your tears are of sorrow, not of joy.

71 Please tell me the cause of your sorrow, and let me share it. Let me partake of your sorrow, and help you to bear it."

72 Annikā's husband, full of distress, gave her no answer, but just stood bathing the letter with the tears from his eyes.

73 Then Annikā took the letter and read it herself. She immediately understood the cause of her husband's distress. She said:

74 "By no means be upset, noble husband. I'll make my brother understand, and get him to do what you want."

75 So she went to her brother, and, pretending to be very angry, said: "What have you done, my clever brother?

76 Your sister's husband is pining because of the separation from his family, and I long to pay my respects to my mother- and father-in-law!

77 Give my husband permission to go to his home town. I will go with him too, since I depend on him, not on you.

78 But if he remains here, true to his oath, and I go alone to pay my respects to my in-laws, then what concern can you have with him?"

79 Over again she obstinately repeated her request, so in the end Jayasiṃha granted permission for Devadatta's journey to northern Mathurā.

80 So the merchant's son departed from that city, and Annikā followed him, like the night following the moon.

81 Now Annikā was pregnant, and her time was very near, so while she was still travelling, she gave birth to a son, who was endowed with auspicious features.

82 The parents did not give a name to their son, thinking that they would let his grandparents name him.

83 As they travelled on their journey, the servants who attended them caressed and fondled the little boy with great happiness, calling him 'Annikā's son'.

84 Eventually, Annikā's husband arrived at northern Mathurā,

where he paid his respects to his parents, and was kissed by them on his head.

85 Saying, "Please take what I have gained in foreign parts!", he presented the little boy to his delighted parents.

86 "This is your daughter-in-law, and this is my son to whom she has given birth"; he explained the relationship in a voice made charming by affection.

87 His grandparents named the child Sandhīraṇa, but the people called him Annikā's son.

88 Annikā's son thrived with loving care. Eventually he reached middle age, the blessed part of the four stages of life.

89 Rich in wisdom, even in his youth he disregarded sensual pleasures, as if they were straw. He was ordained a Jain monk by the monastic teacher Jayasiṃha.

90 An excellent monk, with a vow of asceticism as sharp as a sword, he tore out the dreadful thorns of karma from his soul.

91 The brightly flaming fire of his asceticism burnt the heap of dirt which was his karma, and he purified his soul, like a white cloth purified by fire.

92 In course of time, he developed right belief, right knowledge, and right conduct,* and he became the foremost of the learned Teachers, a sun for the lotus flowers that were his pupils.

93 In his old age Annikā's son, while wandering with his followers, came to the city of Puṣpabhadrā, which was an ornament for the bank of the Ganges.

94 In that city there once ruled a king named Puṣpaketu. His wife was Puṣpavatī; she was like Rati, the wife of Mīnaketu.*

95 Puṣpavatī had a twin son and daughter named, respectively, Puṣpacula and Puṣpacūlā.

96 They grew together and they played together. They had a mutual love for one another.

97 The king thought, "If these two children who have such affection for each other were to be parted, then they surely will not survive, even for a moment.

98 I cannot part them; the best thing will be to marry them to each other."

99 Then the king asked his friends, his ministers, and the citizens,

"Who is the owner of a jewel produced in the royal women's quarters?"

100 They replied, "If a jewel is produced in the middle of the country, then the king is master of it. Why ask about the royal women's quarters?

101 If a jewel is found in the kingdom, the king can do whatever he wants with it. Who would prevent him?"

102 The king seized on the reply of these people, who understood what he had in mind, and effected the marriage of his twin offspring.

103 His queen Puṣpavatī attempted to dissuade him, but the king paid no heed to her, so she became a Jain laywoman.

104 Puṣpacūla and Puṣpacūlā lived together as married householders. They were passionately devoted to each other.

105 In course of time, Puṣpaketu died, and Puṣpacūla became king, ruling with stainless integrity.

106 Queen Puṣpavatī attempted to prevent her offspring from sinning, but they treated her with contempt. Consequently, she became disgusted with existence, and took the vows of a Jain nun.

107 After she died, she was reborn as a god; this was due to her renunciation, for if renunciation does not lead to final emancipation, then it will certainly lead to heaven.

108 By means of his supernatural powers of cognition, the god saw that his daughter was living a sinful life, and with great affection thought:

109 "In my former life she was my daughter, as dear to me as life, so I must take action to prevent her falling into a dreadful hell."

110–11 So in a dream the god showed her all the hells and the hell beings within them, who were screaming from the pain of cuts, piercings, and other tortures that were afflicting them. The hells were gloomy with darkness, as if wrapped in sin.

112 Like a quail escaping from a hawk, like a deer escaping from a forest fire, like a chaste wife avoiding another man's touch,

113 like a good nun prevented from infringing her vows of asceticism, she awoke and trembled in fear of the hells which she had seen in her dream.

114 The sight of the hells frightened her as much as if she were

actually within them. She told her hushand about the whole dream.

115 King Puṣpacūla wished to soothe Puṣpacūlā, so he had an entire ceremony of purification performed by people who were skilled in such matters.

116 But the god whose soul had been Puṣpavatī's had good wishes for Puṣpacūlā's welfare, and continued to display the hells to her in the same manner, night after night.

117 Therefore, the king summoned all the quacks and impostors, asking them, "What is the nature of the hells?"

118 Since they had little understanding, they replied, "Being in the womb, being in prison, poverty, dependence on another: these are actually hells."

119 The queen wrinkled her face as if she had smelled a foul odour, and sent those people away, since their statements conflicted with her dreams.

120 Then the king summoned Annikā's son and questioned him. He described the hells just as the queen had seen them in her dreams.

121 The queen said, "Reverend sir, have you had the same dreams as I? Otherwise, how could you know all this?"

122 The Teacher replied, "Good lady, even without seeing it in a dream, there is nothing in the universe that cannot be known from the teaching of the Jinas."

123 Then Puṣpacūlā asked, "Reverend sir, because of what deeds do embodied beings go to such dreadful hells?"

124 Annikā's son replied, "Through striving too strongly to gain possessions, by hostility to teachers, through harm done through the pleasures of the five senses,

125 or through eating meat—through having sinned in these ways embodied beings go to the hells, and experience pain and torture."

126 But afterwards the god in whom her mother's soul was embodied showed Puṣpacūlā in a dream, in the same way as he had revealed the hells, the heavens, full of blissful joy.

127 When she awoke, she told her husband that she had seen the heavens, so then he asked the quacks and impostors, "What is the nature of the heavens?"

128 Some of them replied, "Heaven consists of union with a loved

one," while others replied, "Heaven is whatever makes one happy."

129 But Puṣpacūlā paid no regard to these descriptions of the heavens, for she had seen their real form in her dream.

130 The king asked Annikā's son, who described the way of life in the heavenly mansions: "They only need to think about what they want, and it is accomplished.

131 Wish-granting trees grow in the gardens, and in the ponds are golden lotuses. Beautiful goddesses, skilled in the arts, fulfil their desires.

132 Servant gods are appointed to arrange whatever they order. If they wish, festivals are held, complete with heavenly singing, dancing, and dramatic performances.

133 There are dwelling places, made lovely with jewels, in everlasting palaces, and there the gods are all-powerful, attended by a constant retinue.

134 How can one describe the blessed condition of the gods who live between the highest heaven and the home of the Interstitial gods?"

135 Puṣpacūlā said, "How do you know all this? Did you see the heavens in a dream?"

136 The monk said, "Since we drink the nectar of the Jinas' teachings, we know the blessed pleasures of heaven and other matters, worthy to be known."

137 Then the queen became convinced that the teachings of the Jinas were true, and asked the sage, "Reverend sir, by means of what actions does one reach the heavens?"

138 The Teacher replied, "The embodied being who believes in the Worthy as a god and in the monk as a teacher is not far from attaining heaven."

139 After the monk had explained true religion and conduct to her, she became disgusted with her poor way of life, and said:

140 "Reverend sir, I will take leave of my husband, and at your feet assume the life of a Jain nun, the fruit of the tree of human existence."

141 She bowed to the monk, and went to take leave of her husband, the king, who said:

142 "I will give you permission, excellent lady, on the condition that, when you become a nun, you accept alms from my house only."

143 She agreed to this. Like a wish-fulfilling creeper, she gave money to needy people, and the king celebrated her departure with a festival.

144 A crest-jewel among women, Puṣpacūlā was ordained at the feet of Annikā's son.

145 Following the path shown by her teacher, she learnt all the teachings; asceticism is the essence of the conduct of pure souled people.

146 One day, Annikā's son realized that there was going to be a famine, so he sent his pupils into foreign parts; one's country is wherever one happens to be living.

147 The pupils were told that the bad times would last twelve years, and in obedience to their Teacher, they departed.

148 But the religious leader, troubled by the infirmity of his legs, remained in the same place, and continued his patient asceticism without the company of his followers.

149 Each day, Puṣpacūlā brought food and drink from the royal women's quarters and gave it to her Teacher. She had as much affection for him as a daughter for her father.

150 Puṣpacūlā always considered that existence was worthless, and she had no other thought than to serve her Teacher.

151 One day, as a result of her wonderful deed, she attained omniscience, the essence of final emancipation.

152 Although she had gained omniscience, she continued to serve her Teacher assiduously, for the religious teachings state:

153 "If a person has been previously instructed to perform a task, then he should do it, even if he has omniscience, as long as the person giving the instructions is unaware of it."

154 Since Puṣpacūlā had omniscience, she was able to accomplish everything her Teacher had in mind.

155 He asked her "Dear nun, how do you know my intentions, which you accomplish as soon as I have thought of them?"

156 Puṣpacūlā answered, "I know your character! When one is constantly with a person, one learns his character."

157 One day when it was raining, the noble nun brought him food. The Teacher scolded her, "You know the teachings. Is this permitted when it rains?"

158 She said, "I went by a path where there were consciousless

water-bodies; for the most part, water-bodies lack consciousness."

159 He asked her, "How did you know that there were consciousless water-bodies on the path?", and she replied, "I have omniscience."

160 The Teacher said, "Because of my hopes of gaining omniscience, I have spoken foolishly", and he wondered, "Shall I gain it, or not?"

161 The omniscient nun said, "Don't lose heart, leader of the monks. You will attain omniscience while you are crossing the River Ganges."

162 So the Teacher, in the company of some other travellers, embarked on a ferry boat to cross the Ganges. Who neglects his own advantage?

163 But no matter on what side of the boat he sat, that side of the boat began to sink.

164 And when the Teacher sat in the middle, then the entire boat began to sink, like iron in water.

165 Thereupon, the people in the boat threw him overboard into the water, where a goddess hostile to the Jain religion impaled him on a stake.

166 Despite being fixed on a stake in the middle of the River Ganges, he thought, "Alas, my body is the cause of misfortune for many living creatures!"

167 Feeling boundless compassion for the water-bodies and for others, he annihilated his remaining karma, and, as he died, gained omniscience.

168 While in the fourth, pure bright, stage of meditation, he suddenly attained final emancipation. The gods thronged around him, praising his glorious attainment of final emancipation.

169 Because his glorious attainment of final emancipation was there celebrated by the gods, the river crossing became a holy place, famous throughout the three worlds as Prayāga,* the place of sacrifice.

170 Annikā's son's skull was torn off by crocodiles and other creatures of the water, and washed to the river bank by the current of the water.

171 As the skull, like a shell, rolled from place to place on the river bank, it fell into a rough hollow and became stuck in it.

172 One day, by an act of fate, a Pāṭala seed fell into the bowl of the skull.

173 Splitting the skull as it grew, out of the right eye-socket sprang up a Pāṭala tree, which in time developed into this extensive tree.

174 This Pāṭala tree is holy because it has grown from the skull of a great monk, and above all, because it has just one embodiment and a root-soul.*

175 So, trusting in the power of the Pāṭala tree, and having witnessed the omen of the blue jay, let us found the city in that place.'

176 One of the interpreters of omens said, 'All interpreters of omens recommend that, when a city is being founded, the measuring tape should be played out until the howl of a jackal is heard.'

177 The king said to the interpreters of omens, 'You're the authorities!', and ordered the measuring tape to be applied to the outline of the city.

178 From the Pāṭala tree they measured to the West, then to the North, then to the East, and finally to the South, until they heard the howl of a jackal.

179 Then they laid down the tape measure. In this way they marked out the rectangular outline of the city.

180 The king had a city built on the land which had been marked out, and named it Pāṭalīputra, after the Pāṭala tree.

181 In the centre of the city, the king ordered a fine Jain temple to be built; it was like an everlasting heavenly mansion.

182 There was a beautiful palace for the king with numerous stables for horses and elephants. It had wide courtyards and lofty turrets, and was decorated with stucco.

183 There were shops, rest-houses, and places for fasting. Then, on an auspicious day, the king held a festival of dedication.

184 In that city King Udāyin ruled, enjoying good fortune and prosperity, spreading the Jain religion and his unbroken authority.

185 Thinking, 'The Worthy is a god, the monk is a teacher, and the Jain religion is true,' the truth about gods, teachers, and religion rested in his heart.

186 Purifying himself by undertaking fourfold austerities* at the four changes of the moon, he fasted in the fasting halls.

187 Without breaking the laws of religion, he increased his military

glory, and by the fourth stratagem* made the other kings his servants.

188 But all the kings who had been defeated by Udāyin thought, 'As long as Udāyin is alive, we can take no pleasure in our kingdoms.'

189 Then, because of some offence committed by one of those kings, Udāyin, the all-powerful wielder of the thunderbolt, deposed him from his kingdom.

190 Deposed from his kingdom, that king ran away and died. His only son escaped, and went to Ujjayinī.

191 This prince, who had been deprived of his kingdom, entered the service of the king of Avanti, since that king was a constant enemy to Udāyin.

192 The attendant prince told the king of Avanti, 'Master, at your command, I shall overcome Udāyin.

193 Approve of this, my companion, and don't make a mistake; what man whose life has been made worthless, miscarries in a bold attempt?'

194 The king of Avanti agreed, so the prince went to Pāṭalīputra, and entered the service of Udāyin.

195 The wicked man was always on the watch for Udāyin's weak spot; like a sorcerer, he did not become weary.

196 In the Jain temple he noticed that Jain monks had free access to Udāyin.

197 So, to gain access to Udāyin's palace, he had a Jain monastic Teacher give him initiation as a Jain monk.

198 Although it was all a deception, he did not infringe his vows, and, since he gave honour and respect to the monks, they believed in him.

199 No one realized that the only object of his asceticism was to deceive; but the one who habitually practises deceit does not go to heaven.

200 On the eighth and fourteenth days of the fortnight Udāyin would fast, and remain in the presence of the Teacher, in order to hear him preach.

201 On a certain day of fasting the sham monk and the Teacher by whom he had been initiated went to the royal palace.

202 The Teacher said to the sham monk, 'Go and beg for food in the royal palace, novice monk.'

203 The sham monk, feigning obedience, went on ahead, pretending to be of service to his Teacher.

204 He drew his iron dagger, which he had long kept hidden, and held it under his robe, with the intention of murdering Udāyin.

205 The Teacher, thinking, 'He's been walking for a long time, he should have a rest,' entered the royal palace, together with the sham monk.

206 When he'd finished preaching, the Teacher felt tired, as did the king. Worn out with reciting the sacred texts, he cleansed the ground and fell asleep.

207 But the wicked sham monk remained awake. Sleep, as if frightened, does not come near evil-minded people.

208 The sham monk laid his dagger on the sleeping king's neck; it looked like the tongue of Death.

209 With it he cut the king's throat, which was like a tender plantain stem. Blood flowed like water from the open wound in the king's neck.

210 Under the pretext of answering a bodily need, the wicked man immediately departed. Because he was a monk, he was not challenged by any of the guards.

211 Splattered with the spray of blood from the king, the Teacher awoke. He saw the severed head; it looked like a lotus flower deprived of its stalk.

212 Not seeing his pupil there, the Teacher thought, 'Surely my pupil must have done this, since he's nowhere to be seen.

213 Your majesty, you are the supporter of religion. What sin did you commit, that caused you to be destroyed and a blemish to appear in the Jain religion?

214 Because the wicked man was initiated as I looked on, and was then brought here by me, I have caused a blemish in the religion.

215 So I shall remove this blemish from the religion by my own death; let people think that the king and the Teacher were murdered by the same man.'

216 So, having determined upon a final denial of life, the Teacher applied the iron knife to his throat, and died.

217 In the morning the guards arose from their beds in the inner rooms of the palace, and came to that place. They screamed and beat their breasts when they saw the horrific sight.

218 The king's servants all gathered together. They thought, 'There's no doubt that the king and the Teacher were both murdered by that novice monk.
219 If the novice had been about to be murdered, he would have screamed first, but that wicked man has committed this act of violence, and disappeared.
220 Someone, either an enemy, or an enemy's son, or perhaps someone sent by an enemy, pretended to be a Jain monk, and murdered the unsuspecting king.
221 The Teacher was like a father to the king, and the king was like a son to the Teacher. Surely the king was either performing a penance or sitting before the Teacher.
222 While the Teacher, whose body was attenuated by his ascetic practices, was doing that, he was felled to the ground and killed by that wicked man, in the same way as the king.
223 The Teacher was deceived by his pretence of morality, and initiated him. Who isn't deceived by cunning swindlers?'
224 Since the sham monk had escaped in the night, in the following morning the king's troops were unable to catch him. He who escapes by just one step escapes by a hundred miles.
225 Then the courtiers and nobles, weeping and loudly lamenting, performed the funeral rites for the king and the Teacher.
226 Udāyin's evil murderer returned to Ujjayinī, and told the king how he had murdered Udāyin.
227 The king of Avanti cried, 'You villain! You who after taking initiation as a Jain monk spent so much time with the monks,
228 and, although you listened day and night to the precepts of the Jain religion, remained evil-minded and then committed such a crime—how can you be well disposed towards me?
229 I don't want to see your face, you wretch! Be off with you, right now!' The king scolded him, and banished him from the city.
230 From that time on, the crest-jewel of those that ought not to be on the face of the earth, he was notorious to all as the murderer of King Udāyin.

231 Now in the same city of Pāṭalīputra lived the son of a barber and a prostitute. He was named Nanda.
232 One morning the barber's son dreamt that Pāṭalīputra was surrounded by his own intestines.
233 When he awoke, Nanda told his teacher about the dream. The

Teacher understood the meaning of the dream, and took Nanda to his house.

234 He affectionately presented Nanda with ornaments and jewels, and married his daughter to him.

235 The Teacher mounted his new son-in-law on a palanquin, and paraded him around the city.

236 Now because Udāyin's male heirs had predeceased him, at that very moment the five divine emblems of royalty were being lustrated by the ministers.

237 The city elephant, the chief horse, the parasol, the ewer, and the two fly-whisks; these five divine insignia were being led through the palace.

238 And when the insignia emerged from the palace, they saw the newly married Nanda being carried in the palanquin.

239 Suddenly the elephant trumpeted with a roar like the thunder of an autumn rain cloud, and with upraised trunk anointed Nanda with the entire contents of the ewer.

240 The elephant raised Nanda aloft, and placed him on its shoulder. The horse neighed for joy, as if hymning with praise an auspicious occasion.

241 The parasol opened, like a lotus flower at dawn, and the two fly-whisks fanned out and flew about, as if they were dancing.

242 Then the nobles, townspeople, and country folk joyfully held a great coronation festival for Nanda.

243 When this Nanda became king, sixty years had elapsed from the year of Lord Mahāvīra's passing away.

244 Afterwards, some of Nanda's vassals, blinded by pride, refused to pay him any respect, because he was the son of a barber.

245 So Nanda, to observe their true disposition while concealing his own intentions, suddenly strode towards the door of the assembly hall, like an elephant striding towards the door of its stable.

246 His mother and the nurse who was carrying his little child followed Nanda, but no one else stood up to escort him in the way that they had done.

247 Then Nanda returned to the assembly hall and ordered his guards to execute his vassals.

248 But the guards just looked at each other, grinning and gesturing, as if they had seen a ghost.

249 Then Nanda knew the minds of his counsellors. His glance

darted towards the two plaster figures moulded on the wall at each side of the door.

250 Thereupon a goddess, impelled by Nanda's merits, placed life into the bodies of these figures, and the two plaster door-keepers stepped from the wall and ran forwards.

251 They killed some of the ill-mannered counsellors, and put the others to flight. From then on, Nanda's authority was unchallenged.

252 King Nanda ruled with great prosperity. He governed his kingdom well, and became learned in the scriptures. Generally, merit and valour are the right standard; a sissy can be born even in a good family.

Here finishes the sixth canto of the scholar-monk Hemacandra's epic poem, the Appendix, or Lives of the Jain Elders. In it were related Yaśobhadra's departure for heaven, the story of Bhadrabāhu's four pupils, the story of Annikā's son, the founding of Pāṭalīputra, the story of Udāyin's murder, and the story of Nanda's accession to the kingdom.

CANTO SEVEN

The subject of Canto Seven is the relationship between King Nanda and his shrewd minister, Kalpaka. Stories about kings and their clever ministers are a frequent motif in Indian folk-tale. The theme of this Canto foreshadows the stories about King Candragupta and his minister Cāṇakya related in Canto Eight, which provide a fuller example of the genre.

1–19 On the outskirts of Pāṭalīputra lived a Brahmin named Kapila, who was converted to Jainism by the preaching of a Jain Teacher. A son was born to Kapila. The child was possessed by goddesses who brought childhood illnesses, but he was cured by some Jain monks who were staying in Kapila's house. The child was named Kalpaka.

20–39 Kalpaka grew to be a pious Jain layman, noted for his learning. Despite being courted by the parents of charming maidens, he persisted in remaining single, until one day a Brahmin tricked him into becoming betrothed to his daughter who was suffering from dropsy. Kalpaka married the girl, having first cured her of her affliction.

40–84 King Nanda, hearing that Kalpaka was a learned man, desired him to become his minister, but Kalpaka refused on the grounds that the performance of the duties of a king's minister would be incompatible with the life of a pious Jain layman. However, Nanda goaded Kalpaka into murdering a laundryman, so Kalpaka, to gain the king's forgiveness, was forced to become minister. Kalpaka's political skills soon enabled Nanda to become the dominant power in Bharata.

85–138 A former minister of Nanda, jealous of Kalpaka's success, brought about his temporary downfall. Then Nanda's enemies began to besiege Pāṭalīputra. The king realized that his difficulties were due to Kalpaka's absence, and had him brought from the well in which he was imprisoned. Kalpaka once more enabled Nanda to dominate his enemies.

1 Now just outside that very city ruled by King Nanda lived a Brahmin named Kapila.

2 One evening, a certain Jain Teacher accompanied by his followers came to the vicinity of Kapila's house. He was like a lion to the elephant of existence.

3 Then, as if through weariness from its journey through the whole sky, the sun became like an elephant, lapped by the waves of the ocean in the West.

4 The twilight sky was flecked with beautiful clouds which has appropriated the magnificent colour of fresh pomegranate flowers; it looked as if it were wearing a fine garment dyed with saffron.

5 Because at every step it was shining with series of lamps in the lofty houses, the earth appeared to have gained its own constellations, in constant emulation of the sky.

6 On all sides, the birds, under the guise of their chattering, asked the begetter of light, as if he were their playfellow, 'When will we see you again?'

7 When the sun sets, I believe, its rays are placed in fire. How else does it become so very bright at that time?

8 Then the space between heaven and earth was filled with dense night like black ink; it became like the spaces between the hells.

9 Because it was difficult to gain entrance to the city at night, the Teacher purified with his feet the courtyard of that Brahmin's house.

10 Having asked the Brahmin's permission, the Teacher, affectionate to all, spent that starry night in his sacrificial enclosure.

11 Since the Brahmin was of opposed views, he did not know any of the things that the Jain monks knew. During the night, Kapila approached the principal Teacher.

12 The Teacher explained the Jain doctrine to him in words which were like waves of the ocean of religious knowledge dancing in his heart.

13 So on that night, because of this explanation of the Jain religion, Kapila became a Jain layman. After that, the Teacher went elsewhere.

14 One day, during the rainy season, at the invitation of that Brahmin who had become worthy of the honour, some Jain monks came to stay in his house.

15 On the next day, a son was born to the Brahmin Kapila, but

as soon as he was born he became possessed by Brilliant goddesses.*

16 The Brahmin, who abounded in faith, placed the child under the monks' bowls as they were arranging them.

17 They sprinkled the child with water from their bowls, and through the power of these ascetics, the cruel Interstitial goddesses immediately departed.

18 Since the child had become healthy through being sprinkled with water from the monks' bowls as they were being made fit for use (kalpa), the Jain layman Kapila named the boy Kalpaka.

19 From that time on, Kapila had no more trouble with Interstitial goddesses in his home, and afterwards he was blessed with an abundance of male offspring.

20 In the passing of time, Kalpaka, bereft of his parents, grew up to be learned in all branches of knowledge, and became a very well-known person in that city.

21 He always delighted in being a Jain layman from birth, and he had no desire to be married.

22 Even though he was courted on behalf of maidens of good family who were charming, beautiful, and admired by all, he did not marry them.

23 When Kalpaka walked about the town, he was thronged by the young men of the city. He was respected by the citizens, for wise men are everywhere respected.

24 Now, by the side of the road along which Kapila's son used to come and go, lived a Brahmin who had a daughter.

25 Although she was very beautiful, no one would marry her, because her beauty was marred by the dropsy.

26 Her body was like a leather water-bottle filled with liquid. Her belly was swollen. She looked as if she were pregnant, even though she was a virgin. She could not even walk.

27 The girl was like a creeping plant, ready to flower, if only manured. The girl's mother informed her husband of this.

28 The Brahmin said to his wife, 'This is a shameful matter for us both, our daughter being unmarried, although she has started to menstruate.

29 Because she has no husband, her blossoming is wasted, and we are in the position of committing the sin of killing a Brahmin.

30 What shall we do? No one will marry her, because she has the dropsy. So we must entrap someone by means of a deceptive statement, and marry her to him.

31 But no one except Kalpaka will agree to be married on the basis of a deceptive statement; he alone is true to his word, so we'll make him the object of our endeavour.'

32 So the Brahmin dug a well in front of his house, and threw his daughter into it, at the time when Kalpaka was passing.

33 As soon as he saw Kalpaka coming, the Brahmin cried, 'Help, help! Whoever can pull my daughter out of this well, to him I shall marry her.'

34 Kalpaka, whose heart was engraved with sympathy, immediately rescued her, without hearing the last part of the Brahmin's sentence.

35 Thereupon the girl's father said, 'Marry my daughter, Kalpaka, since I publicly announced that she would be betrothed to whoever rescued her from the well.

36 Having heard the terms of her betrothal, you accepted them. For a person accepts what he doesn't refuse: that's logic.

37 You know as much logic as if you were the creator of the branches of knowledge. Furthermore, you are true to your word, so do the right thing.'

38 Kalpaka thought, 'I've been deceived by the power of his intelligence. What shall I do?' And, although he had no wish for a broad-hipped one, he decided to marry her.

39 Kalpaka was like the one born in a jar* in his knowledge of all the arts and sciences. He cured her with medicine prescribed in the medical texts, and then married her.

40 Now King Nanda had heard that Kalpaka was a learned scholar, so he summoned Kalpaka and ordered him to become his minister.

41 Kalpaka replied, 'Apart from food and clothing, I have no desire for any other possessions.

42 The business of a king's minister is not fit for pious, religious people, so I'm turning down the job.'

43 With these words Kalpaka flouted the king's command, and went away. But the king began to look for Kalpaka's weak spot.

44 Although King Nanda was constantly on the watch, he could not find Kalpaka's weak spot; indeed, it is generally hard to find faults in religious men who are not ruled by their desires.

45 The king was an ocean of wisdom, so one day he summoned his laundryman, who lived on the street which passed the door of Kalpaka's house, and asked him:

46 'Do you or do you not wash the clothes of your neighbour, the Brahmin Kalpaka?'

47 When the laundryman confirmed that he did, the king ordered him, 'Take Kalpaka's clothes, then don't give them back.'

48 The laundryman agreed to undertake the king's command, and left. Soon after, it became the time of the full moon festival.

49 Kalpaka's wife said to her husband, 'My dear, please get the king's laundryman to wash my fine clothes.

50 Then, when my beautiful multi-coloured clothes are thoroughly clean, I'll perfume them, and wear them at the full moon festival.'

51–2 Kalpaka thought, 'When it's time for the festival, the laundryman who works for the king will take the clothes, but will not return them, so that he can gain a fee for their hire. I will not buy with my own hand this disgrace and its associated annoyance.'

53 This man of supreme foresight, saw this with the eye of his faculty of discernment, and ignored his wife's request; wise men are not dominated by their wives.

54 But Kalpaka neglected to hide his wife's clothes, so she took them and gave them to the laundryman; women have a strong grasp.

55 On the morning of the festival, Kalpaka went to the laundryman, but he, as ordered by the king, did not return the clothes.

56 The laundryman repeatedly deceived him, saying, 'Go away today, come back tomorrow.' He did not fear Kalpaka, since he was acting on the king's order.

57 Pursuing this errand Kalpaka went day after day to the laundryman's house, like a debtor to the house of his creditor.

58 In this way, Kalpaka continued to ask for the clothes for two years, for if one displays patience, eventually one overcomes.

59 But at the start of the third year, Kalpaka said, 'Hey laundryman, you're a thief! You've made my clothes grow old.

60 If I don't take back the clothes dyed with your blood, then my name isn't Kalpaka, and you're not a vile laundryman!'

61 At night, Kalpaka stole from his home alone and went to the laundryman's house, as boldly as if he were going to perform a magic ritual.

62 Learned in all the teachings of Caṇḍikā, Bhṛgu, Vetāla, and others,* he held a concealed dagger; it looked like the goddess of death.

63 Then like a springing leopard, his face contorted in a frown, terrible with anger, Kalpaka entered and shouted to the laundryman:

64 'Like a slave, I've been coming to your house for two years. Speak! Will you return my clothes right now, or not?'

65 As soon as the laundryman saw Kalpaka, who looked like a ravenous demon, he trembled, and told his wife to return Kalpaka's clothes.

66 She did so. But Kalpaka revealed his dagger, brandishing it before him, like a lion shaking its tail.

67 The laundryman's belly went split-splat!, as Kalpaka rent it with his knife, which was like a ploughshare cleaving the earth.

68 True to his promise, Kalpaka dyed the clothes in the blood which flowed from the laundryman's stomach like water from a spring.

69 The laundryman's wife cried, 'Why have you killed this innocent man? He retained your clothes for so long in our home on the orders of the king.'

70 When Kalpaka heard this, he became worried, and thought, 'Ah! This was a stratagem of the king, because I disobeyed his orders.

71 So, rather than be carried before the king by his officers for the crime of killing the laundryman, I'll go to the king myself.'

72 Having decided upon this course of action, Kalpaka went of his own accord to King Nanda. The king was overjoyed and treated him with the utmost respect.

73 Nanda knew why Kalpaka had come, since he understood what his real intention was. He said sternly, 'Accept the office of my minister, as was requested of you.'

74 Kalpaka, wishing to be forgiven for his crime, acceded to the king's request. The man who knows the right moment is wise indeed.

75 Nanda, considering that his purpose was achieved, was overjoyed, and treated Kalpaka like a cloud for the peacock of his mind.*

76 Nanda consulted Kalpaka about problems in affairs of state, which were like thorns in his heart, as if Kalpaka were a long-desired teacher of wisdom.

77 Kalpaka was extremely wise; he pleased the king with his words of advice, which were like hammers smashing the clay clods of the king's problems.

78 When the guild of laundrymen came to complain about the crime, they saw that the king had honoured Kalpaka with the position of royal adviser.

79 Seeing how Kalpaka was situated, the laundrymen departed, their business undone. The king's favour is indeed the only remedy for misfortune.

80 Subsequently, the king appointed Kalpaka prime minister, entrusting him with the seal and the royal elephant, as was proper.

81 With the hands of his political skills he stole the prosperity of all the hostile kings who ruled over the earth as far as the ocean. Then he made it Nanda's entire possession.

82 By means of this new minister, who was a magician who understood how to subjugate the goddess of Prosperity to his will, Nanda's prosperity became as imperishable as a stream of water.

83 The king's tree of victory was sprinkled with the water of his minister's wisdom, and grew branches fragrant with the blossom of glory.

84 The minister's manifold intelligence was like a strong wind fanning the ever increasing fire of King Nanda's glory.

85 But a former minister who had been dismissed from his office wanted to outwit Kalpaka, because he had been placed in a subordinate position.

86 This man won over Kalpaka's favourite maidservant with gifts of clothes and other objects so that he could gain information about Kalpaka's way of life.

87 And she, overcome by greed, informed the former minister of everything that was said and done each day in Kalpaka's house.

88 Now Kalpaka had many sons, for the worshippers of the supreme Worthies usually have many sons.

89 One day, he was about to celebrate the wedding of one of his sons, so he decided to invite the king and his family to the ceremony.

90 In order to welcome the king properly, he ordered a crown, parasol, fly-whisks, and other appropriate things to be prepared.

91 The maidservant reported all this to the dismissed minister, who seized the opportunity and informed the king:

92 'I'm no longer your minister, and I'm not respected. Nevertheless, I come from a good family and I'm very devoted to you, so I'll relate something of benefit to your majesty.

93 Hear what Kalpaka, your favourite minister, is doing: at this very moment he's preparing a parasol and the other insignia of royalty.

94 I'll say no more; your majesty can find out his intentions for yourself. Wise men only need to taste a ball of rice to know that the pot is boiling.

95 I'm telling you this because I lived on your majesty's bread, not because I'm jealous of Kalpaka's position.

96 Would I tell a lie because of jealousy? You can check that it's true by means of spies, for spies are the eyes of kings.'

97 So the king sent spies to Kalpaka's house. They saw the things described by the former minister, and reported back to the king.

98 Consequently, the king berated Kalpaka, and immediately had him, together with his family, thrown into a disused well to serve as his prison.

99 At the king's command, every day two handfuls of kodrava* gruel and a coconut-shell of water were placed in the well for Kalpaka and his sons.

100 Kalpaka saw that there was only a scanty amount of food, and said to his family, 'If we share this out, it will be in little paste-balls; there can be no talk of mouthfuls.

101 It takes a hundred little paste-balls to fill a belly, so if you only eat one paste-ball, you'll all die.

102 So let the one who is able to take adequate revenge on that former minister eat all the kodrava gruel.'

103 His family replied in unison, 'You eat it, father! May you fare well! None of us is able to take adequate revenge.'

104 So each day Kalpaka ate all the food, but the others fasted, died, and went to heaven.

105 When the vassal kings realized that Kalpaka was absent, they besieged Pāṭalīputra, hoping to extirpate Nanda.

106 The gates of Pāṭalīputra were blockaded in every direction. Inside the citizens were driven by fear; pot smashed into pot as they rushed about.

107 Unable to defeat his enemies, Nanda, as if suffering from a fever, could gain no comfort in either sitting or lying down.

108 He thought, 'While Kalpaka was my minister, this city was like a lion's lair; no one attacked it.

109 The city is in this dangerous situation because Kalpaka is not here; by-passers plunder an orchard that is unguarded.

110 If he is still alive, then he alone can relieve the city; an elephant's burden can usually only be drawn by an elephant.'

111 The king enquired of the prison warders, who reported that someone in the well was still eating the kodrava each day.

112 Nanda lowered a platform into the well, placed Kalpaka on it, and then drew him out, as if drawing out his own hidden treasure.

113 Kalpaka was as thin as a withered leaf. The king had him placed in a litter. Then he had him paraded around the city ramparts, like a protective deity.

114 When the enemy saw him, they thought, 'Nanda must be really stupid, if he's trying to frighten us by displaying a substitute Kalpaka.'

115 So the hostile forces fearlessly began to assault a strong point, using siege engines turned against the opposing defences, and other contrivances.

116 Then Kalpaka sent a messenger to the enemy, having ordered him to say, 'Send out a man who is respected by you on a boat to the middle of the Ganges.

117 I too shall come on a boat and speak with that wise man, so that I can make a treaty or some other arrangement that is acceptable to you.'

118 According to this stipulation, the enemy's minister of peace and war and Kalpaka met on their respective boats; they were like two planets, one with a crooked course, the other with a straight one.

119 Then Kalpaka saw a man holding a stick of sugar cane. Kalpaka pointed to him, and by gesturing with his fingers asked the enemy minister:

120 'If the bottom and the top of the stick of sugar cane are cut off, then what will become of the piece in the middle?'

121 Although the minister of peace and war was very wise and learned, he was unable to apprehend Kalpaka's meaning. This is what he meant:

122 'As the sugar cane thrives at its top and bottom joints, so the military man thrives by both kinds of treaty.

123 One is the true treaty which once agreed is not violated; the other is the false treaty which is devised deceitfully.

124 Now you may make either a sham or a true treaty with Nanda. But tell me this, how can you make a sham treaty?

125 If you do not make a binding treaty with King Nanda, you will be consumed like a stick of sugar cane which has had its top and bottom joints cut off.'

126 Then Kalpaka pointed to a herdsman's wife who was carrying on her head a jar of thick yoghurt, which was suddenly smashed by a stick.

127 As before, the enemy minister was unable to apprehend Kalpaka's meaning. This is what the minister Kalpaka had in mind:

128 'If the jar of your collected army is hit by the stick of my arm, then your force will be scattered like the yoghurt, to be eaten by rats and crows.'

129 Then Kalpaka rowed three times around the other's boat, but once again the enemy minister did not understand what he was aiming at.

130 This was his meaning: 'Just as your boat was surrounded by my boat, so shall your glory be surrounded by our glory.'

131 The minister did not understand what Kalpaka was signifying by these three gestures, so without any further consideration he left, his mouth gaping, like a baby crow.

132 Then Kalpaka returned home, and the minister of peace and war, without understanding Kalpaka's meaning, returned, full of astonishment, to his tent.

133 Questioned by his attendants, the minister for peace and war said, 'The Brahmin Kalpaka just prattled some nonsense.'

134 They asked him again and again, but he said nothing more. Then he felt ashamed, and said, 'I didn't understand what Kalpaka meant.'

135 Then the vassal kings were convinced that it was Kalpaka whom he had met, and immediately fled in every direction.

136 Then, as they were fleeing, King Nanda, on Kalpaka's advice, annihilated them, and captured their elephants, horses, jewels, and treasure.

137 Nanda imprisoned that wicked former minister in anger because he had inflicted harm on the faithful Kalpaka.

138 The wise prime minister Kalpaka, a guardian attendant for Nanda's prosperity, an ocean for the rivers of expediency, subdued the earth to Nanda's will.

Here finishes the seventh canto of the scholar-monk Hemacandra's epic poem, the Appendix, or Lives of the Jain Elders. In it was related the story of the minister Kalpaka.

CANTO EIGHT

The first 169 verses of Canto Eight centre on the Jain Elder Sthūlabhadra, a descendant of Kalpaka, while the theme of the remaining verses is the overthrow of the Nanda dynasty and the establishment of the Maurya dynasty be Cāṇakya, the minister of the first Mauryan emperor, Candragupta.

1–10 Nanda was succeeded by his eight descendants, whom the descendants of Kalpaka served as hereditary ministers.

11–66 The ninth king of the Nanda dynasty's minister was named Śakaṭāla. He had two sons; the elder, Sthūlabhadra, lived with the prostitute Kośā, while the younger, Śrīyaka, was the king's bodyguard. The king was induced by the machinations of the Brahmin poet Vararuci to suspect the loyalty of Śakaṭāla, who, to confirm his family's loyalty, was, at his own arrangement, executed by his son Śrīyaka as he bowed before the king.

67–108 Śrīyaka became the king's chief minister, while Sthūlabhadra became a Jain monk, having received initiation from Sambhūtavijaya. Śrīyaka, with the assistance of Kośā and her sister, took mortal revenge on Vararuci.

109–68 Sthūlabhadra vowed to spend the rainy season in Kośā's house, while preserving his vow of chastity. He successfully performed that difficult vow, but the following year another monk, attempting to emulate Sthūlabhadra's feat, was overcome by Kośā's charms and began to lust for her. The monk was persuaded to remain true to his vows by Kośā herself, who had become a Jain laywoman.

169 Sambhūtavijaya died and went to heaven.

170–93 The king bestowed Kośā on his charioteer. By her constant praise of Sthūlabhadra she converted him, and he became a Jain monk. At that time a famine of twelve years' duration set in.

194–226 A Brahmin, who was a Jain layman, and his wife had a son who was prophesied by Jain monks to become the power behind a throne. The child, named Cāṇakya, grew into a learned Jain layman, and married a Brahmin's daughter. One day, she was invited to a wedding, at which she was mocked by her relatives and the other guests for her poverty. Cāṇakya decided to gain wealth by visiting

King Nanda, who had a reputation for generosity to Brahmins. Unfortunately, he insulted the king and was dismissed from the court.

227–326 Then Cāṇakya remembered the prophecy of the Jain monks, and vowed to destroy Nanda. He came to the village of Nanda's peacock breeders, and there assisted at the delivery of Candragupta, the son of the head peacock breeder's daughter, his fee being the right to adopt the child. Cāṇakya left the village, and began to gather wealth by means of alchemy. Eventually, he returned, and saw that Candragupta had grown into a child with the right characteristics to be made king. The two left, and Cāṇakya recruited a band of soldiers with whom he beseiged Pāṭalīputra, but the attack was repulsed. Cāṇakya and Candragupta escaped. Eventually, they changed their tactics, and by attacking Nanda's kingdom from the outskirts, they, in alliance with Parvataka, the king of the Himalayas, eventually captured Pāṭalīputra. Candragupta became king, marrying Nanda's daughter.

There follow several episodes illustrative of Cāṇakya's cunning:

327–39 Parvataka was poisoned, but Cāṇakya, to gain Parvataka's kingdom, prevented Candragupta from aiding him.

340–6 Cāṇakya appointed an efficient city constable.

347–51 Cāṇakya destroyed a village by means of an ambiguous order.

352–76 Cāṇakya taxed wealthy citizens by means of a stratagem.

377–414 Cāṇakya exposed the activities of two monks who, having made themselves invisible, were stealing food from Candragupta.

415–35 Cāṇakya converted Candragupta to Jainism, by demonstrating that the ascetics of other religions lacked self-control.

436–43 One day, the pregnant queen took food from Candragupta's plate in which, to render the king immune to its effects, poison had been placed on Cāṇakya's orders. The queen fell dead, but Cāṇakya split open her belly, and rescued her son, who was called Bindusāra.

444–5 Candragupta died, and was succeeded by Bindusāra, by that time a young man.

446–69 Through the prompting of Subhandu, a jealous minister, Bindusāra began to suspect Cāṇakya, who met his end on a burning dungheap. He was reborn as a goddess.

1 Afterwards, Kalpaka, that ocean of wisdom, had other sons, and bore the office of seal-bearer to King Nanda for a very long time.

2 In course of time, seven descendants of Nanda became king, and their ministers were the abundant descendants of Kalpaka.

3 Eventually, ruling over every portion of the earth, like the husband of the goddess of Prosperity, having eradicated his enemies, the ninth Nanda became king.

4 The king's prime minister was named Śakaṭāla, a descendant of Kalpaka. He was an extensive dwelling place for the goddess of Prosperity, and a wide wagon (śakaṭa) of wisdom.

5 His wife's name was Lakṣmāvatī. She was as beautiful as Lakṣmī, the goddess of wealth. She was bedecked with the ornaments of morality.

6 Their elder son was named Sthūlabhadra. Adorned with good conduct, of refined intelligence, he was a moon for the night of prosperity.

7 The younger son was named Śrīyaka. Grounded in devotion, he was like sandalwood providing the fragrance of abundant joy for the heart of King Nanda.

8 In that city lived a prostitute named Kośā, the dawning of beauty and prosperity, the thought of whom bewitched the universe, a medicinal plant vivifying the world.

9 Sthūlabhadra was devoted to her. Enjoying various kinds of sexual pleasure, he stayed in her home day and night for twelve years.

10 But Śrīyaka was the king's bodyguard. The king placed a great deal of confidence in him; he was like Nanda's second heart.

11 In the city lived a leading Brahmin named Vararuci, the crest-jewel of poets, philosophers, and grammarians.

12 Each day, to entertain the king, he recited a hundred and eight newly composed verses of his own making.

13 But the prime minister never praised Vararuci, because he held the wrong views about religion. Consequently the king, even though he was delighted, never gave the Brahmin a gift to mark his satisfaction.

14 Vararuci knew that the reason for his not receiving a gift lay with the minister, so he ingratiated himself into the favour of Śakaṭāla's wife.

15 She was delighted, and one day asked what she could do for him. He replied, 'See that your husband praises my poetry in the presence of the king.'

16 She repeatedly asked her husband to do this, but he replied, 'How can I praise the compositions of a man who holds the wrong views about religion?'

17 She obstinately continued to ask him, so in the end the minister did what she wanted. The obstinacy of blind people, women, children, and of fools is powerful indeed.

18 So when Vararuci recited his poetry before the king, the prime minister exclaimed, 'Bravo! Well recited!'

19 Thereupon the king gave the minister a hundred and eight golden dinars. One can live by the mere word of the great, provided that it is favourable.

20 Every day Vararuci was given a hundred and eight golden dinars. The minister asked the king, 'Why are you giving him so much?'

21 The king replied to the minister, 'I am rewarding him on account of your praise. If I gave of my own accord, I would have rewarded him before now.'

22 The minister said, 'Your majesty, I did not praise his poetry; I was praising the compositions of other poets.

23 He is reciting before us the verses of other poets, while pretending that they are his own.' The king asked whether there was proof of this.

24 The minister said, 'In the morning I shall show you some girls who will recite the same poems that he recited.'

25 The minister had seven daughters. Their names were Yakṣā, Yakṣadattā, Bhūtā, Bhūtadattā, Eṇikā, Veṇā, and Reṇā.

26 The first of these could recite what she had heard once, the second, what she had heard twice, the third, thrice, and so on.

27 On the following day the minister brought them to the court, and hid them behind a curtain.

28 Vararuci recited his one hundred and eight daily verses which he had composed himself, but the girls repeated them, exactly as he had first recited them.

29 So the king became angry with Vararuci and withheld his pay; ministers have stratagems appropriate for their ill-will or for their favour.

30 After that, Vararuci went and placed in the Ganges a catapult in which he had placed a knotted purse containing a hundred and eight dinars.

31 In the morning he sung a hymn of praise to the Ganges, then triggered the catapult with his foot. The purse of dinars flew up and landed in his hands.

32 He performed the same thing every day. The people were astonished. The king overheard the people discussing it, and told his minister about it.

33 The prime minister said, 'I'll go myself tomorrow morning to see if it is true.' The king gave his assent.

34 The prime minister thought about the matter, and in the evening sent a spy, who hid in a thicket of reeds and remained there unnoticed, like a bird.

35 Vararuci came in secret to the Ganges, hid the purse containing the one hundred and eight dinars, and then returned home.

36 The spy took hold of the purse, as carefully as if it were his own life, and secretly gave it to the prime minister.

37 In the morning the prime minister concealed on his person the purse of dinars, and went with the king to the Ganges. Vararuci soon came.

38 Bursting with pride because the king had come to watch, the deluded Vararuci began to praise the Ganges.

39 As he hymned the river, Vararuci triggered the catapult with his foot, but the purse of dinars did not fly up and land in the palm of his hand.

40 He searched for the bag with his hands in the water. When he failed to find it, he became silent; a cheat when confounded partakes of silence.

41 Then the prime minister said, 'What? Won't the Ganges give you the money which you are looking for, although you hid it there?'

42 Saying, 'Here, take your money!', he placed the purse of dinars in Vararuci's hand.

43 So because of that knotted purse of dinars, which was like a knot of anguish swelling in his heart, he reached a state that was harder to bear than death.

44 The minister told the king, 'To deceive the people, he deposited the money here in the evening, then took it back in the morning.'

45 The king said to his prime minister, 'Well done! His deception has been exposed.' He returned to his palace, his eyes popping with astonishment.

46 Vararuci could not bear this, so he plotted revenge. He questioned the minister's house-servants.

47 One of the maidservants told him, 'The king is coming to dine in the minister's house, at Śrīyaka's wedding.

48 And the minister is preparing weapons to give to the king on that occasion. Kings are fond of weapons, so weapons are an excellent gift for them.'

49 So Vararuci, skilled in deceit, succeeded in outwitting the prime minister. He bribed some boys with chickpeas to recite:

50 'The king does not know what Śakaṭāla intends to do. He's going to kill Nanda, and make Śrīyaka king in place of him.'

51 Everyday the boys recited this everywhere they went. The king overheard the rumours and thought:

52 'The talk of women, the talk of children, and talk of calamities never fails to come true.'

53 To make certain of it, the king sent a servant to the minister's house, who returned and reported everything he had seen to the king.

54 So afterwards, when it was time for the audience, and the minister came to pay his respects to the king, the king angrily turned his back on him.

55 Understanding his position, he returned home, and said to Śrīyaka, 'Someone has slandered me to the king; he refused to receive me, as if I were an enemy.

56 My son, this disgrace which has without reason come upon our family will be averted, if you do what I command:

57 When I bow before the king, cut off my head with your sword, and then say, "He who is not received by the king must be executed, even though he is my father."

58 I want to go to my next rebirth, where old age is already taking me. Soon you will be the supporting pillar of my house and family.'

59 Śrīyaka wept, and sobbed incoherently, 'Father, shouldn't this dreadful deed rather be performed by the public executioner?'

60 The minister replied, 'If you hesitate like this, you'll only please my enemies.

61 The king, his sceptre upraised, like Yama, the god of Death, will not destroy my household along with me. So by means of my death only, protect my household.

62 Before I bow to the king, I shall place in my mouth some poison wrapped in a leaf. Then cut off my head as I die; you'll not be guilty of parricide.'

63 Thus admonished by his father, he assented, and performed the dreadful deed. Wise men perform deeds that appear terrible for the sake of a prosperous outcome.

64 The king said angrily, 'Young man, why have you committed this wicked crime?' Śrīyaka replied:

65 'I executed him because your majesty had discovered that he was a traitor; the actions of servants accord with the thoughts of their masters.

66 When servants themselves discover a fault among their number, they should hesitate about taking punishment, but when the king discovers the fault, there should be no hesitation.'

67 After Śrīyaka had performed the funeral rites, Nanda said to him, 'Accept the seal and all the offices that come with it.'

68 Śrīyaka bowed in refusal, and told the king, 'I have an elder brother named Sthūlabhadra.

69 He left our father's home, and for twelve years has lived in Kośā's house, enjoying sensual pleasures.'

70 The king summoned Sthūlabhadra, and described the duties of the office. Sthūlabhadra said, 'I'll have to think about the job, before I take it on.'

71 The king said, 'Go and think about it right now.' So Sthūlabhadra went to a grove of Aśoka trees, and reflected intelligently:

72 'Ministers, like labourers, do not enjoy couches, meals, baths, and other sources of pleasure, even at the proper time.

73 The mind of a minister is fully engaged with affairs of state;

like a pot full of water, there's no room for thoughts of a mistress.

74 Although ministers abandon their own business to perform that of the king, their detractors attack them, as if they had been hung up to be attacked by crows.

75 Since the endeavour of caring for the king's affairs is performed at the cost of one's own health and property, shouldn't the wise man care for his own affairs?'

76 Having thus reflected, he decided to uproot his hair in five handfuls, and to receive the whisk-broom with the jewel and the fringed garment.

77 Then the blessed man went to the palace, and said to the king, 'This is what I've decided: let religion be my choice.'

78 Then he strode vigorously from the palace, like a lion from its lair, angry with the cause of worldly bondage.

79 But the king did not believe him, thinking that Sthūlabhadra was playing a trick because he wanted to return home, so he spied through a window.

80 The king saw Sthūlabhadra walking in a place full of stinking corpses without even wrinkling his nose. The king shook his head:

81 'This holy man is free from passion; shame on me for my wicked thought.' Thus King Nanda loudly reviled himself while praising Sthūlabhadra.

82 Then Sthūlabhadra received initiation, which consists of calm-minded renunciation, at the hands of holy Sambhūtavijaya.

83 Then Nanda took Śrīyaka by the arm, and entrusted him with the office of keeper of the seal, together with all its associated duties.

84 Śrīyaka, ever attentive, took care of the kingdom. In his wise conduct of policy, he was just like Śakaṭāla himself.

85 Every day Śrīyaka humbly went to Kośā's house. Through affection for a brother, his mistress is highly respected by men of good breeding.

86 When she saw Śrīyaka, she wept, 'Once she has seen the man she desires, a woman afflicted by grief is not able to endure her sorrow.'

87 Śrīyaka said to her, 'What could we do? That wicked Vararuci caused the death of our father.

88 And he made my brother Sthūlabhadra, blazing with the fire of a needlessly raised thunderbolt, part from you.

89 Vararuci is in love with your sister Upakośā, so consider taking revenge on him by some means, intelligent lady.

90 Tell Upakośā to make Vararuci somehow become fond of intoxicating liquor.'

91 So, through the enmity she had because of her separation from her lover, and also through the goodwill she had for her brother-in-law, on that same day she persuaded Upakośā to agree to this.

92 On Kośā's direction, Upakośā induced Vararuci to start drinking alcohol. What won't men who are ruled by women do?

93 In the morning Upakośā told Kośā that she had persuaded the poet Vararuci to drink copious amounts of liquor.

94 Kośā told Śrīyaka all about it. Then Śrīyaka knew that he had found the means of taking revenge upon his father's enemy.

95 Ever since the death of the prime minister Śakaṭāla, the poet Vararuci had taken every opportunity of serving the king.

96 Each day he would attend the court when it was time to pay homage to the king; he looked like Nanda's prime minister to the assembled vassal kings.

97 One day King Nanda was perturbed by the recollection of the merits of his former prime minister. In front of everyone, he shouted incoherently to the minister Śrīyaka:

98 'Śakaṭāla was wise, he was always devoted, and always effective; my prime minister was like Bṛhaspati, the minister of Indra.

99 But he was destroyed by fate. What shall I do now? Without him, I feel that my assembly hall is empty.'

100 Śrīyaka replied, 'Your majesty, we don't disagree about that. All the trouble was caused by Vararuci; he's a drunkard.'

101 When the king asked if it was true that the poet was a drunkard, Śrīyaka replied, 'Tomorrow I shall prove that he is.'

102 On the following day, when everyone had assembled in the court, Śrīyaka ordered his obedient servants to distribute a beautiful lotus flower to each person.

103 But the lotus flower given to wicked Vararuci was impregnated with the syrup of emetic fruits.

104 Exclaiming, 'Where is that lovely fragrance coming from!', the king and his courtiers lifted their lotus flowers to their noses to sniff them.

105 But when the poet put his lotus flower to his nose, he immediately vomited the liquor which he had drunk during the night.

106 As Vararuci fled from the court, everyone cried, 'Shame! A Brahmin who drinks alcohol is worthy of death by hanging.'

107 He asked some Brahmins for absolvement, and they replied that the expiation for the crime of drinking alcohol was to drink molten tin.

108 So Vararuci heated some tin in a crucible and drank it. His vital spirits immediately departed, as if from fear of the heat.

109 Sthūlabhadra, who had seen the far shore of the ocean of religious teaching, preserved his vows in the presence of the monastic teacher Sambhūtavijaya.

110 One day, at the start of the rainy season, three monks bowed their heads before their Teacher Sambhūtavijaya, and made these vows:

111 The first promised: 'I shall retire to the mouth of a lion's lair, and remain there fasting for four months.'

112 The second declared: 'I shall fast for four months standing with upright body before the hole of a snake whose glance is deadly.'

113 The third said: 'I shall retire to a well, and fast for four months while living in the machine for raising water.'

114 As soon as the Teacher, knowing that they were capable, had given his approval to their vows, Sthūlabhadra went before him, bowed, and said:

115 'In the house of the prostitute named Kośā there is a chamber painted with murals depicting the various postures of lovemaking described in the textbooks on erotics.

116 I shall stay in it for four months, eating a six-course dinner every day, while performing a remarkable act of asceticism. This is my vow, master.'

117 The Teacher, knowing from his powers of cognition that Sthūlabhadra was equal to the vow, gave his permission. Then each of the monks went to the place that he had mentioned.

118 When those three, the lion, the snake, and the machine for raising water, saw the excellent monks who were free from passion and intent on harsh austerities, their peace of mind was shattered.

119 When Sthūlabhadra arrived at the prostitute Kośā's house, she stood before him with her hands folded in welcome.
120 She thought, 'His constitution is very delicate. He has come here because he is oppressed by the burden of his vows, as the trunk of a plantain tree is by its fruit.'
121 She said, 'Welcome lover! Tell me, what I can do for you? My body, my wealth, and my servants, all are entirely at your disposal.'
122 He said, 'Let me have this painted chamber to stay in for four months.' She replied, 'Take it.'
123 The holy man entered that room which she had set in order, as if he were Religion taking the place of Pleasure, by virtue of his superior strength.*
124 Then, after the monk had enjoyed a six-course meal, she appeared wearing her most seductive clothes in order to arouse him.
125 She sat before him, as beautiful as a nymph, and continually performed charming and alluring gestures.
126 At the same time she reminded him of their former acts of sexual pleasure and their playful dalliances as depicted in the paintings of sexual intercourse.
127 But she was no more able to arouse that great monk than a scratch with a fingernail is able to mark a diamond.
128 She did the same thing every day, trying to arouse him, but the great-minded ascetic was not in the least bit aroused.
129 Her attempts to change him for the worse had the contrary effect: the fire of his religious meditation was reflected by her, as lightning is by the ocean.
130 She fell before his feet and reproached herself, 'Shame on me, for wanting, through my ignorance, to have sexual intercourse as before.'
131 Astonished by the monk's remarkable self-control, she took the vows of a Jain laywoman:
132 'If the king pleases to bestow me on some man, I promise to keep to him alone, without any other man besides.'
133 When the rainy season was over, the three monks, their vows accomplished, returned, one by one, to the presence of their Teacher.
134 When the monk who had stayed in the lion's den returned, the

Teacher rose from his seat a little, and said, 'Welcome, you have performed a difficult vow.'

135 When the other two returned, the Teacher addressed them in the same way. Having accomplished equivalent vows, the Teacher welcomed them with equivalent respect.

136 But when Sthūlabhadra returned, the Teacher stood up, and said, 'Great-souled one, you have performed an extremely difficult vow. Welcome to you!'

137 The other monks were jealous, and thought, 'The Teacher has only given him such a welcome because he is a prime minister's son.

138 If he performed an extremely difficult vow while eating six-course dinners, then we shall undertake the same vow in the next rainy season.'

139 Thus the great ascetics consoled their spirits, and spent the following eight months practising self-control.

140 When the time came, the monk who had stayed in the lion's den was as happy as a creditor, and vowed before the Teacher:

141 'Reverend sir, I shall spend the four months in the house of the prostitute Kośā, eating a six-course dinner every day.'

142 The Teacher knew from his powers of cognition that the monk had made this vow through jealousy of Sthūlabhadra, and would go astray. He said:

143 'My dear, do not undertake this vow. It is extremely difficult to perform. Sthūlabhadra is equal to it because he is as firm as the Himalaya mountains.'

144 The monk declared once more to the Teacher, 'His vow was not harder than mine. How can he have performed an extremely difficult vow? I shall certainly succeed in performing the vow.'

145 The Teacher said, 'It will spoil your previous acts of asceticism. Too heavy a burden will be placed on your frame.'

146 Disregarding the advice of his Teacher, thinking himself to be a hero, the monk arrived at Kośā's house, where flew the banner bearing the fish emblem of the god of love.

147 Thinking, 'I suppose this monk has come here because of his jealousy for Sthūlabhadra; his descent into existence must be prevented', she rose and bowed to him.

148 The monk asked to live in the painted chamber, and Kośā gave it to him. Thereupon the monk entered it.

149 Then, at midday, after he had enjoyed a six-course meal, Kośā, a treasury of beauty, came to test him.

150 As soon as he saw the lotus-eyed lady, he was immediately aroused. How could such a woman and such a meal fail to arouse passion?

151 Smitten by lust, he importuned her, but Kośā said, 'Reverend sir, we prostitutes can only be enjoyed if we are given money.'

152 The monk said, 'Don't worry, deer-eyes. I have money. Isn't oil found in the sand?

153 The king of Nepal gives a jewelled cape to each monk he sees for the first time.' She said, 'Bring it!', but she said it to make the monk indifferent to worldly objects.

154 Then, like a fool, he set off for Nepal, even though it was the rainy season, stumbling, like his vow, in the muddy ground.

155 He arrived there and received the jewelled cape from the king. He returned by a road that was beset by robbers.

156 The robbers had a bird of omen. It said, 'Here comes a hundred thousand!' The leader of the robbers asked his spy who was keeping watch in a tree, 'Who is coming?'

157 But the man in the tree told the leader of the robbers that no one was coming except a solitary monk.

158 When the monk arrived at that place, the robbers stopped and searched him, but they did not find anything, so they let him go.

159 The bird spoke again, 'There goes a hundred thousand!' Then the leader of the robbers said to the monk, 'Speak the truth; what have you got?'

160 When the monk said that he had a jewelled cape hidden inside his cane with which to pay a prostitute's fees, he was released by the leader of the robbers.

161 On his return, he gave the jewelled cape to Kośā, but she nonchalantly threw it into a muddy house-drain.

162 The monk stuttered, 'Shell-necked one, why have you thrown this precious jewelled cape into the filthy slime?'

163 Thereupon, Kośā said, 'You fool, you grieve for this jewelled cape, but you don't grieve for yourself, as you fall into hell.'

164 As soon as he heard this, a desire for emancipation was produced in the monk, and he said to Kośā, 'Well done! You've enlightened me! Well done! You've protected me from worldly bondage!

165 Faultless one, I shall go eradicate the impurities produced by my transgression, at the feet of my Teacher.'
166 Kośā said to him, 'I treated you badly through good-will for you. I strengthened your vow of chastity, because you were faltering.
167 I kindled your desire in order to enlighten you. It will be forgiven; seek refuge in the guidance of the Teacher. Go quickly!'
168 Saying, 'I will', the monk went to Sambhūtavijaya, confessed and received forgiveness, and performed harsh austerities once more.

169 The following day, the Teacher Sambhūtavijaya died while absorbed in meditation, and went to heaven.

170 One day, the king gave Kośā to his favourite charioteer, but because she had been bestowed by the king, she resorted to him without feeling sexual passion.
171 Day and night, his wife said to the charioteer, 'There's no other man like Sthūlabhadra.'
172 The charioteer decided to please her by showing off his cleverness. He went into the garden and sat on a bench.
173 He shot an arrow into a clump of mangoes and transfixed it. Then he shot a second arrow into the shaft of the first arrow, then a third into the second, and so on, until the chain of arrows reached his hand.
174 Then he cut the stalk with a sharp-edged arrow, and with his hand drew towards him the clump of mangoes by the chain of arrows that was fixed in it. Then he gave the mangoes to Kośā.
175 Kośā said, 'Now see how clever I am!' She made a heap of mustard seed, and danced on top of it.
176 Then she placed a needle in the pile, and covered it with petals. Then she danced on top of it, without being pierced by the needle and without disturbing the petals and the mustard seeds.
177 The charioteer said, 'I'm delighted with this performance of yours. Tell me what you want, and I'll give it to you right away.'
178 She replied, 'What difficult thing have I done that has caused you to be delighted? Practice makes everything easy.
179 Your cutting of the mango clump and my dancing were not difficult. What Sthūlabhadra did was unpractised; that was difficult.

180 Without tasting the pleasures he had enjoyed for twelve years with me here in this painted chamber, he stayed in it without breaking his vow.

181 Just as milk is spoilt by the approach of a mongoose, the concentration of monks is spoilt by the appearance of a woman; except for Sthūlabhadra!

182 Who would be able to stay with a woman for one day as Sthūlabhadra did for four months without breaking his vow?

183 The man who eats a six-course dinner and stays in a painted chamber without breaking his vow has a constitution of iron!

184 Those who are made of metal melt in proximity to a woman, who is like a fire, but the great monk Sthūlabhadra is made of diamond, I suppose.

185 Sthūlabhadra is constant, he performed an extremely difficult vow.' Having said all this, she was ready to recite it again, as if it were branded on her mouth.

186 Then the charioteer asked her, 'Who is this Sthūlabhadra whom you have described in this manner, this crest-jewel of constancy?'

187 She replied that the Sthūlabhadra she had described to him was the son of King Nanda's minister Śakaṭāla.

188 When he heard this, he became excited, and said, with his hands folded in salutation, 'I myself shall become the servant of that great monk Sthūlabhadra.'

189 Realizing that he was spiritually aroused, she gave him instruction in the Jain religion. His faculty of right belief was awakened, and he cast off the sleep of delusion.

190 After she had enlightened him, she told him of her vow. When he heard what it was, his eyes opened in astonishment, and he said:

191 'Good lady, you have enlightened me by your description of Sthūlabhadra's virtues. I shall now follow his path which you have shown to me.

192 May you enjoy good fortune, good lady. Keep your vow.' After saying that, he went to the presence of the Teacher, and received initiation as a Jain monk.

193 Holy Sthūlabhadra continued to perform harsh austerities. At that time a famine of twelve years' duration set in.

194 Now, in a village called Caṇaka in the Golla district, lived a Brahmin named Caṇin and his wife Caṇeśvarī.

195 Caṇin was well known for being a Jain layman since birth, and learned Jain monks frequented his house.

196 One day, Caṇeśvarī gave birth to a son whose teeth had already developed. Caṇin presented the baby in humble greeting to the monks.

197 He informed the monks that the baby had been born with teeth, and the learned monks said that the baby would become a king.

198 Fearing that performing the duties of a king would destine his son for hell, Caṇin ground out the baby's teeth, without heeding the pain he was causing.

199 He told the monks of this, who said, 'Because his teeth have been ground out, he will be a king hidden in a shadow.'

200 Caṇin gave the name Cāṇakya to his son. Cāṇakya became a Jain layman, and reached the far shore of the ocean of every kind of knowledge.

201 His wealth was the satisfaction he gained from assiduously serving the monks. He married the daughter of a Brahmin of good family.

202 One day, Cāṇakya's wife went to her mother's house, because her brother's wedding was being celebrated there.

203 Her other sisters had gathered for the occasion. They were arrayed in fine clothes and ornaments.

204 They all had fine carriages; all were attended by maidservants; all had parasols as indications of their high rank; all had their hair wreathed with garlands.

205 All had their bodies perfumed with heavenly unguents; all carried betel in their hands. They all looked like living images of the goddess of Prosperity.

206 But Cāṇakya's wife wore the same outfit day and night. Her necklace was empty of pearls. Her bodice was dirty.

207 Her saffron-dyed dress was worn out. Her mouth was bereft of betel. The sweat from her body was her only perfume. Her bracelets were made of tin.

208 Her hands were rough with work. Her hair was unkempt. Her rich, well-married sisters mocked her.

209 The other guests who had come to the wedding also mocked her.

She was so ashamed that she crept into a corner, and stayed there until the wedding was over.

210 When she returned to Cāṇakya's house, her face was shadowed with depression, and she spotted the earth with her sprinkling teardrops.

211 When Cāṇakya noticed her dejected countenance which was like a white lotus in the morning, he was pained by her distress, and he said to her sweetly:

212 'Have I or one of the neighbours insulted you, or did something happen in your father's house that has caused you to be so unhappy?'

213 But the disgrace had rendered her incapable, and she was unable to reply. Eventually, at her husband's insistent prompting, she told him everything that had occurred.

214 When Cāṇakya knew the cause of his wife's unhappiness, he began to think of some infallible method of obtaining money.

215 'In the city of Pāṭalīputra King Nanda gives splendid gifts to Brahmins, so I shall go there.'

216 Having thus determined, he went there, and entered the king's palace. Chairs had been laid out in front, and Cāṇakya sat in the foremost of them.

217 But that foremost chair on which Cāṇakya was sitting was adorned by King Nanda only, for it was his throne.

218 Then Nanda entered together with his son. The son said, 'There's a Brahmin sitting there, stepping on the king's shadow!'

219 One of the king's maidservants spoke to Cāṇakya kindly, saying, 'Sit in this second seat, Brahmin.'

220 But he replied, 'My water pot can stand on it', and placed the water pot on the second seat, without rising from the first.

221 In the same way he blocked the third seat with his staff, the fourth with his rosary beads, the fifth with his sacred thread, without rising from the first seat.

222 The maidservant cried, 'Oh! He's so insolent that he refuses to leave the first seat. To add insult to injury, he's covered the other chairs!

223 What can one do with this impudent, crazy, Brahmin!' She kicked Cāṇakya out of the chair.

224 At once Cāṇakya rose up, like a cobra prodded with a stick, and, as everyone looked on, made this vow:

225 'I shall uproot Nanda together with his treasury and his servants, his friends and his sons, his army and his chariots, like a hurricane uprooting a tree.'

226 His face as red as glowing copper, blazing with anger like a fire, knitting his brow, the son of Caṇin straightaway left the city.

227 Then Cāṇakya, the crest-ruby of the wise, remembered that he was destined to be a king hidden in a shadow.

228 Because of the insult he had received, he wandered the earth looking for a man worthy to be king; proud men do not forget an insult.

229 One day, the Brahmin Caṇeśvarī's son came to the place where the keepers of King Nanda's peacocks lived.

230 Wearing the garments of a wandering ascetic, Caṇin's son entered the peacock keepers' village to beg for grain.

231 At that time the daughter of the head peacock breeder was pregnant, and she had a pregnancy-longing to drink the moon (candra).

232 Her family told Cāṇakya of her desire, and asked if he could somehow fulfil it. He said:

233 'Good people, if you give me her new-born child, then I shall fulfil her pregnancy-longing to drink the moon.'

234 Fearing that she would lose her baby if her pregnancy-longing was unfulfilled, her parents agreed to his request.

235 Cāṇakya ordered a thatched pavilion with a hole in its roof to be built. Then he had a man holding a lid concealed (gupta) upon the roof.

236 Underneath the hole he placed a bowl of water. At midnight the full moon was reflected in the bowl.

237 Cāṇakya showed the pregnant woman the full moon reflected in the bowl, and told her to drink it. As she began to drink, her face beamed.

238 As she drank, the man who was concealed on the roof covered the hole with the lid.

239 Her pregnancy-longing fulfilled, in course of time she gave birth to a son. His parents named him Candragupta.

240 Like the moon, Candragupta grew day by day, a light for the lotus-thickets that were the peacock keeper's family.

241 Cāṇakya resumed his wandering, intent on acquiring gold, and began to seek men skilled in alchemy.

242 Meanwhile, Candragupta played with the other boys every day, continually granting them villages and other gifts, as if he were a king.

243 He would mount the backs of the other boys, treating them as his elephants and horses; future prosperity is often manifested by portents.

244 Eventually Cāṇakya in the course of his wandering returned to that village. When he saw Candragupta behaving like that he was extremely astonished.

245 In order to test him, Cāṇakya said, 'Give me something too, your majesty!'

246 Candragupta said, 'Take as many of these village cows as you wish, Brahmin. Who will complain, if they've been given by me?'

247 Cāṇakya smiled and said, 'How can I take these cows? I'm very frightened of their owners. They will surely kill me.'

248 Candragupta replied, 'Don't be afraid. Take the cows which I have given you. The earth is meant to be enjoyed by the brave.'

249 Then Cāṇakya thought, 'Ah! He's intelligent!', and asked the other boys who he was.

250 The boys told him, 'He's the son of a wandering ascetic. He was adopted by the ascetic while he was still in his mother's womb.'

251 Then Cāṇakya knew that he was the boy who had been given to him. He said, 'I'm the one whom you belong to. Come, I shall give you a kingdom!'

252 Candragupta wanted a kingdom so he grasped him by the thumb, and Cāṇakya took him away, as quickly as if he were a runaway slave.

253 With the gold he had obtained by means of his alchemy, Caṇin's son collected a band of foot-soldiers, and concentrated on destroying Nanda.

254 Then, with his entire army of foot-soldiers, he began to besiege the city of Pāṭalīputra on all four sides.

255 But King Nanda issued from the city, and crushed Cāṇakya's paltry siege forces, as easily as if he were driving a herd of goats.

256 Cāṇakya knew that it was time to flee with Candragupta. Although defeated, one should protect oneself; prosperity will return to a good man.

257 Nanda ordered crack horsemen to capture Candragupta; kings do not tolerate those who desire their kingdoms.

258 Acting like a conquering victor, Nanda returned to his city, and the citizens celebrated a festival as befitted their success.

259 One of those horsemen, mounted on a swift steed, came to the place through which Candragupta was proceeding, not very far ahead.

260 But Cāṇakya had seen the horseman coming in the distance, and with presence of mind ordered Candragupta:

261 'Plunge into the water of this pond which is adorned with thickets of lotuses, pretend to be a duck, and emerge at the sound of my voice.'

262 Candragupta immediately dived into the water, as calmly as if he had cast a spell for solidifying water.

263 But Cāṇakya himself sat motionless by the edge of the pond, pretending to be a selfless ascetic sunk in meditation.

264 Then Nanda's crack horseman, carried on his wind-swift steed, the blows of whose hooves were like drumsticks beating on the drum of the earth, rode up.

265 He asked Cāṇakya, 'Tell me quickly, reverend sir, have you seen a man just now, a very young man?'

266 Acting as if he did not wish to break his meditational trance, Caṇin's son hummed and pointed to the pond.

267 The horseman prepared to plunge into the pond so that he could drag Candragupta out, and removed his armour, like a dancing-girl removing her skirt.

268 Thereupon, the cruel son of Caṇin took his sword and cut off his head, as if making a sacrifice to the water goddess.

269 When Cāṇakya shouted, 'Come, come, my boy!', Candragupta at once emerged from the pond, like the moon from behind a cloud.

270 Cāṇakya mounted Candragupta on the horse, and said to him, 'When I pointed you out to the horseman, what did you think?'

271 Candragupta said, 'Master, this is what I thought: master is more intelligent than I am.'

272 Then Cāṇakya thought, 'Surely he will always be obedient, and never stray from me, like a well-trained elephant.'

273 But as they travelled on, behind them followed another of Nanda's horsemen mounted on a wind-swift steed; he was like a zealous messenger of Death.

274 Cāṇakya saw him coming, and at his command Candragupta plunged, like a swan, into a pond.

275 Caṇin's son then said to a laundryman who was sitting by the edge of the pond, 'The king is angry with your guild. Disappear, unless you want to die!'

276 The laundryman saw the horseman approaching in the distance with upraised sword, he thought that it was true, and ran away to save his life.

277 The laundryman had already begun to wash his laundry in the pond. The son of Caṇin started to wash it himself.

278 When this horseman arrived and asked the same question as the first, the son of Caṇin, whose wit was as sharp as a blade of grass, killed him in the same way.

279 Then Cāṇakya and Candragupta hastened from that place. As he travelled Candragupta became weak, and his belly became thin with hunger.

280 Leaving Candragupta behind, Cāṇakya went to a village to fetch food, for there is no food without a village.

281 He saw a learned Brahmin coming from the village; he had just had his dinner, and was walking very slowly, patting his belly.

282 Cāṇakya asked him, 'Do Brahmins get a good allowance of food in this village?' The Brahmin replied, 'Yes, I've had mine just now.'

283 Cāṇakya asked again, 'What did you have to eat, Brahmin?' He replied, 'Rice pudding cooked with fresh milk.'

284 Cāṇakya thought, 'If I go on to the village to get food, it will take a long time. How will Candragupta survive without me?

285 Left on his own, Candragupta will be overwhelmed by Nanda's horsemen, whose strength is irresistible, like a wild boar by dogs.

286 If the young man Candragupta is captured by Nanda's horsemen, then my heart's desire will become a mere dream of kingship.

287 Therefore, I'll take the rice pudding from the Brahmin's stomach, and give it to Candragupta, so that his life will be saved.'

288 Cāṇakya immediately split open the Brahmin's belly, like a cook splitting a pumpkin.

289 Then Cāṇakya quickly took the rice pudding from the Brahmin's stomach, as if taking it from a cooking-pot, and fed Candragupta with it.

290 Taking Candragupta, Cāṇakya travelled on, and at nightfall approached a village, like a partridge approaching its nest.

291 Cāṇakya entered the village. As he walked around, looking for food, he came to the house of a poor old woman.

292 She was serving hot porridge to her children. One of the children was very hungry, and straightaway put his hand in his porridge.

293 He burnt his fingers and began to cry. The old woman said to him, 'Child, you're as stupid as Cāṇakya.'

294 Cāṇakya heard what she said, and entered the house. He asked the old woman, 'How can Cāṇakya be compared to the child?'

295 The old woman explained, 'Dim-witted Cāṇakya rendered himself defenceless when he began to besiege Nanda's capital, without securing the outlying districts.

296 In the same way, this child did not begin by gradually eating his way in from the edges, but put his hand in the middle, and got his fingers burnt by the red-hot rice pudding.'

297 Thinking, 'Aha! This woman is intelligent', Cāṇakya went and stayed in a place in the Himalaya mountains.

298 There, because he wanted his help, Cāṇakya became friendly with a king named Parvataka.

299 One day, Cāṇakya said to him, 'Let's uproot King Nanda, capture his kingdom, and share it out like brothers.'

300 Parvataka agreed to this suggestion, and from that time on, as eager to fight as a lion, allied himself with Cāṇakya.

301 Cāṇakya, Candragupta, and Parvataka began to conquer the outlying districts of Nanda's kingdom.

302 But one town held out against them, although they had blockaded it, so Cāṇakya entered it, disguised as a wandering mendicant begging for food.

303 Carrying the triple staff of a religious mendicant, he strolled

around the town centre, where he saw a group of images of all seven mother goddesses.

304 Cāṇakya thought, 'This group of goddesses must be protective deities. Surely it is due to their power that this town cannot be taken.'

305 As Cāṇakya was wondering how to remove the mother goddesses, the townsmen, who were suffering because of the siege of their town, asked him:

306 'Reverend sir, when will this city be relieved? People like you, good sir, usually know everything.'

307 Candragupta's teacher said, 'Right, townspeople, listen: as long as these mother goddesses are here, from where will relief from the siege come?'

308 The townspeople hastily removed the group of mother goddesses. What won't suffering people do, especially when they have been bamboozled by a swindler!

309 Then Candragupta and Parvataka, at a signal given by Cāṇakya, retreated, and the citizens were extremely happy.

310 But unexpectedly they returned, and, as irresistible as the tide of the ocean, broke into the town, causing pain to their enemies.

311 After they had captured that town, those two great warriors, Cāṇakya's assistants, overran Nanda's kingdom.

312 Armed with Cāṇakya's intelligence, the two valorous warriors besieged Pāṭalīputra on all sides with an immeasurable army.

313 Nanda's treasury was exhausted, his power was exhausted, his intelligence was exhausted, and his valour was exhausted, because his merit was used up;* prosperity only lasts as long as merit.

314 Nanda's vital spirits rose to the tip of his nose, and he begged Cāṇakya for the right to depart in safety; to whom is life not dear?

315 Cāṇakya said, 'Go from here on one wagon, sir. You may place in it as much of what is dear to your heart as you are able.

316 No one will attack you as you leave on that one wagon. Be of good cheer. Like a Brahmin, you will not be executed.'

317 King Nanda loaded the wagon with two wives, one daughter, and as many valuables as he could, and departed from the city.

318 As Nanda's daughter sat in the wagon, she saw Candragupta

passing by, and she immediately fell in love with him; like a goddess, her gaze was unblinking.

319 With her side-glances, like rays flashing from the moon of her face, Nanda's daughter seemed to promise Candragupta the pleasures of love.

320 Nanda said to her, 'Choose your own husband, my child. Indeed, choosing their own husbands is often recommended to maidens of the warrior estate.

321 Long life and good luck to you! Descend from the wagon and leave me. May my sorrow at your marriage leave with you.'

322 Thus addressed, she alighted from the wagon and began to climb into Candragupta's fine carriage.

323 But as she got into Candragupta's carriage, nine of its spokes broke, like sticks of sugar cane passed through a mill.

324 Candragupta thought, 'Who is this inauspicious girl who is climbing into my carriage, trying to break it?', and blocked her way.

325 But Cāṇakya said, 'Don't block her way, Candragupta. This is an auspicious omen; don't think otherwise.

326 My child, this omen indicates that your male descendants will enjoy ever increasing prosperity for nine generations in succession.'

327 Then Candragupta and Parvataka entered Nanda's palace, and began to share out his abundant treasure.

328 In the palace was a girl who was guarded as if she alone were the whole property. King Nanda had caused her to be fed on poison from her birth.

329 Parvataka fell passionately in love with her; it was as if he had placed her in his heart as a deity to be meditated on.

330 Candragupta's teacher bestowed her on Parvataka, and then began to perform the ceremony of the joining of hands.

331 But at that moment their perspiration which was produced by the heat of the sacrificial fire mingled, and the girl's poison entered Parvataka.

332 Parvataka was sickened by the effects of the poison he had absorbed. All his limbs became loose, and he said to Candragupta:

333 'I feel like I've drunk poison; I can barely speak. Help me, my friend. I'm sure that I'm going to die.'

334 Candragupta repeatedly shouted, 'Sorcerers, sorcerers! Doctors, doctors!', but Cāṇakya came and stood by his ear, and whispered:

335 'If your torment leaves you without medicine, then let it leave. Wait in silence. You'll enjoy good fortune without him.

336 He who does not destroy a friend who is about to take half his kingdom will be himself destroyed. So if this man who must be killed dies himself, it is lucky for you.'

337 Having thus admonished Maurya,* Cāṇakya, foremost of the intelligent, indicating his meaning by a frown, prevented him from bringing help.

338 So then the king of the Himalayas died, and Candragupta succeeded to two empires.

339 Thus Candragupta became king after one hundred and fifty five years had elapsed since the final liberation of holy Mahāvīra.

340 But in Candragupta's kingdom were some men, former servants of Nanda, who lived by robbery, holding out in an inaccessible place.

341 Cāṇakya, while searching for someone whom he could make constable of the city, came to the house of a certain low-caste man.

342 The low-caste man was setting fire to some ants' nests, and Cāṇakya asked him what he was doing.

343 He replied, 'I'm completely eradicating these wicked ants because they keep biting my son. What else is fit for the wicked?'

344 Thinking, 'Ah! This low-caste man excels in intelligence and determination', Cāṇakya went to Candragupta.

345 Caṇin's son, experienced in accomplishing his wishes, got Candragupta to summon the low-caste man and make him superintendent of the city.

346 This man won over Nanda's thieving retainers with food and other gifts, and then destroyed them. Cāṇakya's plan did not miscarry.

347 Maurya's teacher had previously failed to receive food from a certain village, so he summoned the householders of that village.

348 Angry with them because of their mean-mindedness, he ordered them to make a mango bamboo fence.

349 Acting on Cāṇakya's instructions, the village householders cut

down their bamboo canes, and with them made a fence for the fragrant mango trees.

350 Then Cāṇakya pretended to be angry, exclaiming, 'Hey, hey! I told you to make a fence for the bamboo canes from the mango trees!'

351 Having caused the householders to make the mistake about the hedge, in his anger Cāṇakya had their village burnt down, children and grown-ups together.

352 One day, Cāṇakya realized that Candragupta's treasury was empty, so he filled a cup with dinars, and said to the people:

353 'Whoever beats me at dice-play can take this cup filled with dinars; that's the prize.

354 But from whomever I beat, citizens, I shall take just one dinar. My promise is as good as if it were engraved in stone!'

355 Then he began to play dice with the people day and night, but Candragupta's teacher always beat them because he played with crooked dice.

356 But because this method of gaining money was slow and not very productive, he thought of another method. He invited all the citizens.

357 Then he dined them, and gave them fine wine to drink. He ordered musicians to play loud dance music at the drinking party.

358 Cāṇakya was skilled in the ways of getting money. He laughed, danced and sang, and did the other things that drunken men are accustomed to do. Then he declared:

359 'I have two robes dyed in red, a triple staff, a water jar made of gold, and a king who obeys my will, so sound the lute!'

360 Then, after the musicians had played their lutes, a drunken citizen raised his hands and said:

361 'If an elephant were to walk for a thousand miles, I could honour each one of its footsteps with a thousand gold pieces.'

362–3 The lutes played as before. Then another citizen said: 'If you were to sow a bushel of sesamum seeds, and all the shoots were to flourish vigorously, the amount of sesamum produced from it would be equivalent to the number of gold pieces that are in my house.'

364–5 The lutes played as before. Another guest said, 'With the butter that it produced from my cows, I could build a high dam against a rushing mountain river swollen with rain in the rainy season, and stop its current flowing from on high.'

366–7 The lutes played as before. Another said, 'With the hair from the manes of my noble colts that are born in just one day, I could envelop the city of Pāṭalīputra on all sides, like a tree enveloped in spiders' webs.'

368–9 The lutes played as before, and another said, 'In my house is a rice plant which, whenever it is pruned, produces grains of rice. There is another plant, donkey-rice, which, whenever it is pruned, bears fruit again and again. These are my two jewels, citizens.'

370–1 The lutes played as before. Another said, 'The money in my house is counted in thousands. I'm free from debt. I smell nice because I've been smeared with sandalwood ointment. My wife always obeys me. No one is as fortunate as I!'

372 The lutes played as before. But by this means the son of Caṇin now knew how much wealth all those wealthy people had.

373 The amount of gold which would fill the footsteps of an elephant going for just one mile; the thousands of gold pieces equivalent to the seeds produced by just one sesamum plant;

374 each month, as much clarified butter as is made from the fresh butter produced in one day; as many fine foals as were born in just one day;

375 and as much rice as would fill the granaries: they had to give all that to Cāṇakya, since that clever man had learnt their secrets.

376 With this wealth, the son of Caṇin enriched Candragupta. A minister who is an ocean of cleverness is indeed a wish-granting cow for kings.

377 During that dreadful twelve-year famine, a religious Teacher named Susthita was living in Candragupta's capital.

378 The scarcity of food was such that it was impossible to live, so he sent his group of monks to foreign parts, but he himself remained in that city.

379 But two junior monks turned back and returned to that place. When the Teacher asked them why they had returned, they replied:

380 'We were unable to bear being separated from our Teacher; as

long as we are with you, we consider it good fortune whether we live or die.'

381 The Teacher said, 'You have not behaved well, for in your next lives you will sink in a fathomless ocean of sorrow.'

382 Having said this, the Teacher gave the pair permission to stay there, and they attended him with devotion, bees for the lotus flowers of his feet.

383 Due to the severity of that famine, the two obtained very little food by begging, and as they only ate after feeding their Teacher, they began to waste away.

384 Unable to assuage their hunger, wasting away through lack of food, the two junior monks secretly took counsel together:

385 'We once overheard our Teacher explaining to some monks who had completed their course of study the use of a magic eye-ointment which renders its wearer invisible.

386 We'll use that spell to fill our bellies. Once they are full, we'll sit at our Teacher's feet, free from care.'

387 So that very day, the two became invisible, and at dinner time entered the presence of Candragupta.

388 The two invisible junior monks ate from Candragupta's plate as freely as if they were his kinsmen, dear as life.

389 Each day, the two continued to eat the king's food, who rose from his dinner with an empty belly, like an ascetic who had conquered his passions.

390 Like he whose wife is Night in the dark half of the month,* King Candragupta gradually wasted away, because he was being deprived of his food by those two.

391 But he did not tell anyone that his appetite was never satisfied, although he was continually oppressed by hunger, like an elephant in rut.

392 One day his Teacher asked Maurya in private, 'My child, why are you getting thinner day by day, as if you had a wasting sickness?'

393 Maurya replied, 'I'm not served with any the less food, but it's as if some ghost is taking it away from me.

394 The nobles who sit below me think that I eat my fill of the food, but I don't eat even half of it. I don't know what to do about it.'

395 Cāṇakya said, 'Are you still so stupid that you've been letting yourself waste away for so long, like an ascetic who desires emancipation but does not know the truth?

396 Never mind. You've done the right thing to tell me about it now. I'll soon catch the plunderer of your food.'

397 After saying that, he sprinkled the floor of Candragupta's dining room with powdered clay, finer than barley meal.

398 So when Candragupta sat down to eat, the footsteps of those two who had come to eat his food became visible on the powdered floor.

399 When the king rose from his meal, the son of Caṇin saw the tracks of their footprints, and thought:

400 'It must be a human being, since his feet have touched the ground. He puts on a magic eye-ointment and takes the food from the king's plate. It's easy for him, since he's become invisible.'

401 At dinner time the following day, Cāṇakya filled the dining room with a smoke so dense that it could be pierced with a needle.

402 So when those two came as before to eat from the same plate as Candragupta, the thickening mass of smoke made their eyes water.

403 The magic eye-ointment which rendered them invisible was dissolved by the water of their tears, and washed away like mud.

404 Without the disappearing-ointment, they immediately became visible eating from the king's plate to the king's servants, who frowned terribly.

405 Through fear of Cāṇakya, no one censured or abused them. Cāṇakya did not want to speak to them disparagingly, but said:

406 'Reverend fathers, you must be gods in the form of ascetics. Grant us the auspicious remnants of your food, and return to your own place.'

407 After the two had left, the king became dejected, and said, 'I've been polluted by eating their leftover food.'

408 But Cāṇakya said, 'Don't make a fault out of a virtue. By sharing your food with monks you've earned religious merit.

409 That man is fortunate indeed who gives to homeless monks; what shall be said of you who have treated a monk as a guest, eating from the same plate?'

410 But after he had instructed Maurya in this way, he went to the Teacher, and complained about the improper actions of the two junior monks.

411 The Teacher said, 'What fault have these two junior monks committed, when lay people like you think only of filling their own bellies?'

412 Then Cāṇakya bowed to the Teacher, asking pardon for his wrong behaviour. He said, 'You have instructed me well. I've been negligent.

413 From this day forth, food, drink, and other provisions which nourish monks, will be found in my house.'

414 Having made that vow, from that time on Cāṇakya, firm in resolution, successfully performed the duties of a householder.

415 But Candragupta was a follower of ascetics who had the wrong views about religion, so Cāṇakya, who was as well disposed to him as a father, began to instruct him:

416 'Those ascetics are wicked. They can't help lusting after women. They're not even worthy to be spoken with, never mind venerated.

417 They are wicked, ungrateful, and trees for the birds of impurity; like rain on barren soil, gifts to them bear no fruit.

418 If you entrust your soul to them, your majesty, you will make it sink like an iron boat in the ocean of existence, so don't pay them any respect.'

419 Maurya said, 'Sir, your opinions carry great weight with me, but convince me that they really lack self-control.'

420 So Cāṇakya had it proclaimed in the city that the king would listen to the religious doctrines of all the heretic teachers.

421 Cāṇakya, solitary in his intelligence, summoned them, and seated them in a solitary place, not far from the royal women's apartment.

422 But Cāṇakya had previously sprinkled powder of fine clay on the ground leading to the women's apartment.

423 After Cāṇakya had conducted them to their seats so that they could give religious instruction there, they realized that the place was secluded, and walked towards the royal women's apartment.

424 Since it was their very nature to lust after women, they were

unable to prevent themselves from peeping at the royal women through the gaps in the lattice windows.

425 Enjoying their evil thoughts, they stared at the royal women until it was time for the king to come. They sat down at his arrival.

426 Then they gave instruction to Candragupta, and departed, hoping to return so that they could look at the ladies in the women's apartment again.

427 When they had gone, Cāṇakya said to Candragupta, 'See the traces of the lust for women of those monks who have the wrong view about religion!

428 While they were waiting for you to arrive, they peeped through the lattice windows into your royal women's apartment; they have not conquered their senses.

429 See their footprints clearly imprinted underneath the window, and be convinced!'

430 The king was convinced, and on the following day his Teacher summoned Jain monks to preach religion in the same place.

431 From the very first, those monks remained in their seats and awaited the arrival of the king, undistractedly performing their religious observances.

432 When they had finished preaching the Jain religion, the monks returned to the place where they were staying, looking only at the ground, because they were intent on following the rule of conduct for care in walking.*

433 Cāṇakya examined the fine clay dust powder underneath the window, and pointed out to Candragupta that it was undisturbed.

434 He said, 'These monks did not come here, as did the monks with the wrong views. Why else are no traces of their footprints to be seen?'

435 Then the king was convinced that the Jain monks were to be respected as Teachers, and he turned from the monks with the wrong views, like an ascetic turning from the objects of the senses.

436 Thus by his many stratagems, Cāṇakya, a tree for the creeper of Maurya's prosperity, displayed the capability of his intelligence. One day he thought:

437 'I shall gradually accustom Candragupta to eating poisoned food, so that it will become like an elixir to him, and no poison will have any power on him.'

438 So each day, Maurya was fed an increasing amount of poisoned food by his Teacher, who was as wise as the teacher of the gods.

439 One day, the queen, who was big with child, began to share Candragupta's food, because she was absolutely devoted to him. Her name was Durdhā.

440 When Cāṇakya saw that she was eating poisoned food, he immediately rushed towards her, fearing that she would lose the baby. He cried, 'What have you done?'

441 As soon as she had tasted the poisoned food, the queen died. Caṇin's son decided that her baby would not die as well.

442 So he sliced open the belly of the dead woman, and prised the baby from it, like a pearl from an oyster shell.

443 A drop (bindu) of poison had passed to the baby's head, so the Teacher named him Bindusāra, meaning 'He whose essence is a drop'.

444 When Bindusāra attained his youth, the time of life dear to the god of love, Candragupta died in meditation and went to heaven.

445 Then Cāṇakya, competent and wise, placed Bindusāra on the throne. Since his success depended on his minister, he became a minister to his commands.

446 Now, previously advised by Caṇin's son, Maurya had appointed, because of his efficiency, a man named Subandhu one of his minister.

447 But Subhandu wanted to be an independent minister, and was jealous of Cāṇakya. In order to ruin him, Subandhu privately spoke in Bindusāra's ear:

448 'Although I'm not the final authority, I shall say something that will have a beneficial outcome; for that's what men of good breeding do.

449 Trust not in Cāṇakya, the destroyer of his trust. That wicked man slit open your mother's belly, believe me.'

450 So Bindusāra summoned the nurses and asked them if it was true. When they confirmed that it was, he became very angry with Cāṇakya.

451 When Cāṇakya found out that the king was angry with him, he thought, 'Ungrateful Subandhu has estranged the king from me.
452 This man, whom I myself previously made a minister, now repays me with slander.
453 I am very near to death, and I have had enough of affairs of state. Nevertheless, I shall still plot my revenge for what he has done.
454 Devoured by the demon of my intelligence, he will not attain power; that will be suitable revenge for his offence.'
455 Cāṇakya recited magic spells over exquisite fragrant substances, and placed them in a casket along with a piece of birch bark inscribed with writing. He was formidable in his intelligence.
456 The clever man covered the casket in lacquer, and placed it in a chest, which he locked with a hundred locks.
457 He deposited the chest in an inner room of his house, as if it contained all his household treasure. Then he distributed his wealth to the poor, widows, and orphans, and to other worthy people.
458 Then he went and sat on top of a dungheap adjacent to the city, and prepared to die by total abstinence from food and drink, intent on destroying his karma.
459 Meanwhile, Bindusāra had learned from his nurse the full story of his mother's death. Full of remorse, he hastened to the place where Cāṇakya was.
460 Candragupta's son begged Cāṇakya's forgiveness, saying, 'Manage the affairs of my kingdom again; I shall follow your advice.'
461 Maurya's teacher said, 'Enough of these entreaties. I've become indifferent even to my body. What advantage would you have with me?'
462 Bindusāra realized that Candragupta's teacher was as fixed in his vow as the sea within its shores, and returned to his palace.
463 As soon as he returned, Bindusāra vented his wrath on Subandhu. Trembling, as if oppressed by cold, Subandhu said:
464 'Your majesty, I did not understand the matter properly when I slandered Cāṇakya. Please grant mercy, while I go to him to beg forgiveness.'
465 With these words Subandhu went and begged Cāṇakya's pardon; but it was all a deception, since he was thinking, 'He must not return to the city!'

466 With this bad intention, he informed the king, 'I shall perform a ceremony of respect before Cāṇakya, because I have wronged him.'

467 The king gave his permission, and Subandhu went and began to pay his respects to Cāṇakya as he fasted.

468 But Subandhu arranged that the ceremony of respect would have an unexpected harmful consequence: unnoticed by any other he placed a smouldering charcoal ember inside the dungheap.

469 Fanned by the wind, the charcoal ember soon set light to the dungheap. Although he was burning like a stick of wood, Maurya's teacher remained motionless. He died, and was reborn as a goddess in that place.

Here finishes the eighth canto of the scholar-monk Hemacandra's epic poem, the Appendix, or Lives of the Jain Elders. In it were related the death of Sakaṭala, Sthūlabhadra's initiation and his performance of his vow, Sambhūtavijaya's passage to heaven, the story of Cāṇakya and Candragupta, and Bindusāra's birth and his accession to the throne.

CANTO NINE

In the first part of Canto Nine the story of Bindusāra's successors is related. In the last part a rationale is provided for the beginning of the gradual loss from the oral tradition of the Original Collections of Teachings.

1–13 Subandhu was forced to live the life of monk because he opened a booby-trapped casket which Cāṇakya had left in his house.

14–54 Bindusāra was succeeded by his son Aśoka. An act of forgery committed by one of Aśoka's wives, eager to promote her own son's advancement, brought about the blinding of Kuṇāla, Aśoka's son and heir-apparent, as if on the king's own orders. His blinding rendered Kuṇāla incapable of succeeding, and he was sent to govern a distant village. Eventually he returned to Pāṭalīputra, and presented Aśoka with his infant grandson, Samprati. Aśoka set Samprati over his kingdom. Samprati, a Jain layman from birth, became a prosperous ruler.

55–111 Sthūlabhadra was learning the Original Collections of Teachings from Bhadrabāhu when he was visited by his sisters, whom he attempted to impress by displaying his supernatural powers. His sister Yakṣā told him that their brother Śrīyaka had become a Jain monk, but that she had encouraged him to fast, and that he had died as a result. To assuage her feelings of guilt, a goddess escorted her to Mahāvideha, a region not normally accessible to residents of Bharata, where a Fordmaker declared that she was free from blame. The Fordmaker gave her a present of four lectures, which she recited to the congregation on her return. After Yakṣā had related this story, she and her sisters took their leave of Sthūlabhadra.

Because Sthūlabhadra had shown off to his sisters, Bhadrabāhu forbade him to teach the last four of the fourteen Original Collections of Teachings to anyone else.

112–13 Bhadrabāhu died and went to heaven, and Sthūlabhadra then wandered the earth, preaching the Jain religion.

1 The following day, Subandhu asked Bindusāra if he could live in Cāṇakya's house, because he wished to obtain the wealth which he supposed to be there.

2 His request was granted by the king, and Subandhu entered the house and saw the chest, locked with a hundred locks.

3 He thought, 'Cāṇakya's entire wealth must be inside it, otherwise it would not be locked with a hundred locks.'

4 Subandhu broke open the locks on the chest, as if breaking the fetters of a released prisoner.

5 He saw the casket inside the chest, and thought, 'This is surely a jewel box, it is so well protected.'

6 He burst open the casket, as if it were a coconut, and saw the fragrant substances, which emitted heavenly perfumes.

7 Subandhu inhaled the fragrant perfumes, like a bee savouring a flower. He shook his head in wonder.

8 Then he saw in the casket the birch bark with the writing on it, and, thinking that it was an inventory of valuables, read it aloud to himself:

9 'Whoever smells these perfumes without leading the life of a monk will immediately become a guest of Death.'

10 After he had read this writing, he became extremely despondent, since he had no doubt that Cāṇakya's magic spell would not fail to work.

11 Nevertheless, in order to test the truth of what was written on the birch bark, Subandhu got a man to smell the perfumes, and then gave him a heavenly dinner.

12 The man immediately died, so Subandhu began to behave like a monk, not wishing to taste sense objects even mentally.

13 But because he was not capable of enlightenment, foolish Subandhu wandered the earth, led a continual dance by his hope of life.

14 King Bindusāra's son was named his highness Aśoka, and when Bindusāra died, he became king.

15 A son named Kuṇāla was born to Aśoka. As an endowment for this prince, the king granted him the city of Ujjayinī.

16 The prince was as dear as life to the king. He stayed in Ujjayinī, looked after by guardians appointed by the king, until he had completed his eighth year.

17 When his guardians reported to the king that he had reached this stage of life, the king was delighted, thinking that he was now ready to begin his studies.

18 Then the king wrote, by his own hand, a letter addressed to the prince. It was written in the local dialect, so that it would be widely understood. It said, 'Let the prince begin his studies (kumāro adhīyau).'

19 One of Kuṇāla's mother's fellow wives happened to be sitting there. She took the letter from the king and read it.

20 She determined that the kingdom should fall to her son and not to Kuṇāla, and while the king was engaged with other matters, she committed the following act of forgery:

21 She moistened with spittle the stick she used for applying her eye cosmetics, dabbed it in the black make-up around her eye, then with it placed a dot under the letter 'a'.*

22 Aśoka carelessly neglected to reread the letter, but sealed it and sent it to Ujjayinī.

23 Since the letter was signed with his father's name and bore his seal at the top, the prince took the letter with both hands, and respectfully placed it on his head.

24 Then the prince gave the letter to his secretary to read. The secretary read it to himself, and immediately became dejected.

25 His eyes filled with tears, and he was unable to read the letter aloud, so the prince took the letter from his hands.

26 Aśoka's son's curiosity and powers of observation had already led him to learn the alphabet, so he read the letter himself.

27 He thought, 'No member of the Maurya family has ever disobeyed his father's orders.

28 If I become the first to disobey the commands of a parent, then others will follow my lead.'

29 An ocean of daring, a moon for the sea of the Maurya family, he immediately branded himself in the eyes with a hot needle.

30 When King Aśoka heard that the prince had committed this act of violence, he reviled himself bitterly, saying, 'Alas, the letter I sent was falsified!'

31 He thought, 'An evil spirit has possessed me and blighted my hopes. That is why the prince is in this dreadful state because of my careless letter.

32 My dear child is now no longer capable of ruling a kingdom or a province. The great love he had for me must now be turned to reproach.

33 After ruling as crown prince, he was to become king; but now my heart's desire will not be fulfilled.'

34 King Aśoka bestowed a prosperous village on Kuṇāla, but he gave Ujjayinī to the son of that co-wife.

35 Now while Kuṇāla was governing that village, his wife gave birth to a son who was endowed with all the auspicious signs.

36 The prince was absolutely delighted, and gave largesse to the midwives and maidservants. He held a festival to celebrate the birth of his son.

37 Thinking, 'Now I shall frustrate the heart's desire of my co-mother', Kuṇāla went to Pāṭalīputra, hoping to gain the kingdom for his son.

38 Then he wandered through the city, delighting the people with his singing. He became very dear to them, since he surpassed Tumburu* in that art.

39 The people hastened to whatever part of Pāṭalīputra he happened to be singing in, attracted, like deer,* by his voice.

40 The king, having heard that he was a divine singer, summoned him, and ordered him to sing. But because he was blind, the king placed him behind a curtain.

41 Kuṇāla sang the following couplet in a melody modulated with the various notes of the musical scale, in the appropriate tones, high, middle, and low:

42 'Here is the great-grandson of Candragupta, the grandson of Bindusāra, and the blind son of Aśoka, begging for a farthing.'

43 When the king heard the blind man sing this couplet, he asked, 'Tell me, singer, who are you?'

44 He replied, 'I'm your own son Kuṇāla, the one who blinded himself after reading the command written in your letter.'

45 The king jerked back the curtain, and as soon as he saw him, recognized his son. He embraced him, his eyes filled with tears.

46 The king said, 'I'm delighted. What shall I give you, my dear boy?' The prince replied, 'I'm begging for a farthing, your majesty.'

47 The king asked his ministers why he was asking for that, and they told him that a farthing was what princes called a kingdom.

48 The king asked, 'My child, what do you want with the kingdom? It is destined for someone other than you, since fate has deprived you of your sight.'

49 The prince replied, 'Father, a son has been born to me. Congratulations, you're a grandfather! Let him be consecrated to the kingdom.'

50 When King Aśoka asked when his son had been born, Kuṇāla replied with his hands folded together in respect, 'Just now (samprati).'

51 King Aśoka immediately had the baby brought to him. He held a festival and named the child Samprati.

52 Ten days later King Aśoka, true to his word, set Samprati over his kingdom, although the child was still drinking from his mother's breast.

53 Samprati thrived in vigour, bravery, and prosperity, and was from his birth a Jain layman.

54 In course of time he subjugated all of Bharata including the southern part of the peninsula, as formidable in his government as Indra.

55 Now during a famine which was as dreadful as the night when the world comes to an end, the congregation migrated to the coast to seek subsistence there.

56 But because they never recited them, the monks forgot the sacred teachings. Even wise men forget what they have learned if they do not repeat it.

57 When the famine was over, the entire congregation of monks assembled in Pāṭalīputra, so that they could then collect the various chapters of the Limbs from whoever happened to remember them.

58 In this way they reassembled eleven Limbs. Then they considered what to do about the twelfth, the Disputation about Views.

59 Then the holy congregation remembered that Bhadrabāhu, who knew the Original Collections of Teachings, had gone to Nepal, so they sent two monks to call him back.

60 When the two monks arrived in Nepal, they bowed to Bhadrabāhu, their hands folded in respectful greeting, and said, 'The congregation commands you to attend its meeting, so that the sacred teachings can be compiled.'

61 He replied, 'I have vowed to meditate while undergoing bodily restraint. The period of meditation will last for twelve years, so I can't come.

62 When I have finished meditating, I shall recite all the Original Collections of Teachings, with their aphorisms and commentaries to whoever comes to me.'

63 The two monks departed, and informed the congregation of what he had said, but the congregation told the two monks, 'Go and summon him again.

64 When you arrive, ask him, "What punishment does that Teacher deserve who does not obey the orders of the holy congregation? Please tell us."

65 If he answers, "He should be excommunicated", then declare emphatically, "You yourself are that Teacher who deserves to be punished."'

66 The two monks returned, and spoke to the Teacher in those very words. He replied, 'The holy congregation should not excommunicate me, but rather take the following course of action:

67 Let the holy congregation be gracious to me, and agree to send me some intelligent pupils; I shall give them seven lessons every day.

68 I shall give one lesson at the time of the daily begging round, and three more lessons at the three daily rest periods.

69 The three remaining lessons will be given in the evening. In this way, the needs of the congregation will not prevent me from accomplishing my needs.'

70 The two monks returned and reported this to the congregation, who agreed, and sent Sthūlabhadra with five hundred monks.

71 The religious Teacher began to teach the monks, but because the lessons were very short they became disheartened and returned home. But Sthūlabhadra persevered.

72 Sthūlabhadra was very intelligent. After eight years had elapsed, he sat at the feet of holy Bhadrabāhu and recited eight of the Original Collections of Teachings without hesitation in a vehement manner.

73 The Teacher asked him if he was discouraged. Sthūlabhadra said, 'I'm not discouraged, but the lessons are very short.'

74 The Teacher replied, 'I have completed the greater part of my vow of meditation. When it is finished, I shall teach you for as long as you wish.'

75 Thereupon Sthūlabhadra said, 'How much remains for me to learn?' The Teacher said that the amount of the remainder was like an ocean of water drops.

76 When Bhadrabāhu had completed his period of meditation, the great monk Sthūlabhadra knew ten Original Collections of Teachings except for two topics.
77 In the course of his wanderings, holy Bhadrabāhu came to Pāṭalīputra, where he stayed in a park on the outskirts of the city.
78 In the mean time, Sthūlabhadra's sisters, Yakṣā and the others,* had become Jain nuns, and they went to pay their respects to Bhadrabāhu.
79 They bowed to the Teacher, and asked, 'Master, where is Sthūlabhadra?' He informed them that their brother was nearby in a small temple.
80 So the sisters set off to pay him a visit. Sthūlabhadra saw them coming, and turned himself into a lion, in order to entertain them with a miracle.
81 But when they saw the lion, they were terrified. They fled to the Teacher, and told him, 'A lion has eaten our elder brother. It's still there now.'
82 The Teacher knew what had happened, and told them, 'Return and pay your respects to him. Your brother's there; there's no lion.'
83 So they returned to the temple, and there saw Sthūlabhadra in his proper form. They paid their respects to him, and then the eldest sister related their story:
84 'Śrīyaka was initiated at the same time as us, but he was always hungry, and unable to withstand the rigours of fasting.
85 I told him to extend his period of fasting to the start of the rainy season, which he did, and then, with my encouragement, he extended it to its end.
86 I told him, "Now complete the next part of the fast. The first half is the most difficult part; the rest of the time will pass very easily in visiting sacred places."
87 Thus he extended his fast for this further period. Then I told him, "Hold firm, take on yet another period of fasting," and he accomplished that too.
88 Then I said to him, "It's nearly night. It will pass easily while you're asleep, so prolong your fast," and he did so.
89 But at midnight, while his mind was fixed upon the teachers of the gods, he was overwhelmed with pangs of hunger. He died and went to heaven.

90 I became depressed thinking that I had caused the death of a monk, so I went before the holy congregation to seek absolution.

91 The congregation declared, "You did this with pure intentions. Therefore there is no need for you to seek any absolution at all in this matter."

92 I replied, "I shall only believe this in my heart, if a Jina confirms this in my presence; otherwise, I shall not believe it."

93 In order to effect this, the entire congregation stood motionless with upright bodies. Then a Jina's attendant goddess came and said, "Tell me, what can I do for you?"

94 The congregation replied, "Take her to a Jina," and the goddess told them, "Stand motionless with upright bodies, so that there will be no obstacle to her going."

95 The congregation did so, and she took me to the Jina. Then I bowed before the blessed Lord Sīmandhara.*

96 The Jina said, "This good woman who has come from Bharata is free from fault." Thereupon, my doubts disappeared, and the goddess took me back to my own country.

97 Full of grace, Lord Sīmandhara sent by my lips a present of four lectures to the congregation.

98 They are called the Clauses, the Liberation, the Rules for Repose, and the Various Observances.*

99 Then, in one lesson, I recited and chanted them to the congregation, just as Sīmandhara had previously communicated them to me.

100 The congregation added the first two lectures as appendices to the Behaviour Rules,* the latter two to the Ten Evening Chapters.'

101 When she had finished telling her story, his sisters took their leave of Sthūlabhadra, and returned to their own lodgings. Then Sthūlabhadra went to his Teacher for his daily lesson.

102 But the Teacher refused to give him the lesson, saying, 'You are not worthy of it.' Then Sthūlabhadra tried to call to mind any sins he had committed since the day of his initiation.

103 He thought it over and said, 'I can't remember any sins.' His Teacher said, 'Do you consider that there was no sin in what you have done?'

104 Then Sthūlabhadra remembered, and fell at his Teacher's feet, saying, 'I shan't do it again. Please forgive me.'

105 The Teacher said to him, 'This is what you won't do again: you've made me refuse to teach you.'

106 Then Sthūlabhadra together with the entire congregation went to pay their respects to their Teacher; for when great people are angry, great people are ready to propitiate them.

107 The Teacher said, 'In the future other weak characters will do the same thing that he has done just now.

108 The knowledge of the remaining Original Collections of Teachings will be confined to me, so that his punishment will be an example to others.'

109 Begged by the entire congregation to reconsider, Bhadrabāhu declared, 'The knowledge of the entire Original Collections of Teachings will not end with me, but with you.'

110 The reverend Teacher made Sthūlabhadra vow that once he had learnt the other remaining Original Collections of Teachings, he would not teach them to anyone else.*

111 Then the great monk Sthūlabhadra learnt all the Original Collections of Teachings, and remained fixed in his attendance on holy Bhadrabāhu.

112 Holy Bhadrabāhu died in meditation and went to heaven, when one hundred and seventy years had elapsed since the final emancipation of Mahāvīra.

113 Thereafter, holy Sthūlabhadra, a treasure hoard of all branches of learning, wandered the earth, awakening living creatures, like a moon awakening blue lotus flowers.

Here finishes the ninth canto of the scholar-monk Hemacandra's epic poem, the Appendix, or Lives of the Jain Elders. In it were related the history of Bindusāra, King Aśoka and Kuṇāla, the birth of Samprati and his accession to the kingdom, Sthūlabhadra's learning of the Original Collections of Teachings, and holy Bhadrabāhu's departure to heaven.

CANTO TEN

In this short Canto Sthūlabhadra, after enabling a friend to find a treasure, died, having appointed his pupils, honourable Mahāgiri and honourable Suhastin, to be his successors.

1 One day, the spiritual leader Sthūlabhadra went to Śrāvastī, and settled in a park on the outskirts of the city, surrounded by his entourage of learned monks.

2 Thrilled with rapture, all the inhabitants of Śrāvastī came to pay their respects to him.

3 Reverend Sthūlabhadra, the creator of blessings for the world, explained the doctrines of the Jain religion. His discourse was as sweet as a shower of nectar.

4 Sthūlabhadra realized that his dear friend Dhanadeva, who lived in Śrāvastī, had not come. He thought:

5 'He is my dear friend. Why isn't he here? All the townspeople have come, but they are not my affectionate friends.

6 He may have gone abroad, or perhaps he is ill. I shall go myself to his house. By all means, I must assist him.'

7 Having decided to do this, he left the grove, his lotus-feet being anointed by the reverential people who bent towards them.

8 His ascetic qualities were hymned by the joyful women of the city. He walked under the parasols of the wealthy citizens as if under an arbour.

9 The lotus of his face was lovingly gazed on by the faithful devotees who went in front, their faces swaying on their necks like lotus flowers on bending stalks.

10 Bowing at every step to the city temples, he went to the home of his old friend Dhanadeva.

11 As reverend Sthūlabhadra entered the house, like a walking wishing-tree, Dhaneśvarī, Dhanadeva's wife, saw him.

12 Dhaneśvarī was of faultless understanding. She immediately rose from her seat, and bowed before Sthūlabhadra, her head touching the ground.

13 Then she brought a large chair for Sthūlabhadra. Religious

teachers are given a respectful welcome in accordance with the devotion of good people.

14 Reverend Sthūlabhadra graced the chair, purifying it with his presence, and then favoured her with a sermon on the virtue of forbearance.

15 Then he asked Dhaneśvarī, who was on her own owing to her husband's absence, 'Lady of excellent disposition, why is your husband nowhere to be seen?'

16 Dhaneśvarī said, 'Reverend sir, my husband has lost all of the money which was not deposited in the house.

17 Deprived of his wealth, he has gone to another city, of less substance than a blade of grass. Everywhere, it is people's wealth that is respected, not their own selves.

18 Although he searched for the treasure deposited by his ancestors, he was not successful. Although wealth remains to a man who has been disinherited, it is in another part of the world.

19 He has gone to another country, hoping to gain wealth by trade. What country is foreign to those engaged in trade?'

20 Through the power of his sacred learning, the religious leader knew that treasure had been hidden in the house. A treasure of compassion, he decided to tell her.

21 Under the semblance of teaching religion, the monk pointed to the post under which the treasure was hidden.

22 He said, 'See the nature of worldly existence! Such is your home, such is your husband's trade, and such is this!'

23 The reverend Teacher repeated this to Dhaneśvarī, and then left to wander in other parts, promoting the Jain religion.

24 Then Dhanadeva returned, having given up the effort of making money. He came just as he had gone, even wearing the same clothes.

25 Dhaneśvarī told him the news of Sthūlabhadra's visit. Full of joy, he asked what the reverend Teacher had said.

26 She told him, 'He gave a sermon, and pointed to that post with his hand.'

27 Dhanadeva thought, 'Sthūlabhadra is an ocean of knowledge; his gestures are never devoid of meaning.

28 Surely his pointing at that pillar indicates that treasure will be found below it.'

29 So Dhanadeva deliberately dug up the base of the post, and

there underneath it found a hoard of treasure, as copious as his own religious merit.

30 This treasure made Dhanadeva a very rich man, and he did not forget that it was due to the kindness of Sthūlabhadra.

31 One day, to give Sthūlabhadra the thanks due to him for his kindness to a friend, Dhanadeva went to Pāṭalīputra.

32 He went to the place where the great monk Sthūlabhadra was staying, and joyfully paid his respects to the great monk and his followers.

33 Dhanadeva, his hands folded in respectful greeting, said to the ascetic Sthūlabhadra, 'By your grace, I have crossed the ocean of poverty.

34 Through your kindness, reverend father, I have become free from debt. You are my teacher and my master, so tell me what you wish me to do.'

35 Sthūlabhadra said, 'Become a Jain layman.' Dhanadeva agreed and returned to his own home.

36 Reverend Sthūlabhadra had two pupils whom he had initiated. Their names were honourable Mahāgiri and honourable Suhastin.

37 'Honourable' was prefixed to the names Mahāgiri and Suhastin because the honourable Yakṣā had brought them up from childhood as their mother.*

38 Having abandoned sinful conduct, rich in forbearance, the two kept their vows of asceticism, which were as sharp as a sword.

39 They were two bees serving the lotus-feet of Sthūlabhadra. Extremely clever, they learnt from him ten Original Collections of Teachings in their entirety.

40 They were free from passion, possessed of extraordinary powers and supernatural perception. They were eloquent and full of vital power. Sthūlabhadra approved of their devotion, and appointed them leaders of the congregation. Then he died and went to heaven.

Here finishes the tenth canto of the scholar-monk Hemacandra's epic poem, the Appendix, or Lives of the Jain Elders. In it were related the initiation of honourable Mahāgiri and Suhastin, and Sthūlabhadra's accession to heaven.

CANTO ELEVEN

The two main topics of Canto Eleven are the spread of Jainism into the uncivilized countries of southern Bharata and the growth of laxity in the conduct of Jain ascetics.

1–4 Mahāgiri handed over his pupils to Suhastin, and began to lead the life of a solitary ascetic.

5–22 Suhastin was visiting a Jain layman, giving his kinsmen religious instruction, when Mahāgiri came to beg for food. The layman was impressed by Mahāgiri's asceticism and ordered leftover food to be set aside for him, although Jain ascetics are not supposed to accept food which had been specially reserved for them. Mahāgiri rebuked Suhastin for encouraging the layman to infringe the rules.

23–82 While visiting Ujjayinī King Samprati saw Suhastin and realized that he had known him in his former life. The king was converted by Suhastin's preaching. The king learnt that in his previous life he had been a beggar who was initiated by Suhastin and who subsequently gorged himself to death. Realizing that he owed his present prosperity to his initiation in his former life, the king became a pious Jain layman, performing charitable works and participating in Jain festivals.

83–102 King Samprati promoted the Jain religion in the uncivilized regions of southern India.

103–22 King Samprati ordered that special food and goods be given to the Jain ascetics, and this was condoned by Suhastin, although he knew it was contrary to the rules. Suhastin's laxity brought about the final breach between him and Mahāgiri.

123–7 Mahāgiri died and went to heaven. King Samprati died and became a god.

128–77 Suhastin initiated a merchant's son, Avantisukumāla. Too tender to bear the rigours of ascetic life, Avantisukumāla decided to fast to death. He was eaten by a hungry jackal, and a temple was built on the place where he had died.

178 Suhastin died, having appointed his best pupil to be his successor.

1 Honourable Mahāgiri and honourable Suhastin wandered the earth, benefiting righteous beings by their preaching of the Jain religion.

2 In due course, reverend Mahāgiri, the befriender of the universe, completed the education of his pupils, having given them numerous lessons.

3 One day Mahāgiri made over his disciples to Suhastin for he was intent on living the ascetic life of a Jina.*

4 The ascetic practice of a Jina was no longer undertaken. Nevertheless, since he no longer relied upon the support of his disciples, the way of life Mahāgiri followed was consistent with the ascetic practice of a Jina.

5 Like rain clouds filling with their showers the ocean of religious instruction, in the course of their wanderings the two came one day to Pāṭalīputra.

6 There lived a merchant named Vasubhūti, who had been converted by Suhastin, and had become a Jain layman, knowing the truth about soul and non-soul.

7 Day and night, Vasubhūti attempted to convert his kinsmen by explaining to them the doctrines of the Jain religion that Suhastin had taught him.

8 Although Vasubhūti strove to convert them, his kinsmen refused to be converted unless they first heard the doctrines expounded by a religious Teacher. They were not very clever.

9 Vasubhūti said to his Teacher, 'Reverend sir, I have not succeeded in converting my kinsmen, but you will be able to convert them.'

10 So Suhastin went to Vasubhūti's house to convert them, and gave them religious instruction which was like a river of nectar.

11 Then honourable Mahāgiri entered the house to beg for food, and Suhastin rose and bowed before him.

12 The merchant exclaimed, 'Who is this man who has come here and is welcomed by you with such respect? Is he senior to you?'

13 Suhastin said, 'Merchant, he certainly is senior to me. He only accepts as alms leftover food and drink.

14 If such food is not offered to him, then he fasts. Even the dust on his feet should be welcomed with honour and treated with respect.'

15 Having thus praised Mahāgiri, Suhastin converted them all, and then returned to the place where has was staying.

16 The merchant was particularly firm in his devotion. He said to his kinsmen, 'When you see that monk coming to beg for food,

17 produce some leftover food and drink to give him. When he accepts, your reward will be great.'

18 His kinsmen accepted Vasubhūti's advice, and on the next day Mahāgiri came to them to beg for food.

19 When the merchant's relatives saw Mahāgiri coming, they did as Vasubhūti had said, hoping that Mahāgiri would accept the food.

20 But Mahāgiri's powers of perceptions enabled him to know that the food was unacceptable, so he did not take it. He returned to his lodgings, and said to Suhastin:

21 'You have acted contrary to the rules of monastic conduct and have committed a great misdeed, for, acting on your instruction, they set aside food especially for me.'

22 Grovelling at honourable Mahāgiri's feet, Suhastin begged forgiveness, repeatedly promising that he would not do it again.

23 Shortly after, King Samprati visited the city of Ujjayinī. Kings are at home wherever they go.

24 Mahāgiri and Suhastin had come to Avanti to see the image of the Living Lord being carried in procession.*

25 The two stayed with their followers in separate lodgings, since the number of their disciples was too large to enable them to gather in one place.

26 The image of the Living Lord was conveyed in a carriage with great festivity. It was a rain cloud for the peacocks of the minds of the devoted citizens.

27 Followed by the two Teachers and the entire congregation of monks, the carriage was safely carried round the city.

28 The carriage passed by the palace gates. There, standing on a balcony, the king saw Suhastin in the distance.

29 He thought, 'That leader of the monks is like a moon for the water-lilies of my mind. I seem to have seen him before, but I can't remember where.'

30 While he was considering the matter, the king suddenly

swooned. His attendants ran forward, exclaiming, 'Ah! What is this!'

31 They wafted him with fans and sprinkled him with sandalwood perfume. Suddenly, the king stood up, and remembered.

32 He remembered that he had known the Teacher Suhastin in his previous life. Straightaway, the king went to prostrate himself before Suhastin, so that there would be no cause for him to forget once again.

33 Touching the ground with his head, hands, and feet, he asked the Teacher, 'Reverend sir, what is the fruit of the Jain religion?'

34 Reverend Suhastin said, 'Final emancipation and heaven are its fruit.' Then the king asked, 'What is the fruit of the attainment of equanimity?'

35 Suhastin said, 'Your majesty, the fruit of one who has attained a state of equanimity is greater than a kingdom.' As he said this, the king was suddenly converted.

36 Snapping his fingers to demonstrate his belief, the king said, 'It's true! There's no doubt about it!'

37 Then the king bowed to Suhastin once more, and asked, 'Do you recognize me, or not?'

38 Through his powers of cognition, the spiritual leader had recognized the king. He said, 'Yes. I recognize you, your majesty. Listen to the story of your previous life:

39 Previously, your majesty, in the course of our wanderings, the spiritual leader Mahāgiri and I came, accompanied by our followers, to Kauśāmbī.

40 We stayed in separate parts of the city, because each of us had a large number of followers.

41 At that time there was a severe famine in the city. Nevertheless, those people who had food continued to give us good quantities of food and drink.

42 One day, the monks went to the house of a merchant to beg for food, and a starving beggar followed and entered the house behind them.

43 There the monks were freely given various kinds of provisions appropriate for monks, such as confectionery and other foodstuffs, while the beggar looked on.

44 After receiving this food, the monks began to return to their

lodgings. The beggar followed them, and begged them to give him food.

45 The monks told him, "Only our Teachers can give permission. We are absolutely obedient to them, consequently, we can't give you anything."

46 Then the beggar followed the monks to their lodgings. Depressed in spirits, he saw me there, and begged. "Give me food!"

47 The monks informed me, "Reverend sir, this image of poverty begged us for food while we were on our way."

48 By applying my powers of cognition, I knew that in his next life the beggar would become a patron of the holy teachings.

49 So I affectionately told the beggar, "You can have some food, if you first become a Jain monk."

50 The beggar thought, "Everything has been very hard for me before, so it is preferable to undertake that extremely hard vow which will enable me to obtain food."

51 After we had initiated him, and he had become a monk, we let him eat as much of the confectionery and other foodstuffs as he wished.

52 He crammed so much of the delicious savouries and sweets down his throat, that his windpipe became constricted.

53 That night he suffocated because of the amount of food he had eaten. He died, and his spirits left his body.

54 Having died in a state midway between beggar and monk, he was reborn as you, the son of Kuṇāla, the king of Avanti!'

55 The king addressed Suhastin once more, 'Reverend sir, it is thanks to you that I have attained this station in life.

56 If you had not initiated me, into what condition of life would I have been reborn, having had no contact with the Jain religion?

57 So please tell me what I can do for you. I shall repay you for your kindness to me in my previous life.

58 You are my teacher in this my present life as in my former. Accept me, and instruct me as your son.'

59 Full of compassion, honourable Suhastin told the king, 'Accept the Jain religion as your refuge here and in the other world.

60 In the next world, heaven or final emancipation belongs to followers of the Jain religion, and in this world, elephants, horses, treasure, and ever increasing prosperity!'

61 At Suhastin's prompting, the king repeated before him, 'The Worthy is a god, the monk is a Teacher, the teachings of the Worthy is my authority.'

62 From that time on, Samprati stood at the head of the Jain laity, free from sin, following the lesser vows, the subsidiary vows, and the vows of instruction.*

63 At dawn, noon, and sunset, he performed an elaborate act of worship to the holy Jinas. He treated his fellow Jain laymen with as much affection as if they were his kinsmen.

64 Full of wisdom, his mind was an ocean of affection for all living beings. Devoted to the performance of good deeds, he gave lavishly to poor people.

65 Abounding in splendour, unwavering in his faith, he adorned the three parts of Bharata as far as Mount Vaitāḍhya with Jain temples.

66 The reverend Teacher Suhastin remained in Avanti for another year, while the congregation held a temple festival.

67 During the temple festival, reverend Suhastin and the holy congregation constantly visited the temple.

68 And Samprati always sat before Suhastin, his hands folded in respectful adoration, as if he were his most insignificant pupil.

69 When the temple festival was over, the congregation performed a carriage procession. For a temple festival is always completed with a carriage procession.

70 Then the carriage was brought from the coach house. It looked like the carriage of the sun, as the light of its rubies and gold shone in all directions.

71 The statue of the holy Worthy which was placed on the carriage was bathed in adoration by wealthy Jain laymen who knew the correct procedure.

72 As the Worthy was being bathed, water from the bath poured down from the carriage, just as it had previously poured from the peak of Mount Meru, at the time of the auspicious birth of Mahāvīra.

73 The image was anointed with fragrant substances by the faithful, their mouths covered with fine muslin cloth, as if they wished to address the Lord.

74 The statue of the Worthy was festooned in adoration with gar-

lands of countless white jasmine blossoms. It looked like the moon surrounded by autumnal rain clouds.

75 The statue was censed with smouldering aloe wood. The streaks of smoke rose up and covered the statue, so that it looked as if it were wearing dark blue clothes.

76 The faithful venerated the statue at night by waving lamps with flames blazing; it looked like a mountain peak encircled by luminous herbs.

77 Then the foremost Jain lay people bowed to the Worthy, who themselves went in front and drew the carriage, as if they were carriage horses.

78 Charming plays were performed before the carriage, and to the sound of four types of percussion, songs and dances were given by the townswomen.

79 The carriage was surrounded on all sides by a large crowd of Jain laywomen who sang hymns and performed various acts of worship, nearby the lofty palace.

80 The ground before the carriage was densely sprinkled with saffron perfume. Eventually the carriage reached the entrance to Samprati's palace.

81 Then King Samprati came, intent on worshipping the carriage. All his body thrilled with joy; it looked as if it were pierced with thorns, like the fruit of the breadfruit tree.

82 The king of Avanti, a swan for the lake of new joy, worshipped the statue on the carriage with the eight substances.*

83 Then the king summoned all his vassals, and caused them to accept the truth about religion, ordering them:

84 'If you vassals respect me as your rightful overlord, then you will richly provide for Jain laypeople and Jain monks.

85 I have no use at all for the wealth you give me, so if you do this, vassals, I shall be very pleased.'

86 Thus commanded, the vassals returned to their own countries, and there, through affection for their master, respectfully served the Jain monks.

87 In their countries, they held carriage processions, in imitation of the festival held in Avanti. Before the carriage, they rained flowers and worshipped the image.

88 Since all the vassals were now living the lives of Jain laymen,

the bordering kingdoms became worthy of being inhabited by Jain monks.

89 One night, Samprati thought, 'I'll arrange for Jain monks to travel in the barbarian countries.'

90 So he said to the barbarians, 'Wherever you see my servants travelling, pay my taxes to them.'

91 Then he sent to the barbarians messengers dressed as Jain monks. On Samprati's orders, they continually instructed the barbarians:

92 'Give us clothes, vessels, food, drink and other things that are free from the forty-two faults.*

93 If you learn to do these things, King Samprati will be pleased with you, but if you do otherwise, he will be angry.'

94 So from that time on, eager to please King Samprati, they always everyday followed the orders of his messengers.

95 So then King Samprati informed the religious Teacher that the four barbarian countries had been made fit for Jain monks to inhabit:

96 'Reverend sir, in whatever part of the barbarian countries these monks travel, it will be just as in civilized countries. So why don't they?'

97 The religious Teacher replied, 'Kings in barbarian countries never promote knowledge, teaching, and correct behaviour.'

98 The king replied, 'You should know that monks have recently been sent to the barbarian countries, and the good conduct of the people there was evident.'

99 So at the king's insistence, the Teacher sent some monks to live in Andhra, Dramila, and the other barbarian countries.

100 When the barbarians saw these monks, they thought that they were Samprati's messengers, and gave them food and drink and other things, just as they had previously been taught.

101 The monks saw that there was a blameless practice of Jain layship even among the barbarians. Full of admiration, they returned and informed their Teacher.

102 In this way, King Samprati, by means of the power of his intelligence, made the barbarian countries fit to be inhabited by Jain monks.

103 The king remembered the hardships of his previous life as a beggar, and had large hospices built at each of the four city gates.

104 Thinking, 'This is my condition now, but that was my condition before', the king enabled those who were in need of food to obtain as much food as they wanted, free from care, in the hospices.

105 The food which was left by those who had eaten was shared out by the royal kitchen workers among those of them who were hungry.

106 The king asked them, 'Who gets the leftover food?' They replied, 'We kitchen workers get it. It is our right.'

107 The king ordered them, 'Give the food that I left over to monks who beg for whatever has been prepared but not used.

108 I shall provide for your subsistence by giving you money. There will be no loss of earnings for anyone who does this.'

109 From that time on, the kitchen workers obeyed the king's orders, and gave the leftover food and drink to those monks whose appearance of purity gave them entitlement.

110 A servant of the Jain monks, the king ordered the bakers, the dealers in clarified butter and yoghurt, and the dealers in clothes:

111 'If anything can be of service to the Jain ascetics, give it to them. I shall reimburse you for its cost; have no fear about that.'

112 They were absolutely delighted to do this, for traders are always full of joy when their goods are being sold.

113 But honourable Suhastin, despite knowing that there was fault in the king's action, permitted it through affection for his pupils, his intelligence polluted by power.

114 Then honourable Mahāgiri said to Suhastin, 'Why have you accepted food from the king, although you knew that such was not to be accepted?'

115 Suhastin said, 'Reverend sir, the subjects do the same as the king. For intent on obliging the king, the citizens also make gifts.'

116 Honourable Mahāgiri cried angrily, 'This is a deception! May your sin be forgiven. Henceforth, we two shall go our separate ways.

117 It is good for monks who follow the path of right conduct to associate together, but you have transgressed the path, since you have broken the rules of right conduct.'

118 Trembling with fear like a child, Suhastin bowed before

honourable Mahāgiri in worship, his hands folded in respectful supplication. He said:

119 'I have done wrong. I have acted very badly through my lack of insight. Forgive my offence. I shall not do the same thing again.'

120 Mahāgiri said, 'Perhaps you are not at fault. For reverend Lord Mahāvīra previously prophesied:

121 "After the passing of Sthūlabhadra from the line of pupillary succession begun by me, the previous excellent conduct of Jain monks will begin to deteriorate."

122 After Sthūlabhadra, we two became the leaders of the monastic order, so his prophecy has been fulfilled by you.'

123 Having thus determined on this course of separation, honourable Mahāgiri bowed to the image of the Living Lord, and left Avanti.

124–5 In the past footprints had been produced by the elephant of Indra, king of the gods, when he was hastening to attend the assembly which gathered when holy Mahāvīra was enlightening Daśārṇabhadra.*

There the footprints remained. Honourable Mahāgiri went to that holy place.

126 And at that holy place, famous as 'The Elephant's Footprints', Mahāgiri abandoned his body by abstaining from food, and went to heaven.

127 King Samprati kept the vows of a Jain layman. When his life was over, he was reborn as a god. Eventually he will become one whose soul is perfected.

128 Now, honourable Suhastin, having spent some time elsewhere, returned to Ujjayinī, to pay honour to the image of the Living Lord.

129 Reverend Suhastin held a preaching assembly in a park on the outskirts of the city, and sent two monks to the city centre to look for lodgings.

130 They came to the house of a merchant's wife. Her name was Bhadrā. She bowed before them, and asked, 'What is your command?'

131 They told her, 'We are pupils of honourable Suhastin. At his command, good lady, we are looking for lodgings.'

132 Thereupon she offered them a spacious shed where the vehicles were kept as lodgings, and Suhastin and his followers adorned it with their presence.

133 One evening, the Teacher began to expound an excellent lecture called 'The Lotus Thickets'.*

134 Meanwhile, Bhadrā's son, Avantisukumāla, was amusing himself like a god on top of their seven-storeyed house.

135 While having fun with his thirty-two wives, he listened to the lecture, an elixir for the ears.

136 So that he could hear it properly, Bhadrā's son, fully endowed with intelligence, quickly descended from the roof of the mansion, and stood by the door of the shed.

137 Wondering, 'Where have I experienced this?', he suddenly remembered his previous life, and entered the presence of the Teacher.

138 He bowed and said, 'Reverend sir, I am Bhadrā's son, and formerly I was a god in the lotus thicket mansion.

139 Since I have remembered my life in the lotus thicket mansion, I now wish to be initiated into the life of a Jain monk, so that I can return there.'

140 He repeatedly begged, 'Initiate me!', but the Teacher replied, 'Young man, you are very delicate.*

141 Although its flames are pleasant to the touch, linseed oil for iron, and productive of bliss, however, the ascetic life taught by the Jinas, the abandonment of wrong conduct, is very difficult to practise.'

142 Bhadrā's son said, 'Very well. But I still long to be initiated, even though I shall be unable to bear the life of a Jain monk for very long.

143 So I shall undertake the life of a Jain monk, depending on my strength of character. The pain will not last for very long.'

144 The Teacher said, 'Excellent one, if you wish to be initiated, then get your parents' permission for your action.'

145 Then Avantisukumāla returned to his home and asked his parents, but they did not give their permission.

146 Thereupon, Bhadrā's son immediately tore out his hair by the roots, and on his own accord assumed the guise of a Jain monk, turning his back on his home.

147 Looking like that, he went to honourable Suhastin.

Avantisukumāla had no thoughts for himself, not even for his own body.

148 So that people would not assume the guise of a Jain monk on their own accord, Suhastin initiated Avantisukumāla, declaring his self-initiation void.

149 Since he was unable to bear the rigours of the ascetic life for very long, he gained his Teacher's permission to go elsewhere, having resolved to abstain from food.

150 As Avantisukumāla travelled, he made the ground seem under Indra's protection with the drops of blood that fell from his tender feet.*

151 He came to a cremation ground. Everywhere, the earth was grey with the ashes from the funeral pyres. It was like the playground of Death.

152 There, in a thicket of thorn bushes, he remained, fasting, his mind concentrated in meditation, while reciting the Fivefold Salutation.*

153 A female jackal accompanied by her cubs came to that place, licking his footprints, meaty with the smell of the blood that had poured from his feet.

154 Following the strong smell of congealed blood oozing from his feet, the jackal and her cubs entered that thicket of thorn bushes.

155 Lapping up the gore, she reached his blood-smeared feet, and began to eat him. She was like the sister of Death.

156–7 As she gorged on him, his skin went crick-crack!, his flesh went rat-tat!, his tendons went snip-snap!, his bones went crick-crack! She gobbled up the whole of one of his feet.

158 Even so, he did not tremble. On the contrary, he had the strength of character to regard the devourer of his foot as if she were its masseuse.

159 In the second watch, she ate his leg. But the monk felt compassion for her, thinking, 'May this being be satisfied!'

160 In the third watch, she ate his belly. But he thought, 'She is not hurting my belly. What business is it of mine?'

161 But in the fourth watch, when it was night, the great-souled ascetic monk died, and was reborn as a god in the lotus thicket mansion.

162 And at that moment, thinking, 'He is mighty! He is courageous! He must be venerated', the gods praised the glory of his corpse.
163 Avantisukumāla's wives missed seeing him, and asked Suhastin, 'Reverend sir, what has become of our husband?'
164 Suhastin knew all about it through his powers of perception. So he told them what had happened in a pleasant voice.
165 Then Avantisukumāla's wives went to Bhadrā's house, and informed her of everything that had occurred.
166 On the following morning, Bhadrā, Avantisukumāla's mother, went to the cremation ground and entered that thicket of thorn bushes.
167 When she saw the pieces of her son's body strewn all over the ground, she cried and became wet with tears, as if she were a spring of water.
168 Accompanied by Avantisukumāla's wives, Bhadrā wept, and lamented, 'Why have you abandoned life and us together?
169 My son you have been a monk for only a year. Why did you not travel with a group of monks when you left our home?
170 When will that auspicious night come, the one that will make us live again, in which we shall see you in a dream?
171 Having become free from illusion, you left us because you wanted to be initiated. But why did you, freed from delusion, leave your Teacher?'
172 Weeping and repeating this over and over again, she performed the funeral rites for his dead body on the bank of the river Siprā.
173 Bhadrā's son's wives also wailed and lamented. They performed a ceremony of pouring water from conch shells into the river Siprā, their clothes wet with tears.
174 Then Bhadrā, rendered formidable by her prodigious sorrow at the death of her son, decided to be initiated as a Jain nun, following that way of life which is an everlasting ocean of tranquillity.
175 Bhadrā went home and was initiated together with Avantisukumāla's wives, who were all of the same mind, with the exception of one who was pregnant.
176 The pregnant wife gave birth to a son. He built a splendid temple on the place where Avantisukumāla had died.

177 Even today that temple remains an ornament of Avanti, famous throughout the world as the temple of Mahākāla.*

178 In course of time holy honourable Suhastin handed over his following of monks to his best pupil. Absorbed in meditation and abstaining from food, he abandoned his body, and went to heaven.

Here finishes the eleventh canto of the scholar-monk Hemacandra's epic poem, the Appendix, or Lives of the Jain Elders. In it were related the deed of King Samprati, honourable Mahāgiri's accession to heaven, Avantisukumāla's accession to the lotus thicket mansion, and honourable Suhastin's accession to heaven.

CANTO TWELVE

Canto Twelve centres on the Jain Elder Vajra and his possession of supernatural powers.

1–20 In a district of Avanti lived a wealthy Jain merchant named Dhanagiri, whose brother Śamita had been initiated by the Teacher Siṃhagiri. Dhanagiri also wanted to become a monk, but he had married Sunandā. When she became pregnant, Dhanagiri left home and was initiated by Siṃhagiri.

21–68 Sunandā gave birth to a boy, who was endowed with precocious understanding. Having learnt that his father had become a monk, the baby resolved to become a monk himself, and irritated his mother into handing him over to Dhanagiri and Śamita. The baby was named Vajra by Siṃhagiri. Vajra grew into such a delightful child that his mother wished to reclaim him.

69–99 Śamita showed that the magic trick performed by a certain ascetic with the wrong views did not depend upon the powers gained by asceticism.

100–36 Sunandā went before the king to demand Vajra's return, but the child made it quite plain that he wished to remain with the monks. His mother then relinquished her claim, and Vajra was then initiated by Siṃhagiri.

137–60 Some Yawning gods who had been friends of Vajra in his former life tempted him with magic food and other goods, but Vajra resisted their temptation and was rewarded by them with magic powers.

161–207 Vajra had learnt the sacred teachings as they were being recited by the monks and nuns. When Siṃhagiri found out about Vajra's facility for learning, he appointed him instructor to the other monks.

208–41 Siṃhagiri sent Vajra to Ujjayinī to learn the ten remaining Original Collection of Teachings from the Teacher Bhadragupta. Vajra learnt them with ease, and returned to teach them to the other monks. Siṃhagiri died, having appointed Vajra to be his successor.

242–306 In Pāṭalīputra lived Rukmiṇī, the daughter of an extremely wealthy merchant. She had overheard some Jain nuns singing Vajra's praises, and had fallen in love with him. When Vajra visited that city in the course of his wanderings, Rukmiṇī's father offered Vajra an immense dowry if he would accept her hand in marriage. Vajra refused, and Rukmiṇī, converted by Vajra's preaching, became a Jain nun.

307–34 Vajra used his magic powers to transport the congregation of monks from the North, where there was a great famine, to Purī, where there was an abundance of food.

335–88 In that city the Jain laypeople were prevented from making offerings of flowers by the Buddhists who had cornered the market in them. Vajra used his magic powers to fly to the gardens of the gods in the Himalayas. Accompanied by his friends, the Yawning gods, he returned bearing an abundance of blooms. The king and the Buddhists were converted to Jainism.

1 In the line of monastic succession headed by Suhastin, Lord Vajra became the mainstay of the holy teachings.* His story is here related in detail:

2 In this Rose-apple Tree Island, in the western part of Bharata, is a country named Avanti which is like heaven in its prosperity.

3 In Avanti is a district named Tumbavana; it is like the blessed district of the majestic gods.

4 There lived a wealthy Jain layman, like a son of the goddess of wealth. He was the son of a rich man. His name was Dhanagiri, and he was famed for his mountain of wealth.

5 Although his body was adorned with the beauty of the prime of life, desire did not enter his heart, for it was guarded by the doorkeeper of tranquillity.

6 It is read in the textbooks of the Analysis school of philosophy* that wealth accrues from the practice of religion, but he esteemed religion more than wealth, and distributed his money to worthy people.

7 Knowing that the reward of chastity was heaven or final emancipation, he had no desire to marry a young lady. He was utterly devoted to the religion of the Worthies.

8 To whatever household his concerned parents visited, seeking a maiden for Dhanagiri to marry,

9 Dhanagiri would himself go, and say, 'I'm definitely going to become a Jain monk. My parents didn't mention this detriment of mine.'

10 But Sunandā, the daughter of the wealthy merchant Dhanapāla, said, 'Let me be betrothed to Dhanagiri; let him be my husband.'

11 So the wealthy merchant gave his daughter, who was fixed upon her choice, to Dhanagiri, even though he intended to become a Jain monk.

12 Sunandā's brother, honourable Śamita, had already been initiated as a monk at the feet of the Teacher Siṃhagiri.

13 One day, Dhanagiri, even though he was chaste-minded, made love to Sunandā, who had just bathed after her monthly courses. The fruit of enjoyment is always karma, never otherwise.

14–15 Previously holy Gautama, while on Mount Aṣṭapada, had related the story of Puṇḍarīka.* The god who had listened to this in company with Vaiśramana fell from heaven, and entered Sunandā's womb.

16 Knowing that she was pregnant, Dhanagiri said, 'Pure-minded one, this will be your only child. Now I shall become a Jain monk.

17 I never really wanted to marry you, for renunciation was dearer to me than that. So farewell!'

18 Having said this, he abandoned her, as if she were a rented house. He went to the Teacher Siṃhagiri and became a monk.

19 Tolerating the twenty-two discomforts,* he performed extremely harsh acts of asceticism, taking no care even for his own body.

20 Endowed with the qualities of a good pupil—determination, sincerity, docility, etc.—he drew from his Teacher the essence of the religious teachings, as if drawing water from a well.

21 When nine months had elapsed, Sunandā gave birth to a son, who was a joy for mankind, as a lotus is for a lake.

22 The young women who, full of affection for Sunandā, had come to the house to assist with the lying-in, said to the little boy:

23 'Little boy, if your father had not been so anxious to become a Jain monk, then an auspicious birth ceremony would certainly have been celebrated for you.*

24 Even though there is a woman in it, a house without a husband does not shine, just as a sky filled with stars does not shine without a moon.'

25 But the baby was endowed with understanding because of the lightness of his knowledge-obscuring karma. He concentrated and overheard their conversation.

26 He thought, 'My father took initiation as a Jain monk.' And as he thought this, he remembered his former life.

27 Remembering his former life, the baby knew the worthlessness of the continuous cycle of death and rebirth, and wanted to travel the same road as his father.

28 He decided to irritate his mother into letting him go. He cried extremely loudly all through the day and night, even when lying in his mother's lap.

29 Not by singing him sweet melodied lullabies, not by playful gestures, not by rocking him in his cradle, not by coaxing words,

30 not by bouncing him up and down on the hip, not by playing musical instruments, not even by kissing him on the head, could the baby be induced to stop crying.

31 The infant cried like this for six months, and even Sunandā began to loath her son.

32 One day, Siṃhagiri came to that village accompanied by his disciples. Among them were Dhanagiri and honourable Śamita.

33 Dhanagiri and honourable Śamita bowed to their Teacher while they were in their lodgings, and asked him:

34 'Reverend sir, our kinsmen live in this village. With your permission, we should like to pay our respects to them.'

35 While they were asking this, the eminent scholar saw a bird of good omen. He said:

36 'Today you will receive a wonderful gift, so accept whatever is offered you, whether or not it is endowed with reason.'

37 The two leading monks went to Sunandā's house. They were ushered in and announced by the other women.

38 All the women said, 'Sunandā, hand your son over to Dhanagiri. Let's see where he will take him.'

39 Joylessly, Sunandā handed over the infant with whom she was disgusted to Dhanagiri. She said:

40 'All the time I've looked after him myself, he's cried continually day and night. I'm sick of him.

41 Although you have become a monk, take your child with you. Don't abandon him, like you abandoned me before.'

42 Dhanagiri, supreme in eloquence, smiled and said, 'I shall do this, good lady. But you will regret it afterwards.

43 So swear before witnesses that you will by no means endeavour to take him back.'

44 Thereupon, Sunandā swore to this before witnesses, and handed her son over to Dhanagiri, who accepted him.

45 Dhanagiri placed the baby in a suitable receptacle, and the child immediately ceased crying, as if at a previously arranged signal.

46 The two monks took the child from Sunandā's house and, obedient to their Teacher's orders, returned once more to his presence.

47 The Teacher saw that Dhanagiri's arms were bending with the burden of carrying his precious jewel of a son. He said:

48 'You seem tired by the burden of the alms you have received. Give him to me, fortunate one. Rest your arms.'

49 With an effort, the monk took the child, that receptacle of good fortune, who looked like a young man being embraced by his beloved, and handed him over to the Teacher.

50 The little boy shone with splendour like the sun in glory, and the Teacher took him in his arms.

51 Straightaway, Siṃhagiri's arms bowed to the earth as if he had been checked in the act of giving a respectful greeting.

52 His arms bent with the weight of the child, the Teacher exclaimed in astonishment, 'A full-grown man is not able to hold this diamond!

53 This boy will become a promoter of the Jain religion, worthy of great merit. He must be guarded with great care, for jewels are prone to loss.'

54 The Teacher gave the child to the nuns, and because his nature was like a diamond (vajra) named him Vajra.

55 The nuns entrusted the child to the faithful laywomen with whom they lodged, saying, 'Look after him, like your own selves.'

56 The women of the household were skilled in the care of young children. They cared for and watched over the baby with as much affection as if he were their own child.

57 The baby was a treasure of good fortune for the ladies of the household. He passed from lap to lap, like a swan passing from lotus to lotus.

58 The ladies of the household went mad as they caressed him with whispered endearments of love.
59 The illustrious ladies vied with each other in offering Vajra treats, giving him baths, drinks, food, and other dainties.
60 In course of time, Vajra began to grow, and although he was still a very young child, he endeavoured not to displease the women with any of the thoughtless actions of childhood.
61 Vajra was intelligent. To keep alive he consumed filtered water, for he possessed true discrimination as a result of his remembrance of his former life and so understood the rules.
62 Whenever the child wished to defecate or urinate, he always gave a timely signal to his nurses.
63 Vajra was like a twin brother to all the other little boys in that house of refuge, showing equal affection to them all.
64 Each day Vajra delighted the ladies by devising childish games from educational material.
65 Sunandā saw that Vajra was handsome and settled in good behaviour, and begged the women in the household for him, saying, 'He's my son.'
66 But they said, 'We do not recognize the relationship of mother and child between you and this boy, for he was entrusted to the Teacher.'
67 The women said that, and refused to return her son to her. So she stood at a distance, and watched Vajra as if he were another's property.
68 With great respect, she entered their house, and cherished her son with milk from her breast, as if she were his nurse.

69 Now the two rivers Kanyā and Purṇā flow through the Acalapura district, splendid in prosperity and of renowned name.
70 In the land between these two rivers lived some monks who had mistaken views. One of those monks with mistaken views had a magic foot ointment.
71 He would smear this ointment on his feet, and then put on sandals. Then he would step on the water, as if on dry land, and begin to walk.
72 In this manner, wearing his sandals, he would daily walk to and from the town by way of the river, to the amazement of the people.

73 He would deride the Jain monks and the Jain laypeople, saying, 'There's no potency in your religion, as there is in ours.'

74 Honourable Śamita, the Teacher, Vajra's maternal uncle, came to that place. In the course of his wanderings, he had practised harsh acts of asceticism, and had gained magical powers.

75 The Jain laypeople told the excellent Teacher that those monks had been laughing and jeering at the Jain religion.

76 When he heard this, honourable Śamita, although he was endowed with the supernatural knowledge of the teachings, knew by the power of his intelligence what was going on. He said to his lay followers:

77 'That monk has none of the powers produced by asceticism. He has deceived you all by some magic.

78 It's a trick, just as out-of-season flowers and other such items are produced at show. It's not like the power produced by asceticism.

79 The things you have seen can only be accomplished by teachings of the Jain religion, so don't be led by your amazement at their tricks to put your faith in those monks.

80 If you don't believe me, then invite him for dinner. When he comes to your home, then wash his feet and sandals.'

81 So the Jain laymen invited that monk, the performer of the magic trick. He went to the house of one of the Jain laymen, followed by the people.

82 When the monk arrived, the Jain layman, in company with his household, feigned devotion, and said:

83 'Reverend sir, I shall wash your lotus-feet. Those who cleanse your feet, cleanse themselves.

84 So please oblige us. You are able to save us. Great-souled ascetics do not hinder the devoted worship of their devotees.'

85 So, although the monk was unwilling, the Jain layman washed his feet and sandals in warm water.

86 He cleansed the monk's feet and sandals so thoroughly that not even a whiff of the ointment remained on them, like passion for a lowly object.

87 The leading Jain layman gave the monk an extremely respectful welcome, and dined him, because even those monks who have the wrong views should be treated honourably.

88 The monk became very worried when the ointment was washed

away. He was unable to enjoy his meal through fear that his means of walking on water would be exposed.

89 After finishing his meal, he returned to the bank of the river, followed by the people, eager to see the miracle of the solidifying water.

90 The fool hoped that some of the ointment would perhaps still remain, and rashly stepped on the water as before.

91 The childish monk immediately sank into the water, making a gurgling sound like a water-jar when it is being filled.

92 Immediately, the respect that even those monks with mistaken views had for him vanished. They thought, 'How long have we been deceived by this performer of magic tricks?'

93 While this was happening, the people stood on the river bank and made a loud commotion. Then the Teacher, most eminent of scholars, arrived at that place.

94 Then, in order to promote his own religion, the Teacher aimed the power of his asceticism at the river.

95 Most eminent of the great-hearted, he said, 'Come here, so that we may reach your opposite bank.'

96 Immediately, the two banks of the river joined together, and the Teacher and his followers passed over to the dry ground on the far bank.

97 When the monks with mistaken views saw this miracle performed by the Teacher, they became agitated with the desire of emancipation, and the people became the Teacher's devotees.

98 With one mind, all those monks, having shaken off their wrong views, took initiation as Jain monks in the presence of the Teacher, honourable Śamita.

99 Because they had originated as dwellers in Brahma's island, from that time on, those monks were known as Brahma's Islanders, and are mentioned in scripture by that name.*

100 Meanwhile, Vajra had remained in that place. When he was three years old, Dhanagiri came there, in company with other monks.

101 Thinking, 'Now that Dhanagiri has come, I'll get my son back', Sunandā was overjoyed at their arrival.

102 Sunandā demanded her son from that great monk, but he refused to hand him over, saying:

103 'You silly woman, you gave that child to us of your own free will. Who would wish to take back what has been given up like vomited food?

104 You no longer own the things you give away, just like the things you sell. So don't demand the son whom you yourself gave away. He was properly made over to another.'

105 Thus each party was of opposed view. The people said, 'The king should settle this dispute.'

106 Thereupon, Sunandā, accompanied by the people, went to the royal court, and the monks, accompanied by the congregation, went there too.

107 Sunandā sat on the king's left, but the entire holy congregation sat on the king's right. Each party sat in its proper place.

108 Disregarding both their arguments, the king announced, 'The child will belong to that party whose call he obeys.'

109 The two parties agreed to this method of deciding the question, but then they asked who should be the first to call the boy.

110 The householders' wives replied, 'This boy has enjoyed the affection of the monks for so long, that he will not disobey their command.

111 The mother should be the first to call the child. She deserves our sympathy, because she has been experiencing difficulties. That's the way it should be, the others should not be first.'

112 So Sunandā repeatedly displayed before her son children's toys and various kinds of sweets, saying:

113 'I've brought these elephants, these horses, and these soldiers for you to play with! Come and take them, my child!

114 Here are boiled sweets, pastry cakes, grapes, and sugared candy! If you want them, come and take them, my child!

115 Long-lived one, my whole body is tormented by your appearance. Enjoy a long and happy life! Come quickly, and delight Sunandā!

116 You are my very god, my son, my life. I'm in distress; revitalize me with your embrace!

117 Don't disappoint me, in front of all these people, or else my heart will be like a slice of boiled cucumber.

118 Come, my child of swan-like gait, decorate my lap! I have not received my payment for your lodging in my womb for such a long time!'

119 But even though he was enticed by these toys, these various kinds of sweet, and these coaxing words, her son made not one step towards Sunandā.

120 Vajra was intelligent. He knew that no man would be able to repay the debt incurred by his mother's benefits. He thought:

121 'If I disobey the congregation through pity for my mother, then I shall be bound in the cycle of death and rebirth for an extremely long time.

122 But she, my good mother, having incurred only a small amount of karma, will become a Jain nun. Her distress at my disobedience will be only temporary.'

123 Vajra was far-sighted. Having thus deliberated, he was as firm as adamant in his decision. He was like a statue; he did not take the smallest step from the place where he was.

124 The king said, 'Give way now, Sunandā. This child has not obeyed your summons, as if he did not recognize you as his mother.'

125 Then the king told Dhanagiri to take his turn. He laid down his broom, and said simply:

126 'If it is your intention to take the vows of a Jain monk, and if you yourself know the true nature of reality, stainless one, then take my broom, the banner of the Jain religion.'

127 Vajra immediately stretched out his hand like a young elephant stretching out its trunk, and quickly ran towards Dhanagiri, while making a gurgling sound.

128 The pure-minded child ran and climbed into his father's lap, grasping the broom, as if it were a beautiful lotus.

129 Vajra raised the broom in his lotus-hands. It shone like the royal fly-whisk of the majesty of the Jain teachings.

130 He smiled, his teeth flashing bright rays like bouncing jasmine blossoms, as he held aloft the broom. He did not lay it down even for a second.

131 Sunandā immediately drooped like a lotus in the evening. She put her hand to her chin, and thought:

132 'My brother has become a monk, and my husband has become a monk. My son will become a monk. Therefore, I shall become a nun.

133 I don't have a brother, I don't have a husband, and now I don't even have a son. So it will be better for me to renounce the world than to remain in my house.'

134 Having made this decision of her own accord, Sunandā returned home, and the monks took Vajra and returned to their lodgings.

135 Thinking, 'Vajra is so desirous of taking his vows that he has not even drunk milk, although he is so young,' the Teacher initiated him, and handed him over once more to the nuns.

136 Her special destiny led Sunandā to become extremely disgusted with worldly existence. She became a nun in the presence of the Teacher's followers.

137 Reverend holy Vajra was an ocean of intelligence. He easily learnt the eleven Limbs from the nuns as they recited them.

138 After Vajra had lived for eight years with the nuns, they handed him over to the joyful monks, and Vajra stayed with them in their lodgings.

139 One day, as Vajra and the Teacher and his followers were travelling to Avanti, an unbroken torrent of rain began to pour from the clouds.

140 Vajra and the Teacher and his followers sheltered in a place adjacent to a Yakṣa's shrine where the rain was not falling.

141 Then some Yawning gods* who had been friends of Vajra in his previous life, came to that place, and transformed themselves into merchants in order to test Vajra's character.

144b Those gods in the guise of merchants created a camp.

142 There were reined and saddled stallions, a herd of wandering camels, a circle of wagons, and a marqueed encampment.

143 There was a series of sacks of goods for sale covered by awnings. There were vessels full of ready-cooked food, and a throng of people eating it.

144a There were workmen moving around with upper garments made of grass.

145 When the rain had almost ceased, the gods courteously invited the Teacher to come and receive alms from them.

146 The Teacher knew that it had stopped raining, so he sent Vajra, who blazed with reverence for his seniors, to collect the alms.

147 Vajra finished performing his religious duties, and, in company with another monk, set off walking, thinking that he would be able to go without harming living creatures on the way.

148 But Vajra saw a thin mist of rain. Even though the rain was as fine as motes of dust passing through a sunbeam, he immediately turned back, lest he injure the water-bodies.

149 The gods put an end to that rain that was only as fine as motes of dust passing through a sunbeam, and called Vajra again, telling him that the rain had stopped.

150 Vajra set off once more when the rain had stopped and arrived at that bazaar, resplendent with the food, drink, and the other goods.

151 As the gods bustled about, inviting him to accept the food and the other things, Vajra inspected the goods, considering the place, the time, and their appearance:

152 'How can these pumpkins and the other goods be produced from nothing? And this place which looks like the city of Ujjayinī is really a barren waste.

153 What can one say of such produce at the start of the rainy season? What's more, the eyes of the donors do not blink, and their feet do not touch the ground.

154 This food is being offered by the gods, so it is definitely not fit for monks; that's the rule. So I shall return to the Teacher, without accepting the food.'

155 Vajra said this, and left without accepting their alms. The gods revealed themselves before him, wondering at his behaviour, and said:

156 'We are Yawning gods, your friends in your previous life. We came to see you, even though you are no longer our companion.'

157 Then those gods, delighted with Vajra, gave him the spell called 'Assuming Transformations', as if in recompense for the illusion they had produced.

158 One Summer's day, Vajra was travelling in the country, when those gods appeared to him once more in the guise of traders, and offered him boiled sweets.

159 Vajra went to their bazaar, but as before knew that the food was being offered by gods, and did not accept it. He was by no means bereft of discrimination.

160 The gods were very pleased with Vajra, their former friend, and gave him the spell for flying through the air. Then they returned to their own place.

161 While Vajra was living among the monks, he learnt by heart the eleven Limbs, by means of his power of remembering what he had once heard.

162 Whenever reverend Vajra, foremost of the intelligent, heard such teachings as the Preliminary Statements recited,* he remembered them.

163 But whenever the elders asked him to recite, Vajra would make a mumbling sound, as if he were half asleep.

164 Fearing that the elders would prevent him from listening, he did not reveal his powers, but would just mumble something, and listen, with averted face, to the person reciting.

165 At noon one day the monks went to seek alms, and the Teacher also went to another place.

166 Vajra remained behind on his own to look after the monks' dwelling place. He arranged the monks' cushions in a circle.

167 He sat in the centre, like a Teacher in the centre of his pupils, and began to expound the teachings in a voice like a thundercloud in the rainy season.

168 The Teacher returned, and from a distance heard Vajra reciting the eleven Limbs and the Preliminary Statements.

169 The Teacher listened to the loud voice from the doorway of the dwelling, and thought, 'The monks must have come back very quickly!

170 They have collected their alms, and have gathered together to await my arrival by reciting the teachings.'

171 When the Teacher found out what was really happening, he paused for a moment, and thought, 'This sound of recitation is being produced by the voice of the child-monk Vajra alone!

172 He's reciting the Preliminary Statements and the eleven Limbs; did he learn them in his mother's womb? I'm amazed!

173 Whenever the elders asked him to recite, he did it very lazily, and knowing that children are prone to be lazy in recitation, we let him be.'

174 The Teacher, thrilled with the capacity of his pupil, went away, lest Vajra be worried or embarrassed by his overhearing him.

175 Then the Teacher made a loud noise to warn of his arrival. Vajra heard the noise, and jumped from his seat.

176 Vajra hurriedly made sure that all the cushions were returned to their proper place when the Teacher came in.

177 Vajra went to the Teacher, took his staff, and wiped his feet, showing high veneration to their dust, while concealing his own splendour.

178 Then, while the Teacher sat in his chair, Vajra washed his feet with warm water, bowing to the dirty water with his head.

179 The Teacher thought, 'This child is great-souled. He is very well versed in the essence of the religious teachings. He must be protected from disrespect by being placed in a position of authority.

180 The other monks are unaware of this child's greatness, so I'll make sure that they do not treat him with disrespect.'

181 In the evening, the Teacher told his pupils that he was going to a certain village, and that he would stay there for two or three days.

182 The monks were taken in by the stratagem, and asked the Teacher, 'Reverend sir, who will be our instructor?'

183 The Teacher told them that Vajra would instruct them. The monks did not quibble. They agreed to it, because of their devotion to their Teacher.

184 The monks placed Vajra in the centre chair, and stood in a motionless position as he expounded the scriptures and led them in the morning acts of devotion.

185 Because Vajra had taken the centre chair at the command of the Teacher, the monks treated him with the respect due to a Teacher.

186 Then Vajra gave a lesson to all the monks. It was clear in its orderly articulation, and was like adamantine cement in the way in which it was retained by the students.

187 Even the monks who were not very bright began to learn the holy teachings, since they were able to understand Vajra's explanations.

188 Vajra's teaching was effective even for the extremely stupid. The monks were all amazed at the young prodigy.

189 Although the lessons had previously been given in a very lucid fashion, when the monks asked Vajra to explain their meaning in private conversation, he did so very gladly.

190 The monks learnt as much from one of Vajra's lessons as they would from several lessons given by the Teacher.

191 The monks said to each other, 'If our Teacher stays away any longer, Vajra will soon teach us all the holy teachings.'
192 The monks considered Vajra to be superior to their Teacher in his qualities. For a group of monks rejoices in the good qualities of one initiated by the same Teacher.
193 The Teacher thought, 'During these few days my followers will certainly have learnt of Vajra's qualities.
194 Whatever new subject I ask Vajra to teach, his pupils learn and master it, because of Vajra's outstanding qualities as an instructor.'
195 The Teacher returned on the appointed day, and Vajra and the monks bowed before his feet.
196 The Teacher asked, 'Did you perform your recitation?', and the monks replied, 'Yes, thanks to you, divine Teacher.'
197 The pupils bowed once more to the Teacher, and said, 'At your command, Vajra taught us the holy teachings.
198 For a long time we treated Vajra with disrespect, because we did not know his qualities, but now we respect the child, just as we respect your worship's feet.
199 Let the child be the instructor of this group of monks, for he is endowed with the qualities of a teacher. The light of the moon, even when it has waned to its thinnest crescent, will illuminate a house.'
200 The Teacher said, 'This will be done, you oceans of asceticism. However, he must not be treated with disrespect. Although he is a child, he is fully grown in learning.
201 I went to that village and appointed him your instructor for that very reason: so that you would come to know his excellent qualities.
202 Nevertheless, he is not yet worthy to be your instructor in the holy teachings, since he learned them by overhearing the Teacher as he was expounding them.
203 If he learns in regular succession the teachings which he learnt section by section, then he will certainly be fit to be an instructor of the holy teachings.'
204 Then the wise Teacher quickly taught Vajra the teachings which had been previously unrecited together with their explanations.
205 The Teacher was merely an onlooker, for Vajra learnt all the

teachings which were presented to him as easily as if he were looking in a mirror.

206 When Vajra was as learned as his Teacher, he became like a hammer for breaking the clods of long-held doubts.

207 He learnt by heart as much of the Disputation about Views as his Teacher knew, as easily as if he were lapping water.

208 One day, while wandering from village to village and from town to town, the Teacher and his followers came to the city of Daśapura.

209 The Teacher thought, 'Now there is a Teacher in the city of Ujjayinī who knows ten Original Collections of Teachings in their entirety. These ten Original Collections of Teachings can be learnt from him.

210 Although my pupils know the eleven Limbs, they only learnt them with great difficulty. How can they possibly master the ten Original Collections of Teachings?

211 Oh, I remember! There's Vajra! There's no need to worry like this, for I have absolute confidence in his ability to learn them by heart.'

212 So the Teacher ordered Vajra, 'Go to Ujjayinī, my son, and there learn the ten Original Collections of Teachings from the Teacher Bhadragupta.

213 All your pupils are extremely stupid. They will be unable to learn there, since they are dull witted even here with me.

214 Go quickly and learn the ten Original Collections of Teachings, obedient to my command. May the gods of learning favour you.

215 Then, let the ten Original Collections of Teachings pour from your mouth onto the monks, as water from a well is poured onto an orchard.'

216 Thereupon, Siṃhagiri sent Vajra to Avanti, together with two other monks, so that a regular course of ascetic life would be maintained.

217 Vajra honoured his Teacher Siṃhagiri's command as highly as if it were an offering. He went to the city of Ujjayinī, which was being purified by the feet of Bhadragupta.

218 At the auspicious moment at which Sunandā's son arrived at Ujjayinī, the Teacher Bhadragupta had a dream.

219 'A stranger took from my hand my bowl, which was full of milk, and drank from it, quenching his thirst.'

220 Thus, in the morning the Teacher narrated his dream to his pupils, and they gave various interpretations of it, each according to his own understanding.

221 The Teacher said, 'A previously unknown guest will come. He will be very intelligent, and will learn from me all the holy teachings, together with their explanations.'

222 Vajra had spent the night on the outskirts of the city. In the morning he went to the Teacher Bhadragupta's dwelling place.

223 When the Teacher saw Vajra coming, it was like when the ocean sees the moon; the Teacher beamed with the reflection of their mutual joy.

224 The Teacher thought, 'Ah, his intelligence is my blessing! Should I embrace him and place him in my lap?

225 This Vajra surpasses the appearance of a diamond in his attainments!' The great monk Bhadragupta decided to do it.

226 Bhadragupta embraced Vajra as he was about to pay his respects. Longing for a loved one by no means waits on good manners, no doubt about it.

227 The Teacher Bhadragupta placed Vajra on his lap and spoke to him. The Teacher's eyes were like bees humming round the lotus of Vajra's face.

228 'I hope that your wanderings have been pleasant, I hope that your body is free from pain, I hope that your practice of asceticism has been unimpeded, and I hope that you abound in well-being.

229 Please tell us, diamond-monk, why you have chosen to delight us by coming here in the course of your wanderings.'

230 Vajra bowed to Bhadragupta, his hands folded in respectful greeting. He laid aside the piece of cloth which covered his mouth, and said:

231 'All the things your reverence has asked me about—were my wanderings pleasant and the other questions—are just as you graciously wished, divine Teacher.

232 I have come to you at the command of my Teacher to learn the ten Original Collections of Teachings. So, reverend sir, please favour me by expounding the holy teachings to me.'

233 So Bhadragupta began to teach the ten Original Collections of

Teachings, and Vajra learnt them without causing any difficulties for his instructor.

234 Thinking, 'I must take leave to return to the place where I began my studies,' Vajra decided to return to the presence of Siṃhagiri.

235 So he took his leave of Bhadragupta and returned to Daśapura, retaining the ten Original Collections of Teachings in his memory, like a cloud retaining water.

236 When Vajra, who was like a swallower of the ocean of the ten Original Collections of Teachings, returned, the Teacher Siṃhagiri commanded him to teach them.

237 Thereupon, the Yawning gods celebrated Vajra's teaching of the Original Collections of Teachings by showering down a rain of heavenly flowers.

238 The Teacher Siṃhagiri handed over his monastic following to Vajra. He then abstained from food and drink, died, and became a god.

239 After that, reverend Vajra wandered the earth with an entourage of five hundred monks, a moon whose light illuminated beings who were capable of enlightenment.

240 The great monk Vajra purified the earth by his wanderings, and everywhere he went, the people said:

241 'Ah, his moral conduct is splendid! Ah, his learning is superhuman! Ah, his grace is faultless! Ah, his beauty is wondrous!'

242 Now in the city of Pāṭalīputra lived a very rich merchant named Dhana, famed throughout the world for his distinguished qualities.

243 He had a beautiful daughter named Rukmiṇī. Like Rukmiṇī herself,* she was also endowed with inner beauty.

244 The nuns who were obedient to the great monk holy Vajra used to lodge in that merchant's wagon shed, stainless in their moral conduct.

245 The nuns used to sing hymns praising Vajra, for hymning the praises of their Teacher is a daily duty of monks and nuns.

246 When Rukmiṇī heard these various stories about Vajra's charm and beauty, she decided that Vajra alone would be her husband. She made this vow:

247 'If Vajra becomes my husband, then I'll enjoy sexual pleasures. Otherwise, I'll have done with them. What use are sexual pleasures without a husband?'

248 Whenever suitors approached her, she repelled them, as easily as if she were repelling mosquitoes.

249 The nuns said to her, 'You're foolish, Rukmiṇī, for wanting to marry Vajra. He is a monk, and he is free from passion.'

250 Rukmiṇī replied, 'If Vajra is a monk, then I'll become a nun. His way of life will be mine as well.'

251 Now at that time, reverend Vajra, a rain cloud full of the waters of the teaching of religion, came in the course of his wanderings to Pāṭalīputra.

252 The king of Pāṭalīputra heard that Vajra was coming, and went to see him, accompanied by an entourage of great magnificence.

253 Everywhere the king looked, he saw multitudes of Vajra's monks, radiant in the splendour of their asceticism.

254 And when he saw them, he thought, 'They all abound in splendour, they all have pleasant expressions, they all have beaming faces.

255 They all speak pleasantly, they are all oceans full of the waters of compassion, they all receive equal respect, and they are all free from thoughts of self.

256 I don't know which of them is Vajra. What shall I do? He is the one to whom I should first pay my respects, for he is the leader of the monks.'

257 So he stopped for a moment and asked the monks, 'Is this man Vajra or is it he or he?'

258 The monks said, 'We are his pupils, your majesty. Don't look for him among us. How can the sun be compared to glow-worms?'

259 In this way the king asked a multitude of monks. Then he saw Vajra, looking like a diamond for the rock of delusion, standing behind the other monks.

260 The king bowed to venerable Vajra, as if bathing Vajra's feet with the rays of light from his jewelled diadem.

261 Sunandā's son, the Teacher, held a preaching assembly in a park, and, surrounded by his disciples, sat in the shade of a tree.

262 Then the king knelt before Vajra's couch and anointed his feet with a fragrant perfumed unguent.

263 Then reverend Vajra, in a voice as sweet as honey, preached a sermon, an excellent lamp for the dispersal of the gloom of delusion.

264 The king's mind was set on drinking this flow of nectar, and his heart was absolutely charmed by holy lord Vajra's teaching of the Jain religion.

265 When the sermon was over, the king returned to his palace. He went to the royal women's apartments, and told the queens:

266 'Lord Vajra is staying in a park in the suburbs, lovely-browed ones. I've just been to pay my respects to that ocean of the milk of religious teaching.

267 Now that they have bowed to him, seen him, and heard his preaching, my legs, eyes, and ears have accomplished their purpose.

268 This day alone I consider to be a real day, beautiful-eyed ones, on which I have seen the sun of the monk Vajra's knowledge.

269 Vajra seems so much richer than I, since from his mouth I have heard the teaching of the Jain religion.

270 You too should go to see the monk Vajra, my queens. Go quickly! Monks are like the wind; they don't stay in one place.'

271 The queens said, 'We are very eager to pay our respects to him, ourselves. Even your command to do this is like a river reached by thirsting people.'

272 The queens took their leave of the king, climbed into their palanquins, and went to the park which was ornamented by Vajra's presence.

273 Rukmiṇī too learnt of Vajra's arrival from the talk of the people. She stood and thought of him only, like a yogic ascetic contemplating her self.

274 The following day Rukmiṇī said to her father, 'Vajra has come here; he's the one I've always wanted to marry.

275 So betroth me to the young man Vajra, father, otherwise death will be my refuge. This declaration of mine is like an engraving on a rock.

276 Abandoning modesty, the companion of nobility, I declare that the reason Vajra has come here is because of my merits.

277 He does not usually remain in one place, and if he does leave, no one knows when he will return again, as with a bird flying up into the sky.

278 Don't delay, father. Betroth me to Vajra! Don't you feel distress to see me pine with love for so long?'

279 Dhana was prevailed up by her perseverance to betroth her to Vajra. Straightaway, he bedecked her with all the ornaments required to be worn at a marriage.

280 Dhana was intelligent. With his daughter he took riches worth tens of millions as an inducement for her prospective husband.

281 The previous day Vajra had given a sermon. The devoted citizens said to each other:

282 'Oh, the eloquence of Vajra! It's as if a state of final emancipation is produced in the people who are sunk in joy at hearing the preaching of the Jain religion.

283 Holy lord Vajra is an ocean of every pearl-like virtue. If his appearance were to conform to his qualities, what would it be like?'

284 On entering the city, Vajra had used his magic powers to diminish his natural appearance, lest it agitate the citizens.

285 Vajra knew what the citizens were thinking and saying through his excellent powers of perception.

286 The following day, Vajra, who had many magic powers, created a lotus with a thousand petals. It was like a lotus-throne.

287 Reverend Vajra sat upon the lotus, and revealed his true appearance. He looked like a benevolent king.

288 When the people saw Vajra's true appearance, like that of a young god, they shook their heads, as if performing a singing exercise.

289 The people said, 'Vajra's natural physical appearance certainly corresponds to that of his virtues, and today they were fittingly united.

290 Worried lest he agitate us, he must have used his magic powers to set aside his splendid natural appearance and make it look ordinary.'

291 The king was full of amazement. He exclaimed, 'The monk Vajra has the power to transform his appearance to anything he wishes!'

292 When the merchant Dhana saw lord Vajra's appearance, he knew why his daughter had set her mind on marrying him.

293 Dhana was intent on making his request, and the meaning of

Vajra's teaching had not settled in his heart, but had passed over it, like spreading water.

294 When the sermon was over, the merchant Dhana folded his hands in respectful greetings, and said, 'Oblige me by marrying my daughter, you god of love.

295 How can this human worm be compared with the godlike appearance of your worship? Nevertheless, please marry her. A request to the great is never made in vain.

296 Immediately after the marriage, Vajra, at the time when you release each other's hands, I shall give you countless tens of millions. Come, agree to it.'

297 Vajra knew that he was ignorant. He smiled and said compassionately, 'Enough of your tens of millions, and enough of your daughter.

298 Beautiful-hipped women are certainly objects of sensual enjoyment, but they are like poison, sweet for the moment, but extremely bitter in the ripeness of time.

299 Sensual pleasures are much worse than poison, since they cause the rebirth of embodied beings, their purpose unachieved.

300 Knowing that sensual pleasures have a bad outcome, how could I agree? Even a weak man is not able to be captured by robbers whom he has previously noticed.

301 If your daughter is firmly resolved in her attachment to me, then let her receive from my hands initiation as a Jain nun.

302 If your daughter's heart desires me only, then she should do this, through her desire to be destined for the other world.

303 Let her obey my command, and with proper judgement, let her receive initiation, which leads to the gaining of final emancipation.

304 Don't let your daughter become attached to sensual pleasures. They produce nothing of value, like the shade of the Vibhītaka tree. I speak for her well-being.'

305 Rukmiṇī's karma was very light, and she was enlightened by reverend Lord Vajra's charming words. She took initiation as a Jain nun.

306 Thinking, 'This is the religion that is the best in which there is such a lack of covetousness as this,' many other people were also converted.

307–8 One day, holy Lord Vajra, who had possessed from birth the power of remembering what he had once heard, extracted from the Great Knowledge section of the Behaviour Rules a spell to enable him fly through the air, because he wished to benefit the holy congregation.*

309 Reverend Vajra said, 'With this spell I have the power of flying from Rose-apple Tree Island to the furthest island inhabited by human beings.

310 I must retain this spell, and not give it to anyone else, for in the future others will be lacking in accomplishments and strength of character.'

311 One day, the great monk holy Vajra went to the northern regions, as the sun, when it passes from Saggitarius to Capricorn, turns from the South to the North.

312 At that time, there was a dreadful famine in those parts, and the people were distressed by the dearth of food.

313 Because of their shortage of food, the householders only made very small meals, so everyday they suffered from unfilled bellies, as if they were monks.

314 The householders and the rulers closed down the shelters and the places where they offered hospitality. Everywhere, the earth seemed filled with incessant howls of lamentation.

315 Half-starved beggars like dogs lapped tiny drops of milk on the ground where vessels of milk had been placed for sale.

316 Beggars, their bodies mere remnants of skin and bone, the tracks of their veins clearly visible, wandered everywhere, like frightful ghosts.

317 When the monks came seeking alms, the laypeople, in their desire to keep their food, offered them food that was unacceptable.

318 Everywhere, the villages were deserted. No smoke came from the houses. There were no travellers walking on the roads.

319 The entire congregation was languishing because of the famine. Feeling great distress, the monks said to the monk who was Sunandā's son:

320 'Remove us by some means from this ocean of distress. It is not sinful to use magic for the benefit of the congregation.'

321 So reverend Vajra used his powerful magic spell to create

an extensive carpet, like the king who made a magic leather purse.*

322 Then, on holy Vajra's instructions, the entire congregation stepped onto the wide carpet, like a company of merchants stepping onto a boat.

323 Through the power of the reverend monk Vajra's magic spell, the carpet flew up into the sky, as if it were being wafted up by the wind.

324 Just then, a man named Datta, who had been the great monk Vajra's host, came by seeking water.

325 When he saw Vajra and the congregation flying through the sky, he immediately tore out his hair, and said:

326 'I have been your host, and now I have become your fellow believer also. Why don't you rescue me?'

327 When Vajra heard his host's reproachful words and saw his plucked-out hair, he remembered a commentary on the holy teachings:

328 Those who are intent on showing affection to fellow believers, those who are intent on studying the teachings, and those who are intent on promoting the Jain religion, should all be rescued by a monk.'

329 Having remembered this comment on the holy teachings, Lord Vajra also placed that excellent host on the carpet.

330 As they flew through the air on the magic carpet, they looked down upon the earth with its mountains, oceans, and cities. It was as clear as a myrobalan fruit lying in one's hand.

331 As he passed, Vajra was worshipped by the Interstitial gods, who bowed in devotion. The devoted Stellar gods gave him a respectful welcome to the sky.

332 He was praised by the masters of magic, who were astonished by his magic powers, and embraced as a friend by the Wind.

333 He provided comfort for the denizens of the earth with the shade of the carpet, which seemed like the shade of a cloud, and, although he was in the sky, paid his respects to many Jain temples as he passed.

334 Although he was on a flying carpet, he continued to expound the holy teachings to the other monks on the carpet. At length he landed in a big city called Purī.

335 Food was easy to obtain in that city in which there was an abundance of wealth and grain. Most of the citizens were Jain laypeople, but the king favoured the Buddhists.

336 In that city, the Jains and the Buddhists vied with each other in making their temple offerings, but the Jains outdid the Buddhists.

337 Whenever the Jains saw some flowers or plants that would be appropriate for their temple worship, they would buy them up at their market price.

338 So, since the Buddhists were unable to offer flowers and plants, the offerings in their holy places were very meagre.

339 The Buddhist laypeople were ashamed. They informed the king, who was a Buddhist devotee, and induced him to prevent the Jains from buying up all the flowers.

340 Although they offered large sums of money in all the flower markets, the Jain laypeople were then not even able to obtain flower stalks.

341 The Abiding festival was at hand. Weeping, their faces downcast, the Jain laypeople went to see the monk Vajra.

342 The Jain laypeople, wetting the earth with the tears from their eyes, bowed to Vajra, and said to him, in voices indistinct with depression:

343 'We have been outdone by the Buddhists, who are unable to bear seeing flowers in the Jain temples. They are like wicked ghosts.

344 The Buddhist laypeople have induced the Buddhist king to prevent the florist from selling us any flowers.

345 We cannot even obtain wild mountain flowers. What are we to do? Although we are rich, no one is willing to transgress the king's orders.

346 The images of the Jinas are receiving unworthy offerings of grass and shrubs, as if they were village Yakṣas! Alas, what point is there in our living!

347 The Buddhists were very anxious to use some trick to prevent us from offering flowers to the Jinas, and now we cannot even obtain artificial flowers made from hair and cloth.

348 Master, are we not constantly counting the days to the Abiding festival, that most excellent of days?

349 When the day of the Abiding festival comes, how can we make

offerings to the Jinas as befits devotees, if we are deprived of flowers?

350 Continually outwitted by these malevolent Buddhists, we are like living dead, even though we have you as our leader.

351 The Jain religion has been humiliated. Make a display of its power, reverend sir. You are able to make us live again.'

352 Saying, 'Take heart, you faithful believers! I shall obtain great glory for you,' reverend Vajra flew up into the air like an eagle.

353 In a twinkling of an eye, Lord Vajra came to the city of Māheśvarī, the consort of the god Śiva, and landed in a garden full of wonderful produce.

354 The garden belonged to the god named Oblation-eater, the god of fire, but in it was the gardener, who was a friend of Dhanagiri.

355 The gardener, whose name was Lightning, saw Vajra descending from the sky like rain without a cloud, and said with joy:

356 'This is the most blessed of auspicious days on which you have come as my guest. I consider myself blessed that you have remembered me.

357 Thank heaven! Your coming as my guest has provided food for my mind, like an auspicious dream. What guest service can I do for you?'

358 Lord Vajra said, 'Let me have as many flowers as you are able to give me, gardener.'

359 The gardener said, 'Oblige me by taking the flowers, for two million bloom here every day.'

360 Reverend Vajra said, 'Arrange the flowers while I go from here and return, gardener.'

361 Having said that, the noble monk Vajra flew up like the wind who rides on a piebald horse, and went through the sky to the lower range of the Himalayas.

365b From the sky, Vajra, like another sun, looked down upon the Himalayas,

362 where the gods' elephants were engaged in playing in the waters of the river Ganges; where the delightful lotus lake looked like the tenth vessel of nectar;*

363 adorned with the resorts of holy sages and gods; where herds of deer followed the What-people goddesses,* attracted by their singing;

364 which had the beauty of twilight clouds through their earth which contained many minerals, whose caverns were reverberating with the bellows of the crazy wandering yaks;

365a whose slopes were burdened with Nameru, Birch, Tagara, and Kimpāka trees.

366 Vajra bowed to the images of the future Worthies in the caves of the holy sages, while his feet were bowed to by the masters of magic.

369 At length, the monk Vajra arrived by way of the sky at the lotus lake, where the goddesses hymn the abode of the goddess of Prosperity.

367 There, the lotuses are performing in a dance with the ripples as their stage; the wind is sluggish as if through bearing the fragrance of the lotuses;

368 and the water is beautified by being made a receptacle for the petals from the lotus flowers, which are blown by the faces of the water nymphs, so that it looks as if it is flowing with lotuses.

370 Then Prosperity, having plucked a lotus with which to worship the gods, saw Vajra as she was on the way to their residence.

371 Prosperity immediately bowed to the princely monk, as if she was bathing his feet with the light from the jewels in her tiara.

372 As the monk stood there, Prosperity expressed a wish to receive religious instruction, and asked what she could do for him, her hands folded in respectful greeting.

373 Reverend Vajra said, 'This is my command to you, lotus-hued one. Give me the lotus which you are holding in your lotus-hand.'

374 Prosperity said, 'Even though this bloom you want has grown in Indra's garden, I am able to give it to you,' and handed him the lotus.

375 Prosperity bowed to Vajra, and he immediately flew up in the air, and returned to Oblation-eater's garden, by the way that he had come.

376 Reverend Vajra used his magic to create a heavenly carriage, like another version of Indra's. It was adorned with various magic powers.

377 In the centre of the carriage he placed the lotus given him by Prosperity, and around it he arranged the two million flowers.

378 Then he remembered the Yawning gods, and they instantly appeared in attendance upon Vajra, who looked like a diamond.
379 The monk, Dhanagiri's son, sat beneath the lotus, as if beneath a parasol, and ordered the carriage to fly through the air.
380 As the carriage flew, the Yawning gods climbed into their own vehicles, and proceeded to the sound of singing and music.
381 Accompanied by these gods in their heavenly vehicles, Vajra arrived at the city named Purī, where the wicked Buddhists lived.
382 When the Buddhist inhabitants of that city saw the heavenly carriages in the sky, they gazed up at them, as if they were preparing to jump. They said:
383 'Ah, the gods have seen the power of the Buddhist religion, and have come to worship the Buddha! Veneration to the Buddha! Veneration to the Buddha!'
384 But as they were saying this, Vajra headed for the Jain temple, and by means of the heavenly vehicles displayed the wealth of the city of the heavenly musicians.
385 Then the Buddhists, as if they had wiped soot from their eyes, thought, 'Oh, this divine manifestation is for the Jain religion!
386 We thought one thing, but another thing happens to be the case.' Then the heaps of flowers were displayed for all to see, held aloft by the wind.
387 Then the gods celebrated the Abiding festival with wonderful festivity, in a way that is not attainable by human beings.
388 When the king and his subjects saw the Yawning gods perform this divine ceremony of worship in honour of the holy Worthy, they abandoned the Buddhist religion, and became Jain laypeople.

Here finishes the twelfth canto of the scholar-monk Hemacandra's epic poem, the Appendix, or Lives of the Jain Elders. In it were related Lord Vajra's birth, renunciation, and magic powers.

CANTO THIRTEEN

The topics of Canto Thirteen are the further gradual diminution of the knowlege of the Original Collections of Teachings, Vajra's death, and the subsequent spread of his lineage of pupillary succession.

1–40 In Daśapura lived Āryarakṣita, a Brahmin's son, who went away to study the sacred teachings of the Brahmins. He became profoundly learned, and on his return he was welcomed with great pomp and festivity by everyone except his mother, who was a Jain laywoman. On being told by his mother that his learning was useless and that he should study the teachings of the Jains, he resolved to find a Jain Teacher.

41–141 Āryarakṣita left home and was initiated by a Jain Teacher, and learnt as much of the teachings as his Teacher knew. He then decided to study the Original Collections of Teachings with Vajra, who knew ten of them. He learnt nine and part of the tenth before he was prevailed upon by his brother to return home, where he converted the king, and his parents and many of his relatives became Jain monks and nuns.

142–79 Signs of incipient loss of memory prompted Vajra to abandon his life. At that time there was a famine, and Vajra took his troop of monks to a mountain, where, prompted by the example of a novice monk, they fasted to death. With Vajra, the fourth section of the tenth Original Collection of Teachings was lost.

180–200 Vajrasena, Vajra's pupil, went to Sopāra, where there was a dreadful famine. Vajrasena successfully predicted its alleviation to the family of a Jain laywoman who were on the verge of poisoning themselves. The laywoman and her relatives became Jain ascetics.

201–3 The lineage of pupillary sucession headed by Vajra flourished and spread in all directions.

1 Now King Audrāyaṇa was ruling in the city of Daśapura. There lived a Brahmin named Somadeva and his wife Rudrasomā.

2 The Brahmin's wife Rudrasomā had become a Jain laywoman. She was adorned with such virtues as compassion, which are the seeds of the tree of religion.

3 They had two sons who were endowed with prudent conduct.

The elder was named Āryarakṣita and the younger Phalgurakṣita.

4 Ever since his investiture with the sacred thread, Āryarakṣita had studied with his father, and had learnt everything his father knew.

5 Then Āryarakṣita received his parents' permission to go to Pāṭalīputra in order to further his studies there.

6 There he learned the four Vedas, the six Limbs of the Vedas, the manual of Enquiry philosophy, the manual of Analysis philosophy, the Tales of Yore, and the Codification of Law.* He was singularly intelligent.

7 When he was able to recite these fourteen branches of knowledge as readily as his own name, he returned to Daśapura.

8 The king thought, 'This man has returned after learning the four Vedas; he must be honoured,' so he ordered that he be escorted into the city while mounted on an elephant.

9 The people thronged him, holding various presents in their hands. No one fails to honour a person who is honoured by a king.

10 Then Āryarakṣita entered the courtyard of his home, giving fresh joy, like a respectful present, to his family.

11 When his relatives saw this treasury of sacred knowledge being honoured by the king, they considered him to be the purifier of their family.

12 The archway at the entrance to his home had been gaily decorated by his servants. It looked like a play swing made ready for long-awaited Prosperity.

13 The women of the household painted the house with luck-bringing svastikas, which were like the letters of a hymn of praise proclaiming Āryarakṣita's excellence.

14 Āryarakṣita remained outside his home for a few days longer, and was made a rich man by the numerous people who came to present him with gifts.

15 Āryarakṣita's thoughts were pure. One day, he thought, 'Ah, I must not neglect to pay my respects to my mother today!

16 Women's life-breath lives outside them in the form of their children. The sorrow which living abroad produces in the children certainly produces sorrow in them also.

17 What effect will my absence have had upon my mother, who

even in her sleep constantly pronounces the syllables of my name?

18 That fortitude of my mother is absolutely remarkable, she who sent me abroad for the sake of my well-being!

19 When I show her my prosperity, the roots of whose obtainment lay in her virtue, I shall gladden my mother, who will be an ocean full of the waters of affection!'

20 Āryarakṣita straightaway put on heavenly garments, and annointed his handsome body with unguents from Kashmir.

21 His hair was bound with garlands of fragrant flowers, and tinkling ornaments were placed around his neck, arms, and ankles.

22 His breath was freshened with betel mixed with flakes of camphor, and his head was shaded by a lucky white parasol. Thus attired, he went to his home.

23 He was well mannered. The first thing he did was to bow to his mother's feet. As he did so, the gold chain hanging from his neck touched the ground.

24 But like a neighbour his mother merely said, 'Welcome back, young man. May you have a long life, free from pain,' and nothing more.

25 Since he did not receive from his mother the usual kind reception accompanied by those words with which she was accustomed to show the strength of her affection for her son, he said:

26 'I have come to pay my respects to you, having mastered all the branches of learning. Why don't you greet me in a way that does not transgress the rules of affectionate behaviour?

27 The king himself has honoured me, as if I were his Teacher. Are you not thrilled to behold the greatness of your son?'

28 Rudrasomā said, 'What use is this acquisition of learning of yours? For this is the knowledge that teaches harmful violence and leads to hell.

29 I'm sunk in depression, like a cow sunk in mire, to see you, who were born from my womb, on the verge of falling into hell.

30 If you love me, and if you consider me well disposed towards you, then study the Disputation about Views,* for it leads to heaven and final emancipation.'

31 Then Āryarakṣita thought, 'What is this knowledge that I have learnt? If it does not delight my mother, what use is the wealth that it produces?'

32 Having thus reflected, noble-minded Āryarakṣita said to his mother, 'I shall study the Disputation about Views, Mother. Tell me who teaches it.'

33 Rudrasomā said, 'You must become a lay follower of the Jain monks, my child. Only the Jain monks teach the Disputation about Views, not the other sorts.'

34 Because the Disputation about Views is a consideration of the teachings, its very name seemed auspicious to Āryarakṣita. Faith was produced in his heart.

35 He said, 'A mother's command must be obeyed. But where can I find a teacher with whom I can study?'

36 Rudrasomā was cheered by her son's respectful obedience. Fluttering the edge of his garment, full of gracious affection, she said to him:

37 'Now I no longer feel shamed by you, my son, since you are ready to follow my instructions which are my heart's desire.

38 Āryarakṣita, there is a Teacher named Tosaliputra. He is now staying in my sugar plantation.

39 Be like a swan worshipping the lotus of his feet, and he will teach you the Disputation about Views, my son.'

40 Āryarakṣita promised that he would do so first thing in the morning, and during that night did nothing but think about the name Disputation about Views.

41 In the morning, Āryarakṣita took his leave of his mother. He was like the one born in a jar;* he was intelligent enough to drink the ocean of the Disputation about Views as easily as drinking a mouthful of water.

42 In a neighbouring village lived an important Brahmin who was a friend of Āryarakṣita's father and was like a father to Āryarakṣita.

43 He thought, 'I did not visit Āryarakṣita yesterday. Today, I must go and visit my friend's venerable son.'

44 So the important Brahmin took nine complete sticks of sugar cane and part of another, and went to Āryarakṣita's house.

45 He saw Somadeva's eldest son coming from his house, but did not recognize him in the twilight.

46 He asked Āryarakṣita in a loud voice, 'Who goes there?', and Āryarakṣita replied, 'It's Āryarakṣita.'

47 The Brahmin said, 'Nephew, I was prevented from seeing you yesterday by family business.

48 Each day on which I do not see you seems like a week to me, you moon for the night-blooming lotus of my heart.'

49 The Brahmin affectionately embraced Āryarakṣita, and said, 'I've brought these sticks of sugar cane as a present for you.'

50 Somadeva's son said, 'Give the sugar cane to my dear mother, uncle. I'm going further on to see to my bodily needs.

51 And tell my mother that I saw you carrying the sticks of sugar cane as I was going by.'

52 The Brahmin did as Āryarakṣita asked. Āryarakṣita's mother was intelligent. She thought:

53 'This is a lucky sign for my son, and he has understood the omen. Surely my intelligent son will learn the first nine sections and part of the tenth.'

54 And as he journeyed, Somadeva's son thought, 'I shall learn the first nine sections of the Disputation about Views and part of the tenth.'

55 When he arrived at the door of the sugar cane shed, firm-minded Āryarakṣita thought, 'I don't know what to do when I go in.

56 I know that one should behave in the presence of Teachers as in the presence of kings, but I don't know what to do on entering.

57 So I shall stay right here for a while, and enter the lodging house with the Jain laypeople when they come to perform their morning act of veneration to the Teacher.'

58 So Āryarakṣita stood like a doorkeeper beside the door of the monks' lodging place. Wise people have a faculty of reflection which is a sure check against hasty action.

59 Charmed by the monks' recitation, which went through modes and pitches, especially mālava and kaiśikī, he became absorbed, like a deer.

60 Then, early in the morning, a Jain layman named Ḍhaḍḍhara came to perform his act of homage to the Teacher, his eyes wide open with joy.

61 Three times he gently attracted the Teacher's notice to prevent his surprise, and then quickly recited the formula for making

atonement for inadvertently treading on any living organisms in a very loud voice.*

62 Then he made fitting obeisance to the Teacher, and sat down, having cleansed the place where he was about to sit.

63 Āryarakṣita was wise. He entered with that layman, bowed, and recited the formula for making atonement for inadvertently treading on any living organisms, just as he had heard the layman recite it.

64 As he recited them, he imitated the gestures which he had seen him make. Then Āryarakṣita bowed to the Teacher's feet and to the monks.

65 But Āryarakṣita did not bow to the layman Ḍhaḍḍhara. Although he was intelligent, he had not been able to learn that much while he was waiting.

66 Seeing Somadevā's son sit down without bowing to Ḍhaḍḍhara, the Teacher thought, 'Who is this lay believer? He is certainly a very recent convert.'

67 The Teacher, a receptacle for the autumn rain of sinlessness, preached a sermon, and then asked Āryarakṣita from whom he had learnt the religious practices of the Jains.

68 Rudrasomā's son answered truthfully, 'I learnt them from none other than this Jain layman.'

69 The monks said, 'Reverend father, this is Āryarakṣita, Rudrasomā's son. He is highly educated, for he has reached the far shore of the ocean of learning.

70 He learnt the fourteen branches of knowledge, and the king had him escorted into the city, seated on the back of an elephant.

71 He is reckoned to be at the head of those who are endowed with excellence. So why does he practise such strange lay observances?'

72 Āryarakṣita said, 'I'm only a recent Jain layman. Why shouldn't human beings have a fresh change of mind?'

73 Then he asked the Teacher, his hands folded in respectful supplication, 'Reverend sir, please teach me the Disputation about Views.

74 Full of wickedness and lacking proper understanding, I learnt all those teachings which promote harm to others and lead to hell.'

75 The Teacher knew that he was capable and free from passions.

He said, 'If you want to learn the Disputation about Views, then become a monk.

76 As soon as you have taken your vows, best of Brahmins, you will begin to be gradually taught the Disputation about Views. What else?'

77 Āryarakṣita said, 'Initiate me as a monk right now. The life will not be difficult for me to follow, for it is a wishing-cow granting my heart's desire.

78 But with kind words granting peace of mind to your pupil, let the place where you are now practising harsh asceticism be removed elsewhere.

79 For if I remain here, the king and the citizens, out of their excessive affection for me, will force me to abandon the life of a monk.'

80 Through regard for him, the Teacher accompanied by his followers went elsewhere, and Āryarakṣita walked before him like a servant.

81 Āryarakṣita was the first in the lineage of monks founded by holy Mahāvīra to be converted by pupil-stealing.

82 Then the Teacher initiated the learned doctor Āryarakṣita, and in a short time the instructor became an onlooker as Āryarakṣita repeated his explanations.

83 Patiently enduring harsh austerities with equanimity, he learnt the eleven Limbs as easily as learning the alphabet.

84 Āryarakṣita learnt as much of the Disputation about Views as his honourable Teacher knew.

85 Then Āryarakṣita was informed by the senior monks that at that time there was a monk named Vajra who knew the rest of the Disputation of Views by heart.

86 Because the monk Vajra happened to be staying in Purī, Somadeva's son proceeded to go there.

87 On his journey, reverend Āryarakṣita visited the Teacher named Bhadragupta, who was staying in Ujjayinī.

88 The Teacher recognized that he was endowed with excellence, had accumulated austerities, and held his former way of life in contempt, and joyfully embraced him.

89 The Teacher said, 'My son, you are blessed, you are successful, and you are intelligent, for you have abandoned the Brahminical religion and become a Jain monk.

90 I am ridding myself of my remaining life-karma. I intend to fast unto death. I beg you, be my assistant, sinless one.'

91 The monk Rudrasomā's son agreed. The Teacher Bhadragupta ceased taking food and drink, and said to Āryarakṣita:

92 'Don't remain under the same roof as Lord Vajra, but stay elsewhere while you are studying with him, my son.

93 That person who, dedicated to his life's work, stays with Vajra for just one night will follow him in death; there's no doubt about it.'

94 Āryarakṣita promised that he would do so, and, having assisted at the Teacher's final moments, went to Purī, where Vajra was staying.

95 That night, Āryarakṣita stayed outside the city, and on the very same night, Lord Vajra had this dream:

96 In the morning someone filled his alms bowl with milk, and a stranger came and emptied it on the ground. Only a drop remained in it.

97 In the morning Lord Vajra explained the meaning of his dream to his monks: 'Someone who has a good deal of knowledge of the ten Original Collections of Teachings will come as my guest.

98 He is intelligent, and will receive from me most of the teachings of the Original Collections of Teachings. But he will leave a small remainder of their teachings with me.'

99 In the morning, Āryarakṣita set out to visit Vajra. He bowed to Vajra, moving his joined hands from left to right twelve times in salutation.

100 The Teacher asked where he had come from, and Āryarakṣita said, 'I have come from studying at the feet of the Teacher Tosaliputra.'

101 Lord Vajra asked if he were called Āryarakṣita, and Āryarakṣita confirmed that he was, bowing in veneration once more.

102 Lord Vajra knew that he was well mannered, and said, 'Welcome. Where are you staying? Please stay here.'

103 When Āryarakṣita said that he would stay elsewhere, Vajra said, 'Great-souled one, how will you learn the things you do not know if you stay elsewhere?'

104 Somadeva's son said, 'I shall stay in separate lodgings from my Teacher on the orders of the Teacher Bhadragupta.'

105 Then the Teacher Vajra understood the reason, and said, 'This

is permissible. The elders must be honoured; nowhere is it stated otherwise.'

106 So Āryarakṣita stayed in his first lodgings, and Vajra began to give him daily lessons in the Original Collections of Teachings.

107 Very soon Somadeva's son the monk easily learnt nine Original Collections of Teachings which he did not know before.

108 Āryarakṣita then began to study the tenth Original Collection, and the Teacher told him to learn its verses with double meanings.

109 So Āryarakṣita began to study the many difficult verses with double meanings of the tenth Original Collection.

110 Then Āryarakṣita's parents wrote to him saying, 'Why don't you return? Have you now forgotten us?

111 We hoped that you would bring us light. While you are away, everything we see is shrouded in darkness.'

112 Even though summoned by his parents' message, Āryarakṣita remained intent on his studies, and did not depart for home.

113 His parents' hearts were set on calling him home. They persevered by sending Phalgurakṣita, Āryarakṣita's younger brother, who was as dear as life to him.

114 Phalgurakṣita travelled quickly, and when he arrived, he said to Āryarakṣita, 'Are you in love with some woman in this household?

115 Affection for one's family is severed by the snare of passion. Nevertheless, you are compassionate. Say goodbye to your ties.

116 All of your kinsfolk are sunk in a mire of depression, but now you are able to raise them.'

117 Addressed by his brother in this way, pure-minded Āryarakṣita bowed to holy Lord Vajra and asked for permission to return home.

118 Vajra ordered him to remain studying, so Āryarakṣita continued to memorize the teachings. But Phalgurakṣita complained, 'Have you forgotten me?

119 Our relatives have set their hearts on my initiation as a Jain monk, but they won't begin the ceremony if you are not present as my guide.

120 So come home and give me the initiation which is honoured by the whole world. Can you listen to this and still be indifferent to the well-being of your relatives?'

121 Āryarakṣita said, 'If what you say is true, then take the vow which provides well-being for sentient beings now, my brother.'
122 When he heard this, Phalgurakṣita's mind was purified by faith, He said, 'Initiate me. Who would turn his face from nectar?'
123 Āryarakṣita was delighted. He initiated him, and gave him instruction in a voice like nectar.
124 One day, Phalgurakṣita asked Āryarakṣita to leave for home, and he, having learnt all the verses with double meanings, once more asked the Teacher for permission to leave.
125 But as before, the Teacher refused to let him go. Depressed, he thought, 'My family is calling me, but I'm prevented from going by the command of my Teacher. Alas!'
126 He continued to study as before, but his learning of the verses with double meanings had defeated him. Putting his hands together in supplication, he bowed to the Teacher, and said:
127 'I have learnt so much of the tenth Original Collection. Please kindly tell me how much of it remains, master.'
128 The Teacher, his face wreathed in smiles, said, 'You have learnt the equivalent of a drop; an ocean remains.'
129 When he heard the Teacher's reply, Āryarakṣita said, 'I'm worn out. I'm not able to learn any more, master.'
130 'You will soon learn the remaining teachings. You are intelligent and you are steadfast. Why lose heart needlessly?'
131 Thus the Teacher, full of compassion, renewed his confidence. Āryarakṣita began to study again. Although his will was broken, he was devoted to his Teacher.
132 The next day, he looked at Phalgurakṣita, regarding him as an embodiment of his parents' entreaties, and became eager to depart. Once more, he said to Vajra:
133 'Although I'm willing to persevere, alas, I want to go home!' Lord Vajra thought the matter over and became favourable to his request.
134 He thought, 'If he leaves, he will not return quickly. My remaining life will be very short, and the remaining part of the tenth Original Collection will die with me.'
135 He gave Āryarakṣita leave to depart, and he and Phalgurakṣita soon arrived at Daśapura.
136 When they arrived, the king, the citizens, and Rudrasomā and Somadeva came to pay their devoted respects to Āryarakṣita.

137 Their eyes filled with tears of joy, they approached him in their proper order, and bowed to the monk, who was like an image of religion.

138 Knowing that they wished to hear about religion, he, an ocean of compassion, preached to them in a voice like the thunder of rain clouds.

139 They washed away the impurities of their minds with the pellucid waters of his teachings, which they drank with the cupped vessels of their ears. They were amazed.

140 The king was converted by Āryarakṣita. He bowed to his subjects, and returned to his palace.

141 Somadeva and Rudrasomā and many of their kinsmen became disgusted with living in the prison of worldly existence, and became Jain monks and nuns.

142 Thereafter, Lord Vajra wandered the earth. In the course of his ascetic wanderings, he came to the southern regions.

143 When the people of the southern regions saw him, a rain cloud for the root of the kandala* plant of bliss, they were as happy as peacocks.

144–5 Sunk in joy at the sight of him, the people said, 'When this monk illuminates the nature of reality, what need is there of the sun? When the eyes of the partridge meet with delight, what need is there of the moon? What need we of karma when we have his efficacious religion or are granted sight of him?'

146 One day, holy Lord Vajra became very troubled by phlegm, so he sent a monk to fetch dry ginger.

147 The monk, whose heart was pure, gave Vajra the dry ginger, and he, intending to eat it after his meal, put it behind his ear.

148 But after he had eaten, the leader of the monks became engrossed in his studies, and completely forgot about the dry ginger behind his ear.

149 Then, in the evening, as he was making his atonement while inspecting his body and holding his mouth-covering in his hand, the ginger fell out.

150 When the supreme monk Vajra saw it fall, he gasped and remembered it. He scolded himself, saying, 'Oh! Alas for my forgetfulness!

151 How can the asceticism one practises be without blemish, if one

is neglectful? Without asceticism, life is inhuman and without any purpose.'

152 So Lord Vajra decided to abandon his life. A dreadful famine of twelve years' duration had set in.

153 'On the morning following the day on which you shall receive alms worth a hundred thousand, you will notice that food has become plentiful.'

154 Thus he informed his pupil Vajrasena, who had passed to the far shore of the ocean of learning, and told him to go elsewhere.

155 Vajrasena, most eminent of monks, began to wander through the forests, towns, and villages of the earth.

156 Then holy Lord Vajra and his monks wandered from town to town, but they did not receive any food.

157 Lacking food, all the monks' bellies became emaciated with hunger. Each day, they subsisted on magic food given them by their Teacher.

158 'If you eat the food which I am giving you for twelve years, your ascetic practices will not be impaired.

159 But wouldn't it be preferable to abandon food and our bodies together?' Thus addressed by the Teacher, the religious-minded monks thought:

160 'Alas, this food is nourishing. Alas, this food provides well-being. Master, help us to abandon its twofold qualities.'

161 Holy Vajra, the companion of mankind, quickly took all the monks to a mountain, in order to await their future life.

162 As the Teacher was climbing the mountain, he prevented a novice monk from going there by sending him to a village on some pretext. But the novice monk did not stay in the village.

163 Thinking, 'I hope I don't cause my Teacher displeasure,' he remained at the foot of the mountain, abandoning food and his body.

164 He clung to the ground at the foot of the mountain, which was being roasted by the blazing heat of the midday sun. He was like a food offering to the dead placed there by someone.

165 Absorbed in pure meditation, he abandoned his body, like a yogic ascetic possessed of power, and was reborn in the residence of the gods.

166 While he was plunged in bliss at having gained the form of a god, the gods honoured to his corpse by joyfully dancing around it.

167 The monks saw the gods descend from heaven, and asked Vajra, 'Why have the gods come here in all their glory, master?'

168 He said, 'The novice monk has just now performed his duty, and the gods are celebrating his glory.'

169 When they heard this, the monks thought, 'If this young monk has performed his duty, why have not we senior monks performed ours?'

170 Then a goddess who had the wrong views about religion disguised herself as a Jain laywoman, and said to the monks, who were intent on final emancipation and possessed of knowledge and moral conduct:

171 'Please break your fast today, reverend sirs. Take my candied sweets and my sugared drinks.'

172 Thinking, 'Our self-restraint is not the reason for her affection. Let's go elsewhere,' they went to another mountain.

173 They mentally paid their respects to the goddess of that place, and stood upright in meditation. The goddess said to them:

174 'You have shown me great favour by coming here. A tree of plenty never grows in a desert.'

175 The monks were delighted by these words. They and holy Lord Vajra vowed to abandon food and drink. Having accomplished this vow, they died and went to heaven.

176 The god Śakra admired their deed, and went to the mountain in his heavenly carriage. He paid joyful respects to the corpses of Vajra and the monks.

177 Then Śakra in his carriage flew around the mountain in veneration, vigorously bowing to its trees, as devotedly as if it were a manifestation of his own body.

178 Even today people pay their respects to that mountain, which is famed throughout the earth as 'The Mountain Encircled by the Carriage'.

179 After holy Vajra, a diamond for the mountain of bad karma, went to heaven, the fourth section of the tenth Original Collection was lost.

180 Thereafter, in the course of his wanderings, Vajrasena, Vajra's pupil, came to the city of Sopāra, which had no equal for prosperity.

181 Its king had the appropriate name of Jitaśatru.* His wife was Dhāriṇī, the possessor of every virtue.

182 In that city lived a wealthy Jain layman named Jinadatta. His wife was named Īśvarī; she was like Umā the wife of Śiva.

183 The morality which she practised was as bright in appearance as the moon; it was her ornament and the earth's.

184 Now at that time the earth was troubled by a dreadful famine. Due to the lack of grain and water, hardships multiplied like fishes.

185 Pre-eminent in religion, Īśvarī said to her kinsfolk, 'We used to live pleasantly until now.

186 How long can we live with the hardship of being unable to buy food? Let us rather resolve to eat poisoned food.

187 Reciting the fivefold salutation, having vowed to abstain from food and drink, let us determine to abandon our bodies; they are abodes of distress.'

188 Then her relatives said, 'Yes, this is the right thing for us. When its time has come, the body has its reward.'

189 She bought some cooked rice for a hundred thousand. As she was about to put the poison in it, the monk Vajrasena came by, like a life-giving drug.

190 When she saw the monk, she thought, 'Intention, goods, and recipient—thank heavens, these three are at hand!

191 If I give this food to this recipient, I shall render my life blessed. Sometimes one happens to meet with a worthy recipient.'

192 Her eyes wide open with joy, she gave him the food. Then she told him all about the cooked rice which she had bought for a hundred thousand.

193 Vajrasena told her, 'Don't resort to such an action, good lady. For tomorrow morning food will be plentiful. There's no doubt about it.'

194 She asked, 'Did you learn this yourself, or did you find out from someone else?' He replied in a voice as loud as a thundering rain cloud:

195 'Holy Lord Vajra told me that when I receive alms of cooked rice worth a hundred thousand, on the following morning food would be plentiful.'

196 His words were like nectar to her ears. The Jain laywoman easily bore the hardships of the famine for the remainder of that day.

197 Next morning, a wagon train loaded with grain arrived from foreign parts; it was like the sun loaded with its rays of light.

198 Thereupon she and the people became cheered in heart, and Vajrasena stayed there with them for some time.

199 Jinadatta, together with Īśvarī and his sons and relatives, worshipped the Jinas and gave money to the poor.

200 On the following day, their minds composed, they took, in the presence of Vajrasena, the vow which is beneficial for both heaven and earth.

201 Thus the stock of pupillary succession begun by the holy monk Vajra pervaded in all directions like a banyan tree consisting of pupils and their pupils.

202 Its leaves were monks, and rich in good scriptures, it got rid of the bonds of settled habitation. Who did not long for the stock of the blessed monk Vajra?

203 Whichever lineages have ever been seen or heard of, have all had initial tender sprigs, but firm roots too. That stock of holy Vajra the Teacher, who knew the ten Original Collections of Teachings, is a new one which first was slender, but later spread out.

Here finishes the thirteenth canto of the scholar-monk Hemacandra's epic poem, the Appendix, or Lives of the Jain Elders. In it were related Āryarakṣita's taking of his vows, his learning of the Original Collections of Teachings, Lord Vajra's departure for heaven, and the spread of his lineage of pupillary succession.

May this Appendix, a garland plaited with the flowers of the various deeds of the Jain elders from Jambū to Vajra, the head of the troop of monks, hang around the necks of the learned.

APPENDIX
The Jain Universe

The Jain universe is distinctive and complex, and the numerous treatises in which it is described and illustrated attest its central importance in the Jain system. The geography of its various regions is measured with remarkable mathematical precision. The following description of its most important features is based on information taken from Hemacandra's *The Lives of the Sixty-three Illustrious People* and from commentaries on the *Tattvārtha Sūtra*.[1]

The dimensions of the Jain universe are measured in ropes (*rajjus*); a rope is the distance travelled by a god flying for six months at a speed of approximately ten million miles per second. The universe is three dimensional and has the shape of a man standing with his arms akimbo. It measures fourteen ropes in height, but its width varies; it is seven ropes wide at its base, one rope wide at its centre, at the level of the cosmic man's waist, five ropes wide at the level of his chest, and one rope wide at the top. It is eternal and uncreated; it has always existed and will never cease to exist. Outside the universe there is nothing but empty space.

The universe is divided into three worlds: below the level of the man's waist is the Lower World, where the hell grounds are situated, at the level of his waist is the Middle World, a disc on which are situated the continents inhabited by human beings, and above his waist is the Upper World, where the heavens are situated. Above the Upper World is an upturned crescent, 'the slightly curving place', in which the liberated souls live in a state of eternal bliss and omniscience. Within the universe, a soul can have one of four possible embodiments: a god, a human being, a hell being, or an animal or plant (animals and plants form a single class of embodiment). Human beings and animals and plants are confined to the Middle World; the animals and plants which are found in the heavens and hells are gods or hell beings which have assumed animal or plant form.

In the Lower World lie seven hell grounds. They are shaped liked bowls, and are stacked on top of each other, being separated by cushions of air and water. They take their names from the element that predominates in them: at the top is the Jewel hell ground, below is the Pebble hell ground, then in descending order come the Sand, Mud, Smoke, Dark, and the

[1] Hemacandra describes the universe in Book Two of *The Lives of the Sixty-three Illustrious People*. See Johnson, *Triṣaṣṭiśalākāpuruṣacaritra*, ii. 104–27. For a beautifully illustrated description and detailed bibliography, see C. Caillat and R. Kumar, *The Jain Cosmology* (Basle, 1981: Ravi Kumar).

Extremely Dark hell grounds. The individual hells are situated within the hell grounds, stacked on top of each other in stories; there are thirteen stories in the Jewel hell ground, eleven in the Pebble, and thus decreasing by two in progression down the hell grounds so that there is just one story in the lowest hell ground. There are 3,000,000 hells in the Jewel hell ground, 2,500,000 in the Pebble hell ground, 1,500,000 in the Sand, 1,000,000 in the Mud, 300,000 in the Smoke, 99,995 in the Dark, and just five in the Extremely Dark hell ground. The hells come in various shapes; they can be circular, triangular, pot-shaped, and jar-shaped. Their floors are sharp, being serrated like diamond-edged knives.

The lower one descends in the hell systems, the more unpleasant conditions are, and the more unpleasant life is for the hell beings. As are gods, hell beings are born spontaneously, without need for parents. They have the power to transform themselves, but unfortunately for them, whenever they transform themselves in an attempt to alleviate their condition, they actually change themselves into a form which is productive of more pain. Life for the hell beings is harsh, since the hells are characterized by terrible pains, heat, cold, hunger, and thirst. The hell beings hate one another, so they are forced to attack and to fight each other continually. To make matters worse, the hells are visited by some gods known as 'the extremely unjust ones'. They are like sadistic prison guards, and they delight in torturing the unfortunate hell beings.

Gods live not only in the heavens of the Upper World, but also in the Middle World, in the highest hell ground, and in the spaces between the Middle World and the highest hell ground and the lowest heaven. There are four classes of god, each divided into subclasses: the Interstitial, who live in the highest hell ground and in the spaces between the Middle World and the highest hell ground and the lowest heaven of the Upper World; the Peripatetic, who live in the Middle World; the Stellar, who live in the suns, moons, and stars; and the Palace-dwelling gods, who live in the heavens of the Upper World.

Just as the descending hells become progressively gloomier and more unpleasant, the heavens of the Upper World become progressively brighter and more auspicious. The heavens are divided into two: the paradise heavens, and the heavens beyond the paradise heavens. There are twelve paradise heavens stacked in the region of the cosmic man's chest, the first and the last four being grouped in pairs. There are fourteen heavens beyond the paradise heavens, nine in the neck region of the cosmic man, and five more above them, the unsurpassed heavens. The heavenly palaces in which the gods live are arranged in sixty-two layers.

A hierarchy subsists among the gods of the paradise heavens; there are kings, each of whom has his retinue of ministers and servants. However, there is no distinction of rank among the gods of the heavens beyond the paradise heavens, each of whom enjoys the rank of king; devoid of passion, they are conceived on the pattern of advanced Jain ascetics.

Goddesses live only in the first two paradise heavens, but they are capable of making fleeting visits as far as the eighth. Interstitial, Peripatetic, Stellar, and the gods in the first two paradise heavens enjoy bodily sexual activity with goddesses in the same way as human beings. The sexual needs of gods in the third and fourth paradise heavens are satisfied by a mere touch of a goddess, those in the fifth and sixth by merely looking at a goddess, those in the seventh and eighth by a mere sound produced by a goddess. Since goddesses do not venture beyond the eighth paradise heaven, the needs of the gods in the remaining paradise heavens are satisfied by the mere thought of a goddess. Lacking all passion, the gods in the heavens beyond the paradise heavens have no sexual desires.

The Middle World is a flat disc, at the centre of which stands Mount Meru surrounded by the central, circular land mass, Rose-apple Tree Island. Around Rose-apple Tree Island lie countless concentric islands, separated from each other by oceans. Proceeding from the centre to the rim of the Middle World, each island is double the size of the preceding one. Each island is surrounded by a rampart of diamonds, on which rests a fence of jewels topped by a coping of lotuses made from gems. Rose-apple Tree Island is surrounded by Grislea Tormentosa Tree Island, which in turn is surrounded by Lotus Island. A range of mountains runs along the centre of Lotus Island dividing it into an inner and an outer half. This range of mountains marks the limit of the Middle World that is inhabitable by human beings. Thus human life is confined to the inner two-and-a-half islands of the Middle World: Rose-apple Tree Island, Grislea Tormentosa Tree Island, and the inner half of Lotus Island. These two-and-a-half islands are known as the Human World. The eighth island, the Island of Rejoicing, is worthy of note as the place where the gods congregate to celebrate Festivals, in particular the birth of Fordmakers. Above the islands inhabited by humans are 132 suns and 132 moons; they are, of course, Stellar gods and are each surrounded by a retinue of planets and stars.

Rose-apple Tree Island is divided into seven continents by six mountain ranges which cross the island from east to west. The names of the continents are, from south to north, Bharata, Haimavata, Ramyaka, Mahāvideha, Hari, Hairaṇyaka, and Airāvata. The area of the continents increases by a factor of two as they approach the centre of Rose-apple Tree Island; thus the central continent, Mahāvideha, is sixty-four times the size of Bharata and Airāvata, respectively at the extreme south and extreme north of the island.

Bharata is bounded from Haimavata by the Himavat mountains, from which two rivers flow through Bharata to the ocean; the Sindhu to the south-west and the Gaṅgā to the south-east. Bharata is itself divided by a range of mountains which run from east to west: the Vaitāḍhya mountains with their nine peaks. The areas to the north of Vaitāḍhya mountains, to the west of the Sindhu, and to the east of the Gaṅgā are inhabited by barbarians. The remaining area of Bharata, bounded to the north by Vaitāḍhyas and to the west and east by the Sindhu and Gaṅgā, is civilized (*ārya*); here is where the action of *The Lives of the Jain Elders* takes place. Airāvata is a mirror image of Bharata. At the centre of Mahāvideha is Mount Meru, from the foothills of which two rivers flow into the surrounding ocean, one to the east and one to the west. Within Mahāvideha are two crescent-shaped enclaves, one to the north and one to the south of Mount Meru, known as Northerly Kuru and Kuru of the Gods.

The geography of the other islands of the Human World, Grislea Tormentosa Tree Island and the inner half of Lotus Island, mirrors the geography of Rose-apple Tree Island. These ring-shaped land masses are each divided into halves by mountain ranges running from north to south, and within each half are seven continents separated from each other by six mountain ranges, just as in Rose-apple Tree Island. The continents of Grislea Tormentosa Tree Island and Lotus Island have the same names as the continents of Rose-apple Tree Island.

The Haimavata, Ramyaka, Hari, Hairaṇyaka continents and the Kuru enclaves of the Mahāvideha continents are Places of Enjoyment, where conditions are blissful; it is not possible for the soul to gain liberation from further embodiment in these areas. The soul can only be liberated in the Places of Action, in which the law of karma operates: these are the civilized parts of the Bharata and the Airāvata continents and the parts of the Mahāvideha continents which are not within the Kuru enclaves. Fordmakers are born only in the Places of Action, and it is only within these areas that human beings can benefit from their preaching.

Within the civilized portions of the Bharata and Airāvata continents a time cycle operates, envisaged as the perpetual turning of a wheel; as the wheel ascends, conditions become progressively more favourable, as it descends, conditions gradually deteriorate. It takes billions of years for the wheel of time to complete a turn. The ascending and descending turns are each divided into six eras, as follows:

The ascending turn

1 Extremely unhappy
2 Unhappy
3 More unhappy than happy

4 More happy than unhappy
5 Happy
6 Extremely happy

The descending turn

1 Extremely happy
2 Happy
3 More happy than unhappy
4 More unhappy than happy
5 Unhappy
6 Extremely unhappy

The duration of the eras is unequal: the first four eras of each turn last for millions of years, whereas the happy and the extremely unhappy eras each last for 21,000 years.

In the last three eras of the ascending turn and the first three eras of the descending turn all the needs of human beings are satisfied by wishing-trees, which provide wine, food, concerts, light, flowers, ornaments, houses, and clothes. Human beings are born as pairs of male and female twins who live as man and wife, each pair giving birth to another pair. In the extremely happy eras human beings are 6 miles tall, live for hundreds of thousands of years, and eat only on every fourth day. As conditions deteriorate, their height and the duration of the lives decrease, and they have to increase their intake of food. The power of the wishing-trees gradually decreases, so that in the last three eras of the descending turn and the first three eras of the ascending turn human beings have to live by their own efforts. In these eras they procreate indiscriminately. By the time of the extremely unhappy era, their height has decreased to 1½ feet, and they live for only sixteen years.

Liberation from further rebirth can only be achieved in the more unhappy than happy and the more happy than unhappy eras; it is only in these eras when conditions are sufficiently balanced between bliss and wretchedness that human beings are able to conceive of the possibility of gaining final liberation, and it is in these eras that the twenty-four Fordmakers whose preaching provides the ford which enables human beings to gain final liberation are born.

Seventy-five years and eight and a half months after the birth of Mahāvīra, Bharata, the setting for the action of *The Lives of the Jain Elders*, passed into the unhappy era of the descending turn. Some 80,000 years must pass before Bharata passes into the more unhappy than happy era of the upward turn when conditions will be once more propitious for the birth of Fordmakers and the gaining of final liberation. However, this does not mean that a soul at present embodied in Bharata will have to endure the process of death and re-embodiment until then; it only has to be reborn in, or even to visit by means of a supernatural agency, one of the continents in Rose-apple Tree Island, Grislea Tormentosa Tree Island or Lotus Island where a Fordmaker is living. There is always a minimum of four Fordmakers in Rose-apple Tree Island. This is because the time cycles do not operate in the Places of Action of the Mahāvideha continents; there conditions are always equivalent to the end of the third eras. There are always four Fordmakers in the Mahāvideha continent of Rose-apple Tree Island, and at times as many as thirty-two. Likewise, there are always Fordmakers in the other islands of the Human World. One only needs to be reborn in, or to visit, one of those places to have an immediate chance of liberation!

EXPLANATORY NOTES

Canto One

6 *holy beings in the highest stages*: the beings in the highest stages are the Worthies (Arhats), the Liberated Souls (Siddhas), the Teachers (Ācāryas), the Preceptors (Upādhyāyas), and the Monks (Sādhus). The Fivefold Salutation addressed to the beings in the highest stages is the most popular and well-known prayer in Jainism. It may be translated:

> Homage to the Worthies!
> Homage to the Liberated Souls!
> Homage to the Teachers!
> Homage to the Preceptors!
> Homage to all the Jain monks in the world!
> This Fivefold Salutation destroys all sins. It is the foremost auspicious thing of all auspicious things.

8 *fourfold congregation*: the fourfold congregation which attends, and is created by, the preaching of a Fordmaker consists of monks, nuns, laymen, and laywomen.

9 *atmosphere became its own characteristic*: each of the five elements has its own characteristic quality or qualities as well as its own organ of sense. The characteristic of *ambara*, atmosphere or ether, is sound and its sense organ is the ear.

His two arms . . . perfected souls: the Jain universe is shaped like a gigantic man. The liberated souls live above a brilliant canopy at the top of the universe. See the account in the Appendix on the Jain universe.

10 *the lion's backward look*: this is a military maxim: when a lion is about to attack, it is supposed to cast a backward look as it advances forward.

13 *the third stage of life slaughtering youth*: the three stages of life are childhood, maturity, and old age.

14 *an illiterate man*: a pun: *mātṛkā* 'mother' also bears the meaning 'alphabet'.

15 *Viśvakarman*: a divine artist and craftsman, the founder of the science of architecture.

24 *first and last ages of the world*: in Hindu thought, the world passes through four ages (*yugas*). The first age is the Perfect Age (*kṛta yuga*) in which conditions are absolutely blissful. The last age is the present age, the Age of Discord (*kali yuga*) in which conditions are dreadful. It is traditional Jain belief that parts, but not all, of the world inhabited by mankind are subject to a perpetual cycle of decay and renewal. According to this belief, the present age is the age of discord, which will in turn be followed by a further era in which conditions will be even worse. See the Appendix on the Jain universe for details.

five highest stages: see note to p. 6.

27 *the beauty of Rāhu . . . swallowed the moon*: Rāhu is a demon whose swallowing of the moon is thought to be responsible for its eclipse. The point of the simile is that Rāhu is glossy black.

29 *'cakra'-cawing bird*: the cakravāka bird, *Anas casarca*, known as the Brahmany Duck, or Red Shieldrake. They are usually found on the banks of rivers in single pairs, standing some distance apart. The couples are thought to be forced to separate during the night and to mourn over their separation.

30 *three jewels*: the three jewels of Jainism are an encapsulation of the Jain path to liberation. They are: right belief, right knowledge, and right conduct.

32 *first paradise heaven*: the first paradise heaven is Saudharma; its Indra, or king, is called Śakra. See the Appendix on the Jain universe.

fulfilment . . . pregnancy-longing: Sāgaradatta means 'given by the ocean'.

Mount Meru: Mount Meru is situated at the centre of the Middle World, surrounded by Rose-apple Tree Island. See the Appendix on the Jain universe.

34 *sidelocks of hair on his temples*: a characteristic hairstyle of young men of the royal estate.

36 *formula . . . living organisms*: the name of the formula is the Airyāpathīkī. The Prakrit text and an English translation can be found in R. Williams, *Jaina Yoga* (Oxford, 1963: Oxford University Press), 203–4. It is recited by Jain laypeople when they begin the worship of an image of a Jina.

Canto Two

40 *kataka plant*: the seeds of this plant are rubbed on the inside of water jars to precipitate any particles of dirt which may be in the water.

49 *Aryaman, the rising sun*: Aryaman also presides over marriage contracts.

50 *the god, the lord of Rose-apple Tree Island*: this is the god Anādṛta; see 1. 267.

54 *a master of magic*: see note to p. 82.

53 *the life-taking brother*: Yama, the god of death.

61 *the god whose emblem is a sea-monster*: the god of love.

63 *kodrava*: a kind of rough grain eaten by poor people.

71 *'cakra'-cawing birds*: see note to p. 29.

baldhead: Jain monks and nuns pluck out their hair at their initiation ceremony.

72 *annoyed*: *vilakṣita* meaning 'annoyed' or 'confused' also carries the meaning 'marked'.

73 *glancing*: Hemacandra is probably punning here: *paśyantī*, the word I have translated as 'glancing', can also mean 'prostitute'.

75 *Yakṣa Śobhana*: Yakṣas are a kind of demigod. Their powers are usually confined to particular localities, their shrines being often situated in the outskirts of settlements; Durgilā vows to pass between the legs of an image of such a Yakṣa. Usually benevolent, Yakṣas have a fairly low ranking in the hierarchy of supernatural beings.

80 *an Interstitial god*: for information about the various classes of god, see the Appendix on the Jain universe.

81 *elephant . . . hands*: 'kara', meaning 'hand', also has the meaning 'elephant's trunk'.

82 *master of magic*: the masters of magic, or *vidyādharas*, live in the Himalayas, where they have their own kings and cities. They are endowed with supernatural powers. In Jain literature, they are often represented as Jain devotees, and they often travel in their heavenly carriages to visit Jain holy places in the Himalayas. They are usually benign to human beings, often intermarrying with them, but on occasions they can become hostile. As a result of a curse put upon them because of their maltreatment of a Jain monk, the masters of magic were forced to make efforts to gain the magic powers with which they had previously been endowed at birth.

85 *Lake Mānasa*: a sacred lake on Mount Kailāsa in the Himalayas to which swans are supposed to migrate in their mating season.

87 *a naked field watchman*: a pun: *kṣetrapāla*, field watchman, is a name of the god Śiva, one of whose manifestations is that of a naked ascetic.

88 *pān*: a stimulating preparation of betel-nuts, spices, and limes, rolled together in a leaf.

Canto Three

93 *Revanta*: a son of Sūrya, the sun god. He was born mounted on a horse, and he is a patron of horses and hunting.

98 *out of control . . . consummating your marriage*: I have expanded one of Hemacandra's puns: *asaṅgraha* 'out of control' can also mean 'not taking to wife'.

100 *The chaplain had a friend . . . whenever he happened to see him*: the Sanskrit names of the three friends are Sahamitra, Parvamitra, and Praṇamitra.

104 *Vajrayuddha*: literally 'the god whose weapon is a thunderbolt'; a name of the god Indra.

Kusumāyuddha: literally 'the god whose weapon is a flower'; a name of Kāma, the god of Love. His arrows are tipped with flowers.

105 *another son . . . of Prosperity*: her son is Kāma, the god of Love.

Canto Four

111 *King Kūṇika*: Kūṇika was the son of Śreṇika king of Magadha. He transferred his capital to Campā because of his grief at his father's death. See 6. 32.

114 *had previously related it to King Śreṇika*: Mahāvīra's narration of Jambū's former lives was the main subject of Canto 1.

After Jambū passes away . . . range of the senses: shortly after Mahāvīra's death Bharata entered into the present era of time, in which conditions are too adverse for human beings to gain omniscience. See note to p. 24, and the Appendix on the Jain universe.

threefold restraint: the progressive restraint of mind, body, and speech practised by Jain ascetics.

Canto Five

116 *Ten Evening Chapters*: the most readily available version of the text is: K. C. Lalwani (trans. and ed.), *Ārya Sayyambhava's Daśavaikālika Sūtra* (Delhi, 1973: Motilal Banarsidass). Lalwani's edition contains the Prakrit text and translations in English and Sanskrit. For the composition and transmission of the Jain canonical texts, see the discussion in the Introduction.

117 *meditation-sleep*: Prabhava was in a state of *Yogānīdrā*, a state of half-sleep and half-meditation in which the mental faculties remain fully alert.

Canto Six

129 *six flavours*: sweet, sharp, sour, bitter, mixed, and salty.

132 *right belief, right knowledge, and right conduct*: these are the three jewels of Jainism. See 1. 370.

Rati, the wife of Mīnaketu: Mīnaketu, meaning fish-bannered, is one of the names of Kāma, the god of Love. Rati, the personification of sexual pleasure, is his wife.

137 *Prayāga*: Prayāga, near modern Allahabad, situated at the confluence of the Ganges, Yamunā, and mythical Sarasvatī rivers, is one of the holiest pilgrimage places of Hinduism; every twelve years the famous Kumbha Mela festival is held at the site. Hemacandra's account is an example of Jain appropriation of Hindu mythology.

138 *one embodiment and a root-soul*: plants and vegetables can contain many souls; this tree was holy because it was embodied by just one soul throughout its life.

fourfold austerities: the fourfold austerity consists of fasting for three days, and taking food again on the fourth day.

139 *fourth stratagem*: these are the stratagems for success against an enemy: the fourth is open assault. The others are: creating dissension, bribery, and negotiation.

Canto Seven

146 *a son was born . . . possessed by Brilliant goddesses*: Brilliant (Revatī) goddesses are a type of Interstitial goddess. They are bringers of childhood disease.

147 *the one born in a jar*: an epithet of Agastya, a sage proverbial for his learning. He is credited with the remarkable exploit of swallowing the ocean.

149 *Learned in all the teachings . . . and others*: Caṇḍikā is identified with the fearsome goddess Durgā, Bhṛgu is the name of several sages skilled in all branches of learning, and Vetāla is the name given to a kind of demon that inhabits and animates corpses. The point seems to be that Kalpaka was skilled in black magic.

150 *like a cloud for the peacock of his mind*: when a peacock sees a monsoon cloud, it sings a song of joy.

151 *kodrava*: see the story of the farmer related in 2. 355 ff.

Canto Eight

165 *as if he were Religion . . . superior strength*: this is a reference to the Indian concept of the three aims of life: wealth (*artha*), sensual pleasure (*kāma*), and religion (*dharma*). Of the three aims, religion is considered to be the highest, and its claims are superior to those of the other two.

177 *his merit was used up*: that is, the merit he had earned by his good actions in his former lives.

179 *Maurya*: Hemacandra suggests that Maurya, the surname of Candragupta and his successors, derives from Sanskrit *mayūra*, meaning 'peacock'; according to Hemacandra, Candragupta's father was a royal peacock breeder. Other sources state that Maurya is derived from Murā, the name of a low-caste woman who bore Candragupta to the last of the Nanda rulers.

182 *Like he whose wife . . . dark half of the month*: the moon is married to the night; Candragupta is being compared to the waning moon.

185 *looking only at the ground . . . care in walking*: a Jain monk should walk slowly, with his gaze fixed on the ground, so that he can avoid treading on plants and small creatures, and so that he will not be unnecessarily distracted by sense impressions.

Canto Nine

191 *placed a dot under the letter 'a'*: 'kumāro adhīyau' was thus changed to 'kumāro aṃdhīyau' meaning 'let the prince be blinded'.

192 *Tumburu*: a heavenly musician, proverbial for his fine voice.

attracted, like deer: deer are supposed to be attracted by the human voice; compare 3. 194.

195 *Sthūlabhadra's sisters, Yakṣā and the others*: these are the sisters named in 8. 25.

196 *Sīmandhara*: a Fordmaker who lives and preaches in Mahāvideha, a region of the Rose-apple Tree Island that is not normally accessible to people who live in Bharata. Mahāvideha is not subject to the time cycle of progressive decay and improvement which operates in Bharata. In Mahāvideha conditions always have the right balance between good and bad to enable Fordmakers to live there. Although there will not be another

Fordmaker in Bharata for some 80,000 years, it remains possible to use supernatural methods of travel to visit Mahāvideha and other parts of the Middle World where Fordmakers are still preaching. See the Appendix on the Jain universe for more detailed information.

the Clauses . . . Various Observances: the Sanskrit names of the lectures are Bhāvanā, Vimukti, Ratikalpa, and Vicitracaryā.

the Behaviour Rules: the *Ācārañga Sūtra*, containing the rules of monastic discipline and a biography of Mahāvīra. An English translation can be found in H. Jacobi (ed.), *Jaina Sūtras*, Part I, Sacred Books of the East, 22 (Oxford, 1984; repr. Delhi, 1989: Motilal Banarsidass).

197 *he would not teach them to anyone else*: thus the knowlege of all fourteen of the Original Collections of Teachings died with Sthūlabhadra, since he only taught ten of them to his two pupils; see 10. 39.

Canto Ten

200 *honourable Yakṣā . . . as their mother*: Sthūlabhadra's sister, mentioned in 8. 25 and 9. 78.

Canto Eleven

202 *the ascetic life of a Jina*: an ascetic who follows the ascetic practices of a Jina (a Jinakalpin) is one who leads a solitary life, naked in a forest. The more usual practice of White Clad (Śvetāmbara) ascetics is to wear a white robe and to live in monastic communities.

203 *image of the Living Lord . . . in procession*: this image of Mahāvīra, known as Jīvantasvāmin, was carved in his own lifetime. Its story is told in Hemacandra's *Lives of the Sixty-three Illustrious People*. See Johnson, *Triṣaṣṭiśalākāpuruṣacaritra*, vi. 288 ff.).

206 *the lesser vows . . . vows of instruction*: there are twelve lay vows. It is not obligatory for Jain laypeople to take them, but once taken they have to be followed for the period of the vow.

The five lesser vows (*aṇuvratas*) are adaptations for lay life of the five Great Vows taken by Jain ascetics. The first, the vow of not-harming, recognizes that lay life necessitates some degree of harm, but seeks to minimize it by ensuring that laypeople do not follow occupations which involve committing premeditated destruction. The second, the vow of truth, is not only a vow to tell truth but also to ensure that one's words do not have harmful consequences for others. The third, a vow of not-stealing, means that one should only take what has been bought or given, and that one should not wantonly waste natural resources. The fourth lesser vow, chastity, does not demand the complete chastity of the ascetic, but is rather an undertaking to restrict one's sexual activity to one wife, renouncing sex with mistresses or prostitutes. The layman may renounce sexual activity completely after the birth of a son. The fifth vow mirrors the ascetic vow of non-possession. Rather than abandon all his worldly goods, the layman should cultivate an attitude of non-attachment to them, leading a simple life, while making substantial religious donations.

The three subsidiary vows (*guṇavratas*) involve voluntary limitations on the distance one travels, the food one eats, and a ban on purposeless activities, such as digging in the ground for amusement and sitting around moping.

By taking the four vows of instruction (*śikṣāvratas*) the layman pledges to engage on a regular basis in ritual activities, such as temporarily restricting the range of his activities, fasting, meditation, and religious giving.

207 *eight substances*: the eight substances offered in worship to an image of a Jina are: water, sandalwood paste, uncooked rice, flowers, sweets, a light, incense, and fruit.

208 *the forty-two faults*: food should not be accepted by a Jain monk in the following situations:

1 When a layman has prepared food for ascetics of any religion.
2 When a layman has prepared food for a particular monk.
3 When food is mainly pure, but parts of it are impure on account of the first fault.
4 When part of the food has been prepared for a particular monk.
5 When a layman sets aside food for a particular monk.
6 When the food has been prepared for a celebration or festivity.
7 When the layman has to light a lamp in order to fetch the monk's food.
8 When the layman has to buy the food especially for the monk.
9 When the layman has to fetch spoons especially to serve the food.
10 When the layman replaces bad pieces of food with good ones.
11 When the layman has to fetch the food from a distance.
12 When the layman has to open locks before he reaches the food.
13 When the layman has to take the food from a raised or underground storeroom.
14 When the layman has taken the food by force from someone.
15 When the layman has taken the food from a common store without gaining the others' permission.
16 When the monk calls while the food is being cooked, and more food is prepared especially for him.
17 When the monk plays with the layman's children in order to be given food.
18 When the monk brings news in order to be given food.
19 When the monk praises giving in order to be given food.
20 When the monk boasts of his birth and family in order to be given food.
21 When the monk boasts about his asceticism in order to be given food.

22 When the monk cures the sick in order to be given food.
23 When the monk indulges in threatening behaviour in order to be given food.
24 When the monk tells the layman that he has bet other monks that he will receive food from him.
25 When the monk performs magic tricks in order to gain food.
26 When the monk goes begging in the hope of receiving fine food.
27 When the monk flatters the layman in order to receive food.
28 When the monk makes a show of his learning in order to gain food.
29 When the monk performs a favour for the layman in order to gain food.
30 When the monk makes himself invisible, and then takes away the food.
31 When the monk teaches the people spells and magic tricks in order to gain food.
32 When the monk teaches people how to obviate harm by means of roots, spells, and amulets in order to gain food.
33 When a monk is offered food by a layman who is frightened.
34 When the food is smeared by dead or living matter.
35 When the food has been placed among living things.
36 When food consisting of living matter has been covered by dead matter, and vice versa.
37 When the layman takes the food to be offered to the monk from one vessel and places it in another.
38 When the occupation or status of the layman forbids the acceptance of food from him.
39 When the layman mixes pure and impure food.
40 When the joint owner of food makes a donation against the will of the others.
41 When the hands or ladle of the layman who is donating food are smeared with milk, butter, etc.
42 When the layman spills milk or food while making his donation.

Four further faults are usually given in the texts, making a total of 46:

1 When the monk collects various food donations and puts together the ingredients of a good meal.
2 When the monk accepts more than the prescribed quantity of food.
3 When the monk praises a rich layman for his good food, or blames a poor one for his bad food.
4 When the monk eats good food on occasions other than those prescribed in the rules for monastic life.

See H. Jacobi, *Jaina Sūtras 2* (Oxford, 1895: Sacred Books of the East), 131–4.

210 *Daśārṇabhadra*: king of Daśārṇa. The story of his conversion and

renunciation is told by Hemacandra in his *Lives of the Sixty-three Illustrious People*. See Johnson, *Triṣaṣṭiśalākāpuruṣacaritra*, vi. 251–9.

211 *'The Lotus Thickets'*: The Lotus Thickets (Nalinīgulma) is the eighth chapter of the *Garlands of Behaviour* (*Kalpāvataṃsikāḥ*), the ninth Subsidiary Limb of the sacred canonical texts of the White Clad Jains.

you are very delicate: the name Avantisukumāla means 'very tender one of Avanti'.

212 *the drops of blood . . . tender feet*: one of the god Indra's functions is to provide rain; the drops of blood are being compared to raindrops.

the Fivefold Salutation: see note to p. 6.

214 *temple of Mahākāla*: actually a temple to the Hindu god Śiva. This story provides an example of Jain appropriation of Hindu mythology.

Canto Twelve

216 *line of monastic succession . . . holy teachings*: Hemacandra omits the details of the line of succession between Suhastin and Siṃhagiri, the initiator of Vajra. According to the list of elders in *The Guide Book* (*Kalpa Sūtra*), the succession passed from Suhastin to the joint leadership of Susthita and Supratibuddha, then to Indradatta, then to Datta, who initiated Siṃhagiri, Vajra's Teacher.

the Analysis school of philosophy: the Analysis (Nyāya) school is one of the six orthodox schools of Hindu philosophy. As its name suggests, the main concerns of the school are with logic and epistemology. These concerns are not merely theoretical; when correctly practised, they are a means to the soul's salvation. However, the belief that wealth accrues from religious practice is more usually associated with the Enquiry (Mīmāṃsā) school of philosophy.

217 *Puṇḍarīka*: the story of King Puṇḍarīka, the fat ascetic, is told in Hemacandra's *Lives of the Sixty-three Illustrious People*. See Johnson *Triṣaṣṭiśalākāpuruṣacaritra*, x. 242–5.

Tolerating . . . discomforts: the twenty-two discomforts (*parīṣahas*) are listed in the *Tattvārtha Sūtra* IX, 8–9. They are: hunger, thirst, cold, heat, insect bites, the discomfort of nakedness, avoiding feelings of distaste, not being aroused by women, ignoring the pain of constant walking, the discomfort of being seated in meditation, the discomfort of uncomfortable sleeping places, bearing insults, bearing threats and beatings, willingness to beg for one's subsistence, being content if one does not receive what one begs for, bearing sickness and disease, the discomfort of the touch of sharp grass or straw, the discomfort of one's bodily filth, the failure to receive the reverence due to an ascetic, the avoidance of conceit about one's possession of knowledge, the avoidance of despair at one's lack of knowledge, the avoidance of the view that the path of asceticism brings no benefit. See the discussion in P. S. Jaini, *The Jaina Path of Purification* (Berkeley, 1979: University of California), 249 f.

birth ceremony . . . celebrated for you: at this ceremony the new-born baby is induced to lick a gold coin smeared with honey and clarified butter.

222 *Brahma's Islanders . . . mentioned in scripture by that name*: the Brahma's Islanders appear in the lists of pupillary succession given in *The Guide Book* (*Kalpa Sūtra*).

225 *some Yawning gods*: the Yawning (Jṛmbhaka) gods are a kind of Interstitial god. They are servants of Kubera, the god of wealth.

227 *the Preliminary Statements recited*: the Preliminary Statements (Pūrvagata) formed the third section of the now extinct twelfth Limb of the canon, the *Disputation about Views* (*Dṛṣṭivāda*).

232 *Rukmiṇī herself*: a wife of the god Kṛṣṇa, won by him in battle. She is revered as an incarnation of Lakṣmī, the goddess of prosperity.

237 *holy Lord Vajra . . . benefit the holy congregation*: this is not consistent with verse 143, where we are told that the Yawning gods gave Vajra a spell to enable him to fly. There is no spell for flying in the text of *The Behaviour Rules* (*Ācārāṅga Sūtra*) as it exists today.

238 *king who made a magic leather purse*: this may be a reference to an episode in *The Adventures of the Ten Princes* (*Daśakumāracarita*) by Daṇḍin, a Sanskrit prose author of the seventh century AD, in which the story of the theft of a supposedly inexhaustible purse is related.

240 *the tenth vessel of nectar*: the meaning of this allusion is unclear to me. It may have some connection with the fourteen dreams Fordmaker has on his conception: the tenth dream is of a lotus lake.

What-people goddesses: the What-people (Kimpuruṣa) gods are similar in form to the centaurs of Greek mythology. They are a type of Interstitial god.

Canto Thirteen

244 *six Limbs of the Vedas . . . Codification of Law*: the six Limbs of the Vedas (*Vedāṅgas*) are ancilliary subjects necessary for their understanding. They are: the performance of sacrifice, phonetics, metre and prosody, etymology, grammar, and astronomy. The Enquiry philosophy (*mīmāṃsā*) holds that the Vedas are self-created and contain all knowledge. For the Analysis philosophy, see the note to p. 216. The Tales of Yore (*Purāṇas*) are vast compendia of mythological and semi-historical material. The Codification of Law (*Dharmaśāstra*) contains instruction on law, human conduct, and ethics.

245 *Disputation about Views*: in this Canto the *Disputation about Views* (*Dṛṣṭivāda*) is synonymous with the Original Collections of Teachings (Pūrvas).

246 *the one born in a jar*: see the note to p. 147.

248 *the formula . . . in a very loud voice*: see 1. 452.

253 *kandala*: a plant with white flowers which suddenly appear in great abundance in the rainy season.

255 *Jitaśatru*: the name means 'he who has subdued his enemies'.

INDEX OF PRINCIPAL CHARACTERS AND PLACES

ANĀDṚTA 'Unregarded': a god, the lord of Rose-apple Tree Island. 1. 268–85.

ANNIKĀ 'Bestower of Food': a maiden of southern MATHURĀ who married DEVADATTA and was the mother of ANNIKĀ'S SON. 6. 45–87.

ANNIKĀ'S SON (ANNIKĀPUTRA): a Jain ascetic who gained omniscience while impaled on a stake in the middle of the Ganges. The pāṭala tree after which the city of PĀṬALĪPUTRA was named grew from his skull. 6. 81–175.

ĀRYARAKṢITA 'Protected by the Noble': a learned Brahmin who converted to Jainism. 13. 1–141.

ĀŚOKA 'Free from Sorrow': Mauryan emperor, the son and successor of BINDUSĀRA. He was succeeded by his grandson SAMPRATI. 1. 15–54.

AVANTI: a country in western India. Its capital was UJJAYINĪ.

AVANTISUKUMĀLA 'The Very Tender One of Avanti': a young monk, who, unable to bear the rigours of the ascetic life, decided to fast to death and was eaten by a jackal. 11. 128–77.

BAKA 'Crane': a foolish farmer, the subject of the story told by SAMUDRAŚRĪ at 2. 355–78.

BHADRĀ 'Excellent Lady': mother of AVANTISUKUMĀLA. 11. 128–77.

BHADRABĀHU 'Auspicious-armed': a Jain elder, with SAMBHŪTAVIJAYA joint successor of YAŚOBHADRA. He initiated four merchants of RĀJAGṚHA, who each died of cold. 6. 3–21; 9. 59–112.

BHADRAGUPTA 'Protected by the Good': a Jain monk, one of VAJRA'S Teachers. 12. 209–35.

BHARATA: the Indian subcontinent. See the Appendix on the Jain universe.

BHAVADATTA 'Given by Prosperity': a Jain monk who tricked his brother BHAVADEVA into becoming a monk. Previous embodiment of Prince SĀGARADATTA. 1. 286–418.

BHAVADEVA 'Lord of Prosperity': a reluctant Jain monk. Brother of BHAVADATTA, and former embodiment of ŚAKRA, Prince ŚIVA, VIDYUNMĀLIN, and JAMBŪ. 1. 286–389, 419.

BINDUSĀRA 'He whose Essence is a Drop': Mauryan emperor, the son and successor of CANDRAGUPTA. He was succeeded by his son AŚOKA. 8. 439–69; 9. 1–14.

BUDDHI 'Intelligence': one of two old ladies, the subjects of NABHAḤSENĀ'S story told at 3. 1–43.

CAMPĀ: a city in the eastern Ganges valley. King KŪṆIKA made it his capital.

CĀṆAKYA 'He who is sustained by Chickpeas': unscrupulous minister of CANDRAGUPTA, whom he helped to the throne. He was destroyed by the plotting of SUBANDHU, a jealous minister of Candragupta's successor, BINDUSĀRA. 8. 194–469.

CANDRAGUPTA 'Protected by the Moon': a young man whom CĀṆAKYA raised to the throne after deposing the ninth King NANDA. He was the first ruler of the Maurya dynasty and was succeeded by his son, BINDUSĀRA. 8. 227–444.

CAṬṬA: a Brahmin's son, betrothed to NĀGAŚRĪ, the subject of the story told by JAYAŚRĪ at 3. 185–213.

DAŚAPURA: a city in AVANTI, not far from UJJAYINĪ.

DATTA 'Given': a layman rescued by VAJRA. 12. 324–9.

DEVADATTA (1) 'God-given': father of Davadinna and father-in-law of DURGILĀ, a leading character in the story told by PADMASENĀ at 2. 444–641.

DEVADATTA (2) 'God-given': a merchant's son, husband of ANNIKĀ and father of ANNIKĀ'S SON. 6. 42–87.

DEVADINNA 'God-given': husband of DURGILĀ, a character in the story told by PADMASENĀ at 2. 444–641.

DHANA 'Wealth': a rich merchant, the father of RUKMIṆĪ. 12. 242, 274–80, 292–305.

DHANADEVA 'God of Wealth': a merchant whom STHŪLABHADRA enabled to find a buried treasure. 10. 4–35.

DHANAGIRI 'Mountain of Wealth': a wealthy Jain layman who became a Jain monk, receiving initiation from SIṂHAGIRI. He was the father of VAJRA. 12. 4–20, 32–48, 100–34.

DHANEŚVARĪ 'Goddess of Wealth': wife of DHANADEVA. 10. 11–26.

DHĀRIṆĪ (1) 'The Earth': wife of SOMACANDRA and mother of PRASANNACANDRA and VALKALACĪRIN; she died giving birth to the latter. 1. 93–119.

DHĀRIṆĪ (2) 'The Earth': wife of ṚṢABHADATTA and mother of JAMBŪ. 2. 1–165, 3. 278.

DURGILĀ 'Mistress of the Fort': cunning, adulterous wife of DEVADINNA. One of the chief characters in the story told by PADMASENĀ at 2. 444–641.

GAṄGILĀ 'Mistress of the Ganges': adulterous wife of MAHEŚVARADATTA, the subject of the story told by JAMBŪ at 2. 314–54.

ĪŚVARĪ 'Supreme Mistress': Jain laywoman who gave food to VAJRASENA during a famine. 13. 182–200.

JAMBŪ 'Rose-apple Tree': Jain elder, the story of whose former lives is related by MAHĀVĪRA to King ŚREṆIKA in Canto 1. The story of his conception, birth, early life, and marriage is related in 2. 1–188. The stories told by Jambū and his eight wives, SAMUDRAŚRĪ, PADMAŚRĪ, PADMASENĀ, KANAKASENĀ, NABHAḤSENĀ, KANAKAŚRĪ, KAMALAVATĪ, and JAYAŚRĪ, are recounted at 2. 189–3. 275. His gaining of omniscience and his final liberation are related in Canto 4.

leader of the monastic order by STHŪLABHADRA. He practised rigorous asceticism at a time of increasing laxity. 10. 36–40; 11. 1–126.

MAHĀVĪRA 'Great Hero': twenty-fourth Fordmaker. In Canto 1 he holds a preaching assembly at RĀJAGṚHA, after which he recounts to King ŚREṆIKA the former lives of King PRASANNACANDRA and of JAMBŪ.

MAHEŚVARADATTA 'Given by the Supreme Lord': a cuckolded merchant, the subject of the story related by JAMBŪ at 2. 314–54.

MAṆAKA 'Short-timed One': short-lived son of ŚAYYAMBHAVA, for whom his father composed an epitome of the sacred teachings. 5. 55–105.

MATHURĀ: the northern city of Mathurā was situated on the river Yamuna, not far from the modern city of Delhi. The southern Mathurā is the modern city of Madurai in the state of Tamil Nadu.

MEGHARATHA 'He who has Cloud-chariot': brother of VIDYUNMĀLIN. 2. 642–92.

NABHAḤSENĀ 'Power of the Sky': one of JAMBŪ's eight wives. She relates the Story of SIDDHI and BUDDHI at 3. 1–43.

NĀGAŚRĪ 'Beauty of the Snake-maiden': a Brahmin's daughter, a teller of beguiling stories, the subject of the story told by JAYAŚRĪ at 3. 185–213.

NĀGILĀ 'Best of Snake-maidens': jilted bride of BHAVADEVA, who, in later life confirmed his resolve to remain a Jain monk. 1. 312–87.

NANDA 'Joyful Prosperity': the name of a dynasty of kings of MAGADHA. There were nine NANDAS. The first was the son of a prostitute and a barber; the ninth was deposed by CANDRAGUPTA with the aid of his minister CĀṆAKYA. 6. 231–52; 7. 40–138; 8. 1–108, 170, 214–326.

NŪPURAPAṆḌITĀ: see DURGILĀ.

PADMASENĀ 'Power of the Lotus': one of JAMBŪ's eight wives. She tells the Story of NŪPURAPAṆḌITĀ and the Jackal at 2. 444–641.

PADMAŚRĪ 'Beauty of the Lotus': one of JAMBŪ's eight wives. She tells the Story of the Pair of Monkeys at 2. 406–30.

PARVATAKA 'Owner of the Mountains': king of the Himalayas, an ally of CANDRAGUPTA and CĀṆAKYA, but nevertheless left to die by the latter. 8. 298–312, 327–39.

PĀṬALĪPUTRA 'Offspring of the Pāṭala Tree': capital of MAGADHA and, later, the Mauryan empire. Its foundation is described in Canto 6. It was situated at the confluence of the Ganges and the Sone, near the site of the modern city of Patna. The name of the city is usually written 'Pāṭaliputra', but Hemacandra always refers to 'Pāṭalīputra'.

PHALGURAKṢITA 'Protected by Ginger Powder': brother of ĀRYARAKṢITA. 13. 3, 113–35.

PRABHAVA 'Distinguished': a Jain elder. Formerly a robber, he broke into JAMBŪ's house on his wedding night and was converted by him. He was initiated by SUDHARMAN and became Jambū's pupil. On the latter's death he became leader of the monastic order. He initiated ŚAYYAMBHAVA, who became his successor. 2. 166–88; 3. 279–81; 4. 61; 5. 1–54.

PRASANNACANDRA 'Clear Moon': king of Potana, brother of VALKALACĪRIN. Seen standing in meditation by King ŚREṆIKA, his story is related by MAHĀVĪRA in 1. 46–261.

PURĪ: a city situated in eastern India, in the modern state of Orissa.

PUṢPACŪLA and PUṢPACŪLĀ 'Flower-crested': royal brother and sister who married each other. Puṣpacūlā later became a Jain nun and was initiated by ANNIKĀ'S SON, gaining omniscience through her devoted service to him. 6. 93–161.

PUṢPAKETU 'He whose Ensign is a flower': king of Puṣpabhadrā who encouraged his children to engage in an incestuous marriage. 6. 93–105.

PUṢPAVATĪ 'Having a Flower' (meaning flower-like beauty) mother of PUṢPACŪLA and PUṢPACŪLĀ. After her death, she became a god, and in a dream warned her daughter Puṣpacūlā of the consequences of her way of life. 6. 93–126.

RĀJAGṚHA 'Seat of Kings': early capital of MAGADHA. Described at 1. 13–21.

ROSE-APPLE TREE ISLAND: the central island of the Middle World. See the Appendix on the Jain universe.

ṚṢABHADATTA 'Given by Ṛṣabha': a wealthy merchant, father of JAMBŪ. 1. 268–85; 2. 1–165; 3. 278.

RUDRASOMĀ 'Moon of Rudra': mother of ĀRYARAKṢITA. She was unimpressed by her son's Brahminical learning. 13. 1–53, 136–41.

RUKMIṆĪ 'Adorned with Gold': daughter of the merchant DHANA, she fell in love with VAJRA, but was converted by him and became a Jain nun. 12. 242–50, 273–306.

SĀGARADATTA 'Given by the Ocean': a prince of VIDEHA, who becomes a Jain monk. Re-embodiment of the soul of BHAVADATTA. 1. 390–469.

ŚAKAṬĀLA 'Wagon of Excellence': minister of the ninth King NANDA, the father of STHŪLABHADRA and ŚRĪYAKA. He was destroyed through the machinations of his rival, the Brahmin poet VARARUCI. 8. 4–66.

ŚAKRA 'Mighty': a regal god. A future embodiment of BHAVADEVA and a previous embodiment of Prince ŚIVA, VIDYUNMĀLIN, and JAMBŪ. 1. 389–91.

SAMBHŪTAVIJAYA 'Attained to Victory': a Jain elder, initiated by, and, with BHADRABĀHU, joint successor of, YAŚOBHADRA 6. 3–4; 8. 109–10, 169.

ŚAMITA 'Calmed': brother of SUNANDĀ, he was initiated by SIṂHAGIRI. He had supernatural powers. 12. 12, 69–99.

SAṂPRATI 'At the Right Time': Mauryan emperor, the son of KUṆĀLA. He fostered the spread of Jainism in the southern districts of BHARATA. 9. 35, 49–54; 11. 23–127.

SAMUDRAŚRĪ 'Beauty of the Ocean': one of JAMBŪ'S eight wives. She tells the story of the farmer at 2. 406–30.

	The Bhagavad Gita
	The Bible Authorized King James Version *With Apocrypha*
	The Koran
	The Pañcatantra
	Upaniṣads
AUGUSTINE	**The Confessions** **On Christian Teaching**
BEDE	**The Ecclesiastical History**
HEMACANDRA	**The Lives of the Jain Elders**
ŚĀNTIDEVA	**The Bodhicaryâvatâra**

	The Anglo-Saxon World
	Lancelot of the Lake
	The Paston Letters
	The Romance of Reynard the Fox
	The Romance of Tristan
GEOFFREY CHAUCER	The Canterbury Tales Troilus and Criseyde
JOCELIN OF BRAKELOND	Chronicle of the Abbey of Bury St Edmunds
GUILLAUME DE LORRIS and JEAN DE MEUN	The Romance of the Rose
WILLIAM LANGLAND	Piers Plowman

A SELECTION OF OXFORD WORLD'S CLASSICS

	An Anthology of Elizabethan Prose Fiction
	An Anthology of Seventeenth-Century Fiction
Aphra Behn	**Oroonoko and Other Writings**
John Bunyan	**Grace Abounding** **The Pilgrim's Progress**
Sir Philip Sidney	**The Old Arcadia**
Izaak Walton	**The Compleat Angler**

A SELECTION OF OXFORD WORLD'S CLASSICS

JANE AUSTEN	Catharine and Other Writings
	Emma
	Mansfield Park
	Northanger Abbey, Lady Susan, The Watsons, and Sanditon
	Persuasion
	Pride and Prejudice
	Sense and Sensibility
ANNE BRONTË	Agnes Grey
	The Tenant of Wildfell Hall
CHARLOTTE BRONTË	Jane Eyre
	The Professor
	Shirley
	Villette
EMILY BRONTË	Wuthering Heights
WILKIE COLLINS	The Moonstone
	No Name
	The Woman in White
CHARLES DARWIN	The Origin of Species
CHARLES DICKENS	The Adventures of Oliver Twist
	Bleak House
	David Copperfield
	Great Expectations
	Hard Times
	Little Dorrit
	Martin Chuzzlewit
	Nicholas Nickleby
	The Old Curiosity Shop
	Our Mutual Friend
	The Pickwick Papers
	A Tale of Two Cities

A SELECTION OF OXFORD WORLD'S CLASSICS

George Eliot	Adam Bede
	Daniel Deronda
	Middlemarch
	The Mill on the Floss
	Silas Marner
Elizabeth Gaskell	Cranford
	The Life of Charlotte Brontë
	Mary Barton
	North and South
	Wives and Daughters
Thomas Hardy	Far from the Madding Crowd
	Jude the Obscure
	The Mayor of Casterbridge
	A Pair of Blue Eyes
	The Return of the Native
	Tess of the d'Urbervilles
	The Woodlanders
Walter Scott	Ivanhoe
	Rob Roy
	Waverley
Mary Shelley	Frankenstein
	The Last Man
Robert Louis Stevenson	Kidnapped and Catriona
	The Strange Case of Dr Jekyll and Mr Hyde and Weir of Hermiston
	Treasure Island
Bram Stoker	Dracula
William Makepeace Thackeray	Barry Lyndon
	Vanity Fair
Oscar Wilde	Complete Shorter Fiction
	The Picture of Dorian Gray

	Oriental Tales
William Beckford	Vathek
James Boswell	Boswell's Life of Johnson
Frances Burney	Camilla Cecilia Evelina The Wanderer
Lord Chesterfield	Lord Chesterfield's Letters
John Cleland	Memoirs of a Woman of Pleasure
Daniel Defoe	Captain Singleton A Journal of the Plague Year Memoirs of a Cavalier Moll Flanders Robinson Crusoe Roxana
Henry Fielding	Joseph Andrews and Shamela A Journey from This World to the Next and The Journal of a Voyage to Lisbon Tom Jones The Adventures of David Simple
William Godwin	Caleb Williams St Leon
Oliver Goldsmith	The Vicar of Wakefield
Mary Hays	Memoirs of Emma Courtney
Elizabeth Haywood	The History of Miss Betsy Thoughtless
Elizabeth Inchbald	A Simple Story
Samuel Johnson	The History of Rasselas
Charlotte Lennox	The Female Quixote
Matthew Lewis	The Monk

A SELECTION OF **OXFORD WORLD'S CLASSICS**

ANN RADCLIFFE	The Castles of Athlin and Dunbayne The Italian The Mysteries of Udolpho The Romance of the Forest A Sicilian Romance
FRANCES SHERIDAN	Memoirs of Miss Sidney Bidulph
TOBIAS SMOLLETT	The Adventures of Roderick Random The Expedition of Humphry Clinker Travels through France and Italy
LAURENCE STERNE	The Life and Opinions of Tristram Shandy, Gentleman A Sentimental Journey
JONATHAN SWIFT	Gulliver's Travels A Tale of a Tub and Other Works
HORACE WALPOLE	The Castle of Otranto
GILBERT WHITE	The Natural History of Selborne
MARY WOLLSTONECRAFT	Mary and The Wrongs of Woman

A SELECTION OF OXFORD WORLD'S CLASSICS

Blaise Pascal	Pensées and Other Writings
Jean Racine	Britannicus, Phaedra, and Athaliah
Edmond Rostand	Cyrano de Bergerac
Marquis de Sade	The Misfortunes of Virtue and Other Early Tales
George Sand	Indiana The Master Pipers Mauprat The Miller of Angibault
Stendhal	The Red and the Black The Charterhouse of Parma
Jules Verne	Around the World in Eighty Days Journey to the Centre of the Earth Twenty Thousand Leagues under the Seas
Voltaire	Candide and Other Stories Letters concerning the English Nation
Émile Zola	L'Assommoir The Attack on the Mill La Bête humaine Germinal The Ladies' Paradise The Masterpiece Nana Thérèse Raquin

TROLLOPE IN OXFORD WORLD'S CLASSICS

ANTHONY TROLLOPE

An Autobiography
Ayala's Angel
Barchester Towers
The Belton Estate
The Bertrams
Can You Forgive Her?
The Claverings
Cousin Henry
Doctor Thorne
Doctor Wortle's School
The Duke's Children
Early Short Stories
The Eustace Diamonds
An Eye for an Eye
Framley Parsonage
He Knew He Was Right
Lady Anna
The Last Chronicle of Barset
Later Short Stories
Miss Mackenzie
Mr Scarborough's Family
Orley Farm
Phineas Finn
Phineas Redux
The Prime Minister
Rachel Ray
The Small House at Allington
La Vendée
The Warden
The Way We Live Now

A SELECTION OF OXFORD WORLD'S CLASSICS

	The Bhagavad Gita
	The Bible Authorized King James Version *With Apocrypha*
	The Koran
	The Pañcatantra
	Upaniṣads
AUGUSTINE	The Confessions On Christian Teaching
BEDE	The Ecclesiastical History
HEMACANDRA	The Lives of the Jain Elders
ŚĀNTIDEVA	The Bodhicaryāvatāra

A SELECTION OF OXFORD WORLD'S CLASSICS

	The Anglo-Saxon World
	Lancelot of the Lake
	The Paston Letters
	The Romance of Reynard the Fox
	The Romance of Tristan
GEOFFREY CHAUCER	The Canterbury Tales Troilus and Criseyde
JOCELIN OF BRAKELOND	Chronicle of the Abbey of Bury St Edmunds
GUILLAUME DE LORRIS and JEAN DE MEUN	The Romance of the Rose
WILLIAM LANGLAND	Piers Plowman

MORE ABOUT OXFORD WORLD'S CLASSICS

American Literature

British and Irish Literature

Children's Literature

Classics and Ancient Literature

Colonial Literature

Eastern Literature

European Literature

History

Medieval Literature

Oxford English Drama

Poetry

Philosophy

Politics

Religion

The Oxford Shakespeare